Destinations

Spencer Morrissey And Corenne Black

Inca-pah-cho
Wilderness Guides

First edition
First printing

10 9 8 7 6 5 4 3 2

Published by Inca-pah-cho Guides
Lake Placid, New York
www.incapahchowildernessguides.com

ISBN 978-1-4675-1534-4

Printed in the United States of America by King Printing, Massachusetts

Copy editing by Nathan Brown and Corenne Black
Layout by Spencer Morrissey and Corenne Black

Routes are hand drawn by the author with maps created by the United States Geological Survey unless otherwise noted.

Photographs: Spencer Morrissey
Cover: Typical Adirondack High Mountain Trail System
Back cover: Spencer Morrissey chillin' on a summit, Corenne Black on Roostercomb Mountain

for

All of those who feel like someone is chasing them!!

Contents

The High Peaks Region of the Adirondack Park was rated a top five trail running destination in the United States!

"Adirondack Park in upstate New York is the nation's largest trail system with more than 2,000 miles of hiking and running trails spread out on 6.1 million acres. The combination of waterfalls, mountains, lakes and streams makes the Keene Valley and Lake Placid region a true trail runner's paradise."

Courtney Johnson
Women's Running Magazine

About the Authors

Spencer Morrissey grew up in the Hamlet of Long Lake and took to the beauty of the mountains a bit later in life. Spencer later graduated from the Ranger School in Wanakena, New York with a degree in Forest Technology; which only grew his passion and knowledge of his surroundings.

After finishing the Adirondack 46 High Peaks in all seasons including winter he moved on to complete the Adirondack 100 Highest and created a guide book to those peaks named "The Other 54." That however wasn't enough he also decided to bushwhack all 46 High Peaks to become only the second person to do so. An active member of the Champlain Valley Search and Rescue K9 Unit, the New York State Outdoor Guides Association, and the ADK, he keeps fresh on all aspects of the Adirondacks.

Now, trail running, a hidden passion and a past closet trail runner, he broke free and started to take on more adventurous endeavors. With the help of Corenne Black they found some of the best Trail Running destinations in the Adirondack Park. Who knows you may swap dust in a future trail race.

Corenne Black grew up in Cherry Valley, New York and spent many months in the Adirondacks volunteering with the Student Conservation Corps. While doing this she fell in love with the Adirondacks and swore she would be a permanent fixture here someday - be careful what you wish for.

Corenne also attended the Ranger School. She is Adirondack 46er, a member of the Champlain Valley Search and Rescue K9 Unit and the ADK. There aren't too many others out there that know their surrounding like Corenne. Be careful, her small stature is nothing to mess with; she can hold her own on the trail.

Adirondack Blue Line

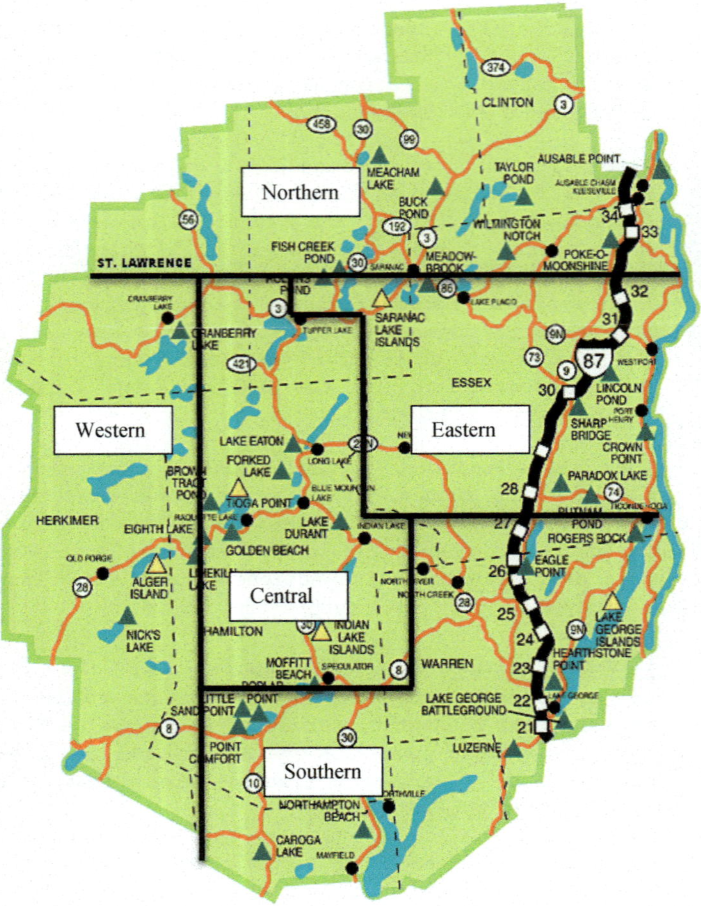

Introduction

Adirondack Regions

This is how I define the 6 regions of the Adirondacks. Others may define and outline them differently but for the purpose of this guide I used these boundaries. Boundaries are built by quad not by geographic feature. Each region is defined by the quads it contains and each quad contained within is listed below. However quads on the boarder of the Adirondack Blue Line may only contain small portions of the Adirondack Park, only routes located within the said Blue Line are considered for this guide.

Northern Region;

Parishville, Nicholville, Rainbow Falls, Sylvan Falls, West Pierrepont, Albert Marsh, Stark, Carry Falls Reservoir, Chasm Falls, Brainardsville, Ellenburg Center, Ellenburg Mountain, Saint Regis Falls, Santa Clara, Lake Titus, Owls Head, Ragged Lake, Lyon Mountain, Moffitsville, Dannemora, Plattsburgh, Lake Ozonia, Meno, Meacham Lake, Debar Mountain, Loon Lake, Alder Brook, Redford, Peasleeville, Peru, Keeseville, Augerhole Falls, Saint Regis Mountain, Bloomingdale, Wilmington, Ausable Forks, Willsboro Bay

Southern Region;

Schroon Lake, Pharaoh Mountain, Graphite, Ticonderoga, Orwell, North Creek, Chestertown, Brant Lake, Silver Bay, Putnam, Benson, Johnsburg, The Glen, Bolton landing, Shelving Rock, Whitehall, Piseco Lake, Wells, Harrisburg, Stony Creek, Warrensburg, Lake George, Putnam Mountain, Morehouse Mountain, Three Ponds Mountain, Hope Falls, Conklingville, Lake Luzerne, Glens Falls, Stratford, Canada Lake, Caroga Lake, Jackson Summit, Northville, Edinburg, Porter Corners, Corinth, Oppenheim, Lassellsville, Peck Lake, Gloversville, Broadalbin, Galway

Central Region;

Childwold, Mount Matumbla, Piercefield, Tupper Lake, Little Tupper Lake, Kempshall Mountain, Forked Lake, Deerland, Raquette Lake, Blue Mountain Lake, Dutton

Mountain, Wakely Mountain, Indian Lake, Thirteenth Lake, West Canada Lake, Page Mountain, Bakers Mills

Eastern Region;
Upper Saranac lake, Saranac lake, Lake Placid, Lewis, Willsboro, Ampersand Lake, Keene Valley, Elizabethtown, Westport, Santanoni Peak, Mount Marcy, Witherbee, Port Henry, Newcomb, Blue Ridge, Paradox Lake, Eagle Lake, Crown Point

Western Region;
South Edwards, Degrasse, Tooley Pond, Brother Ponds, Harrisville, Fine, Oswegatchie, Newton Falls, Cranberry Lake, Remington Corners, Oswegatchie SW, Oswegatchie SE, Five Ponds, Wolf Mountain, Belfort, Stillwater, Beaver River, Crystal Dale, Number Four, Eagle Bay, Brantingham, Thendara, Old Forge, Port Leyden, McKeever, Honnedaga Lake, North Wilmurt, Morehouseville, Hinkley, Ohio, Middleville, Salisbury

Maps, Distances, Routes and Elevation Profiles

The routes that we have provided on the maps in the following pages are all hand drawn. No GPS routes are included; but the hand drawn routes are similar to those recorded on a GPS recorded route. Some of the maps used are older than others and may vary or lack key features. Some trail systems may have been rerouted slightly since the printing of the map. Our outlines follow the routes closely to what is available now, but in some cases may not be exact. There are a handful of maps that have been reproduced with the permission of the designers (VIC, NYSDEC, and The Uihlein Foundation).

The distances we have provided at the beginning of each route description may not be exact and in no way can we guarantee you that any one is. A surveyor may be able to give you exact ground distance from point A to point B; surveyors we are not, runners we try to be. But, the distances are as close to accurate as we can be. When referencing these distances they are not an accumulating total, but are recorded as distances between two points. The total distance is recorded at the end and in some cases may be round-trip (RT) or one-way totals.

Any time reference that is made in the route descriptions are based on our opinion of an intermediate runner, closely to that of us. Time references should not be used as a basis for planning your day. Time can be changed my many factors such as weather, physical conditions, injury, size of group, experience of runners, etc.

Any reference we make to elevation change is based on GPS and/or mapping software estimations. Elevation change is noted with a + and/or - sign to better differentiate a slope's direction. Be aware if you follow one of our routes in the opposite direction than it is described, the elevation change will be opposite of that expressed. If a loop is presented, we inform you of the direction the route is described (clockwise vs. counter-clockwise). By no means are these calculations a means for expressing slope and runs.

The Adirondack Blue Line map on the previous page is a rough outline of the regions developed by Inca-Pah-Cho Wilderness Guides. Regions outlines in black. It can be used as a reference in conjunction with the below list of quads in those regions. Original map developed by the New York State Department of Environmental Conservation.

Types of Routes

There are several different forms of routes, such as snowmobile trail, cross country ski trail, etc. We don't feel it necessary to bore you with their descriptions, but here's a few that might be useful to know about for this guide, in conversation at the local pub and/or everyday life in the outdoors.

Trail…is a route involving a well-established path. This route is marked using foot trail disks placed by DEC, ATIS, or other organizations.

Herd Path…is a route where less traffic is apparent but enough to bed down a route to follow. A herd path can be intermittent and at times hard to follow. Not everyone believes this and some may exist. Herd paths can also be developed by wild game such as beaver and deer. Most herd paths you will encounter are those made by game; do not count on these to get you where you need to go.

*****Side note*****

No herd paths should be maintained, flagged, blazed or otherwise marked

---

Unmaintained Trail…is a route that was once used heavily and maintained, but is no longer. This route is generally easy to follow but may have brush, deadfall, or overgrown sections to impede travel. These routes may have a scattering of old markings.

Logging Road…is a route that can be followed where logging was done, in recent years. These routes can be very muddy with deep ruts.

Jeep Road…is a route that is off road and passable by high clearance vehicles only. Usually sections need to be traveled on foot.

Woods Road…is a route very similar to a logging road, but may be more overgrown or not a logging road at all. Some woods roads once led to hunting camps, logging camps, etc.

Gear thoughts and ideas

You might be thinking - exactly what kind of gear could you possibly need to trail run? Granted, you don't typically need too much on most trail runs, unless of course, you are doing a long-distance outing or marathon.

Keep in mind your destination, terrain and estimated time on the trail. These factors can change what you might consider carrying.

No matter what gear you decide to bring, you really do need to pay special attention to your feet. To do this you need to invest in the proper trail running shoes and running socks. Be sure to seek out a reputable retailer that knows trail running.

Running socks are very vital. Stay away from cotton - when cotton gets wet it stays wet and then blisters and hot spots develop. Synthetic sock work well, but they don't breathe as well and can become very unpleasant to anyone around you. Merino wool socks are the best option. Merino wool is soft, comfortable, breathe well, wicks moisture and works well when wet.

Running shoes should be designated as trail running shoes and not road running shoes. The cushion and support is different in a road shoe. Trail shoes have different support in key areas and tend to be a little stiffer. Trail running shoes typically have less-cushion to allow the foot to be closer to the trail, offering better feel of the terrain and added stability. Tread on a trail shoe is slightly more aggressive as well; while not always the case, it helps to have deeper and adequately developed lugs.

Trail gaiters are very important to some and not even considered by many. A low-cut neoprene gaiter will cover the top of your running shoe and give a gasket like seal around your lower calf or ankle. This will help in keeping out additional moisture when running in mud. Gaiter will also help keep out small rocks, scree, wood particles, insects, ice and snow.

Water is one of the most important pieces of gear you can have and it's free. You can choose from a hydration pack to a handheld version. Our point is, just have some water to keep you hydrated. Hydration packs are a great addition to any trail runners gear closet. Many companies make outstanding hydration packs, some specifically for running. Camelbak®, Golite®, and Nathan® are three reputable brand names with a wide selection. If you do decide to try a hydration pack, try many on before you make a hasty purchase. Some fit better than others and all have different construction. Consider one that fits tightly to your back and doesn't bounce around as you run. Never buy too big or too small - consider the maximum amount of gear and water you will bring and purchase a pack that has the appropriate amount of cubic-inch capacity without having too much dead space.

Problems with chaffing? I think everyone has from this from time to time. Consider some Body Glide©. This roll-on piece of genius gold is a runner's best friend. Roll it on in the problem areas before you head out and it will aid you in the avoidance of runners chafe. Now swamp butt, we have no cure for.

Energy gels are a runner's friend. These little packets of goo can give you that extra boost of energy needed to finish off a run. Energy bars are a good option as well, just much harder to eat while setting a pace. On longer runs, bars are good while on a short break.

Below we have made a short list of gear you might want to consider for certain outings. Do not consider this to be a guideline of items but a reference; you decide what it safe and needed and adjust it to that.

Short runs of 4 hours or less

- **1-2 liters of water**
- **4-6 packets of energy gel**
- **Small pocket map of the area**
- **Watch**
- **Small first aid/safety kit**

Longer runs of over 4 hours

- **2-3 liters of water/hydration pack**
- **4-6 energy gels**
- **2-3 energy bars**
- **Small pocket map of the area**
- **Watch**
- **Headlamp**
- **Small first aid/safety kit**
- **Light shell jacket**

One of the key things with running with a pack, is it needs to be light and tight. Meaning, not too much weight to hold you back and weigh you down, and the pack needs to be tight to your back so it doesn't shift around and do any extensive bouncing.

Trail running with kids

Trail running with kids is a real challenge - they're just so damn fast! But seriously, I'm not going to get into this too much, it similar to hiking with kids.

There are so many traits and eccentricities to kids and the outdoors that only the parents really know about and have any control over. Just simply put, if they are having fun and are comfortable than you will as well.

Trail running at night

This can be a great way to get some exercise late in the day, after work or just as a regular course of excitement. Running at night has a totally different feel as it is; then throw in a trail rather than asphalt and you got a recipe for thrills. While thrilling it can also be dangerous - choose the trail that best suits a night time run. Pick one with less aggressive footing, lose the rocks and roots and pick yourself up a very bright headlamp - one with no less than 80 lumens. Your depth perception and reaction time is lessened - be prepared for anything. Falls, trips and quite possibly worse are more likely to happen at night.

Trail running in the winter

Winter trail running really isn't as far-fetched as you might think. It's done and it's possibly done more often than you might think. I'm not gonna lie, I'm not a politician - winter trail running is a challenge. You have body temperature regulation, traction on ice and snow, shorter days, and people looking at you funny. I think I might be able to set your mind at ease a little.

Temperature regulation isn't that hard - run cool, take short to no breaks and rest when you get back to the car. To do this you can't bite off more than you can chew, as the old cliché goes. This is especially true with winter safety. You should carry more in winter and have everything you need to safely spend the night in the woods. This is very tough to do when running. Keep you trails short and do loops on shorter trails to avoid being too far from civilization.

Maybe you are thinking, "You can't trail run in winter, snowshoes are required on the trails when snow pack exceeds 8 inches." This is true. However, there are alternatives in the form of running or racing snowshoes. Snowshoe running and racing has become much more popular in recent years, with weekly racing all over the northeast. Snowshoe running takes a little practice and once it's realized, it can be one amazing workout. Be sure to check out Atlas® Snowshoes and Crescent Moon® Snowshoe companies for just a couple examples of running and racing snowshoes available.

Now let's talk traction on the trails where snowshoes are not required. These trails are mostly private easement trails as well as snowmobile trails. In cases like this foot traction is the best remedy against slipping while running. Be sure to check out Kahtoola MICROspikes® for an excellent source of strap-on boot traction. Traction can not only save you energy from not slipping but will also protect you from bodily injury due to sudden uneven terrain and slippery conditions.

Give winter running a shot; you do not have a thing to lose from trying.

Hunting Season

Hunting is a popular sport and hobby in the Adirondack Park, one not to be taken lightly. Hunters come from all around the North Country in hopes to take home a trophy, fill their freezer or otherwise. It is, however, unfortunate that getting a hunting license is almost as easy as getting a season's pass to a ski resort. I have nothing in the least against hunting but as runners you should be aware there are many different types of hunters out there from the very cautious to the trigger happy and you should be prepared for anything. Hunters are out there and in many cases you won't even notice them.

Hunting accidents do happen and as an outdoors enthusiast you should protect yourself from being mistaken for game. Avoid highly hunted areas near or around hunting club land during hunting seasons. Wear bright colors such as red and orange. Your pet should be protected as well, if not more so. If you run with a dog they are more prone to being mistaken. A bear bell on your pet is a good indicator for a hunter that this is not a game animal.

There are many different laws in place to protect bystanders from hunting accidents, but most of these laws are generated around highly populated areas, roads and trails.

Some areas are restricted for use during hunting season, i.e. Elk Lake Trails. Keep this in mind when you are planning your outing. You should also be aware of the hunting seasons in the area you will be exploring. Open seasons vary from area to area as well as the game sought after.

Bears and Other Animals

There are hundreds, even thousands of different living creatures out there, many of which you will never see, hear or even know about. The amazing thought is that you are wandering, camping, sightseeing and visiting their home whenever you set foot in the woods. This is their home and to them you are a curiosity and in some case a trespasser. While most you will never see, there are a handful you have a very good chance to encounter. Below are a few such creatures.

American Black Bear- While not usually an issue, they have a bad reputation amongst hikers and outdoor adventurers. Sure, they are large and love to eat, but I have had many people say that about me. You will have a more likely chance of seeing me on the trail than a black bear. So don't be alarmed if you do catch a glimpse of one; this is a rare treat. Just don't approach the bear and try to offer it a picnic basket. Oh, in winter, they do hibernate, sort of, they do on occasion come out, but it's rare.

Coyote- This creature is one you hear howling in the distance at night. Sure to be mistaken as a werewolf, be assured it is not. This is just a wild canine whose interest lies in small mammals and rodents as its main source of food.

Wolf- This large canine has been a source of many debates, including talk of reintroduction, but they haven't been. The wolf, if such a creature still exists in the Adirondacks should not be a thought in your head.

Cougar or mountain lion- Like the wolf, the cougar is believed to still be roaming the forests of the Adirondacks. While sightings of the mountain lions exist, their habitat is generally not the Adirondack Park and could simply just be passing through. Most sightings are of a similar species, the lynx or bobcat.

Bobcat or Lynx- While very similar to one another they are the most abundant of wild cats in the park. These creatures, which feed on small birds, mammals and rodents, will rarely be seen.

Porcupine- This highly known creature is a very poplar one with your canine pets. They arm themselves with quills to protect themselves from predators. A fisher is the only real predator of a porcupine - oh, and a fast-moving motor vehicle. These little creatures dwell in rocky outcropping and caves and in winter will only stray from their dens a short distance to feed on the bark of a nearby tree. Don't worry; they don't shoot their quills at passersby.

Moose- Yes, they are on a comeback in the Adirondack Park and you have an increasingly good chance of seeing one. A moose in most cases is a harmless animal from a distance. However, during rutting season or around their young they can be very aggressive. These creatures can be seen grazing the plant life of the bottom of a shallow pond.

Whitetail Deer- Beautiful creatures; be sure to enjoy their gracefulness.

Hare- Also known as the rabbit or varying hare. If you see one it will be for a split second and then they are gone. They are definitely not a threat to your well-being. They appear white in winter and brown in other seasons. This is how they got the name varying hare. Their color varies in the seasons for camouflage and protection from predators.

Beaver- This is the New York State mammal and rightly so, they are everywhere. You don't see them a bunch because they spend most of their time in the water or in their lodges, but their signs are everywhere. I don't mean a "beware of the beaver" sign, but their cuttings and ponds they create. While they have amazing craftsmanship, beavers tend to raise havoc with trail systems. Most of the beaver ponds in winter will be frozen over and the beavers are tucked away warm in their lodges.

Rodents- This is a general term for field mouse, squirrel, chipmunk, mole, etc. These little guys are seen everywhere and are usually pests around the campsite. You should avoid feeding them and protect your food from them as they are worse than bears for stealing you meals.

Insects- There are a great many of these from the mosquito to the hornet. Hornets and bees will be the only life threatening insects and this only if you have allergies for their stings. Most others are just annoying little creatures that test your patience. There aren't many insects in the winter, except for an occasional few million snow fleas on a warm day. On warm days they come out of the soil and out onto the snow, usually in areas that have been disturbed, like animal tracks or boot tracks.

I could go on forever talking about creatures of the forests, from pine martens to snow geese and from black capped chickadees to brown trout, but this book is about trail running and not wildlife. But you should be aware they are out there. In most all situations you are a walking interest in their daily routine.

Private Property

Private property is in abundance in the Adirondack Park. Simply put, don't impose on someone else's land. This book covers trails and routes that are located on public land; either owned by the State of

New York or privately owned parcels with user easement access.

In either case, some of the trails and routes described are bordering private land where access is prohibited. When this is the cases please remain on the trails specified under the easement agreement - these trails are easily recognized, prohibited trails should be marked with a private or posted sign.

Failure to remain on public land could impose many consequences. Aside from possible charges being raised against the trespasser there are fines that could also be written. When easement land is bordered by private land owned by the same persons, easement rights for that particular parcel could change. Please follow the easement rules and regulations set by the land owners and no problems will arise.

Injury Hazards

Trail running is actually quite a high risk activity. Consider trail running as hiking at an increase rate of speed. The same obstacles you come across while hiking will need to be reacted to much quicker.

Keeping that in mind the probability of a twist, pull, break or sprain to a part of your body increases.

Twisted knees and ankles are not uncommon - pulls in you quads or hamstrings are easy to imagine - sprains to a joint or ligament are almost guaranteed, and breaks to a bone are not totally unimaginable. Scrapes, scratches, bruises and deep lacerations are all part of the game - you'll just have to deal with it.

If any serious accident or injury does occur be sure to seek attention as soon as possible. Emergency contact phone numbers and a place to enter your personal emergency contact information are located in the back of this guide. Minor scrapes and bruising should be cleaned and attended to appropriately.

Obtaining a course in basic CPR and first aid is highly recommended. This will give you the basics on how to deal with certain injury situations until adequate help arrives. Advanced levels of training, such as Wilderness First Aid or Wilderness First Responder are also available to the public and require a longer commitment for course work.

Also, be aware of the area you are running. While many of the areas in this guide avoid too serious of terrain, there are small situations where cliffs and drop-offs come into play. Trail running in some destinations bring you close to large cliffs, raging rivers and other dangerous natural features. Be extra cautious in these areas.

Injury hazards live in everyday life and a complete book can and I'm sure has been written about them - the back-country is no different. While urban hazards don't exist in the back woods, the natural ones do. Avoid running in electrical storms, wind storms, ice storms, nuclear fallout, December 2012 and any other conditions where probability of serious injury is increased.

Remember, any activity you involve yourself in, especially one in the back country at a high rate of speed, has a risk for injury or even death.

Physical Fitness and the Physician

Trail running isn't just for the hardcore runner or adventure athlete. Saying that, there should be some sort of commitment to staying in good physical shape.

It is understood that many runners begin running to get into shape and that is great. But if this is the case with you or someone you are with, start small and slow and build up your tolerance and physical condition before taking on too much.

It would be a good idea to consult your family physician before you begin an exercise program of any type.

Some Common Sense and Trail Ethics

- All human waste should be buried at least 8 inches deep and 150 feet from any water source or trail.

- All dogs need to be leashed while on hiking trails and at public camping areas, when in the Eastern High Peaks Region.

- Most important - leave no traces. If you can carry it in, you can carry it out. Don't litter. If you see litter, pick it up. Always leave the area as nice, if not nicer than you saw it. That way the next person can enjoy it as much as you did. No disposing of anything into the water.

- Do not cut trees, alter views, or deface any mountain to better your experience. You may like it, but the next person may take offense and it's just wrong.

- Be considerate of others. Be polite, courteous and respectful as it all comes back in the end.

- If you are going on private property remember its illegal, to do so without the land owner's or manager's permission. Plan your hike and get permission first. If you get caught you could be arrested and fined, and it would be no one's fault but your own. Just consider this another friendly warning.

- During hunting season be prepared to hear gun fire with the possibility of it being in the region you are in. It can be common to jump a hunter or even walk by one and not even know it. Be considerate to them as well and move away from their hunting area if you can.

- Don't consider any water to be safe to drink. Always carry a filter, purifier or some sort of chemical water purification in case of emergency.

- Take care of others in need. If you see someone injured or lost, offer a hand.
- Be courteous to others on the trail, whether it is hikers, skiers or riders.
- Leave wildlife wild. If you encounter wildlife leave it alone. Don't feed it, pet it, hug it, poke it, corner it, capture it or try and take your picture with it.
- Follow all local rules and regulations, on and off trail. These differ from region to region; be sure to know what they are.

Northern
Adirondacks

Paul Smith Visitors Interpretive Center

Quad:

Saint Regis Mountain

Directions to Trailhead:

From the intersection of Routes 86 and 30 in Paul Smiths, follow Route 30 north. Continue for around 0.25 miles to the VIC Road on the left. A sign marks the road.

Trail Conditions:

Aside from the upper portion of the Jenkins Mountain Trail and the Woods and Waters Loop near Black and Long Ponds the trails can be expected to be mostly graded and in stellar condition. Originally many of them were built to be handicapped accessible. But recently, new trails have been added and are very new to the area. These new trails offer unique looks into the area and at times can feel very new.

****Side Note****

Day Use Fees may be required

Paul Smith's College has developed a varied and exciting program of events and activities at The VIC. The emphasis is on engaging the college community with all phases of VIC operations; open access to the public; a stronger connection to the Arts and increased entrepreneurial opportunities with an eye toward making The VIC self-sustaining. Plans include continued development of the trail system, as well as creating and enhancing partnerships with supporting organizations to broaden the scope of The VIC as a regional economic engine.

The State of New York officially transferred ownership of the VIC Center building to Paul Smith College on January 1, 2011 and was officially released from the lease on the VIC Center acreage wholly owned by Paul Smiths College. Paul Smith's has expanded usage of The VIC following 4 guiding princi-

ples: A) Programs, events and activities linked to Paul Smith's Academic mission; B) The facilities and trails will continue to be accessible to the public; C) An expanded connection to the broad interpretation of "The Arts;" D) Expanded opportunities for entrepreneurialship.

The VIC is also continuing their trail run series through the summers. They also expand to offer interpretive hikes and canoe paddles on and off site, live music events, Armchair Traveler Lecture Series, monthly art exhibits, a native species butterfly house and family nature activities. Please visit their webpage for more in-depth details.

Information supplied by
Sarah Keyes, Paul Smith's VIC

The map provided for the VIC trails was created and produced by the VIC and Paul Smith's College. The map is under reconstruction currently due to newly revised and built trails. The trail system is expected to change over the next few years to include more trails for recreation. The map has been reduced in size to fit these pages. For a larger copy of the map stop into the Interpretive Building and pick up a copy free of charge.

The profiles that were created in the following trail descriptions were created by the author and should be expected to be of limited accuracy. They were produced with GPS tracking which can be temperamental and inaccurate, at times up to 25 linear feet. 25 Linear feet can mean the different between a steep slope and a moderate slope. Please use the profiles as a guide but not a Bible.

The trails in the VIC have different trail markers for each loop. There are five different colors and three designs. Each of the three designs designates a different trail type. While this is not a ski book, the trail markers were designed for winter recreation.

- Snowshoe Hare Track = Snowshoe Trail
- Heron Track = Skate Ski Trail
- Bobcat Track = Classic Ski Trail

A picture of each trail marker will be included in each of the trail descriptions to alleviate any confusion. All trails are open for all activities but certain trails are better for a particular outing. All trails are built in loop fashion and all but four leave and finish at the interpretive center. The Woods and Waters Trail and the Silviculture Trail both start off different trails and the Eskar Trail and the Jenkins Mountain Trail start from the interpretive building but loop back upon themselves.

The VIC trails were built with snowshoeing, skiing, walking, hiking, trail running, bird watching, wildlife viewing, exercise and relaxation in mind - so please be aware you will be meeting all types of outdoor enthusiasts, from the athletic to the leisure walker and of all age groups. With this in the back of your head be respectful to all you meet and hopefully they will return with the same gratitude.

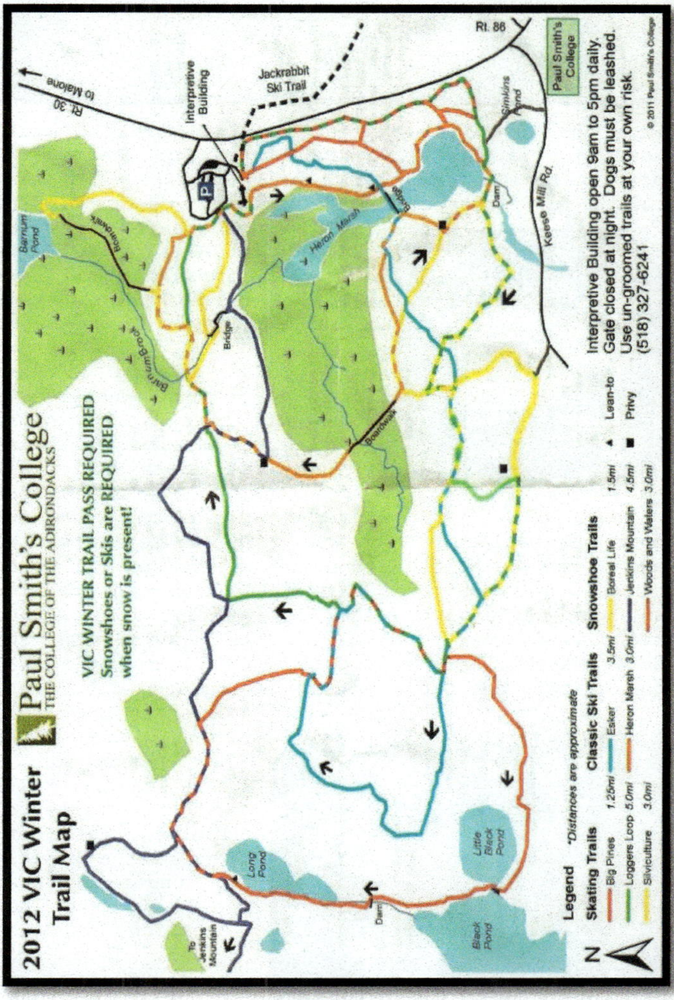

Map created by Paul Smith's College and the VIC

Jenkins Mountain Trail

Trail Conditions:

You will be running along an old woods road for a large portion of this route, keeping you dry and comfortable. As you approach the summit you will find yourself in muddier and wetter conditions. Footing can be very slippery on the steeper slopes.

From the gazebo at the VIC you will see the trail heading straight out toward the marsh. The central portion of the trail has a small lollipop loop that can be incorporated. Below is a brief description of this in a counter-clockwise direction. Be sure to follow the **Blue Snowshoe Hare Track Trail** markers for this trail.

The first portion of this run brings you downhill at a moderate pace to the shore of Heron Marsh. Following along the marsh the trail goes through a mature forest with outstanding views out over the wetland. There are a few different patios and viewing stations along the marsh. You will soon come to a bridge over Barnum Brook before entering an open hardwood forest. On a slight incline you eventually come to a major intersection with the Heron Marsh Trail. From here you will run up a hill and quickly descend down to the Loggers Loop. Cross directly over this trail and enter the woods on a very narrow trail with interrupted footing. The footing is a little under-developed due to the new creation of the trail. This section cuts back and forth through open

hardwoods and eventually comes out to an old logged area where the trail is narrowed by berry bushes and is a bit overgrown. Beyond the logged area you will descend slightly on what looks to be an old logging road and come eventually out on to what is referred to as the Jenkins Mountain Road.

Following here to the right you will be on a very packed-out trail with great footing. You will pass by the northern end of the Jenkins Mountain Loop on your left as you proceed - a sign marks the intersection. You will remain on this old woods road for a while longer, and you will have ample time to relieve yourself - that is, because there is a well-positioned privy sitting right there at the end of the road.

As you begin to transition from woods road to foot trail you will begin to see many signs of beaver activity on both sides of the trail. Fortunately for you, you will be well above them as you run along a glacial esker. Only at one point do you have to drop below the waterline and there is a beaver dam and bridge helping you stay dry as you make your way.

Climbing back up after the bridge you will be on a much narrower esker. As this one weaves through the area, you can see parts of Jenkins to your right. If you ever get the thought. "Am I on the correct trail?" - you really are. This trail meaders through open maple forest and skirts Jenkins only to eventually climb up the opposite side.

You will leave the esker to the left and drop slightly into the hardwoods and run on a trail that was cut into a side hill. There are several very small dips and rises as you approach the first steep climb. This climb, though steep, is very short. You will then be side hilling for a while longer as thoughts of the wrong trail come to mind again. Just don't think about it; it will drive you mad. You will pass by the southern intersection with the Jenkins Mountain Loop on your left; if you wish to summit Jenkins, pass this intersection by. If you could care less about summit at this very moment, hang a left here.

Lollipop Loop Section

Following this trail to the left you will switchback and drop down behind the lean-to on Long Pond. From the lean-to there is a split in the trail. Right brings you along Long Pond on the Woods and Waters Trail and left is the continuation of the Jenkins Mountain Trail. Follow left along a narrow trail with sporatic footing. Running through a mixed forest you will come back out to the Jenkins Mountain Road rather quickly. Follow the trail right and retrace your steps to return to the pavilion at the VIC.

Jenkins Mountain Summit Section

This setion is an out and back portion of the trail that gets you to the summit of Jenkins and the supurb views it does offer.

This portion starts from the southern intersection of the lollipop loop mentioned above. Up to this point you have been very patient in your run of Jenkins Mountain and it will soon pay off. At some point you will be at the base of the climb for the summit of Jenkins and when that time comes, you will know it. The climb starts off a little steep but mostly slippery and a tad bit unstable, especially when wet. With small breaks in the steep terrain you will top out on the ridge and be running a much more moderate slope. Just before the summit you will be in a high elevation col with a short, steep climb ahead that exits you out on to the summit rock.

Once you have soaked in all the views and had a quick, refreshing drink of tepid H_2O and a goo packet, retrace your steps either back to the VIC or to the southern end of the lollipop loop to finish off the trail. You could also invest a little time and visit some of the other trails along the way to add a new flavor to your day.

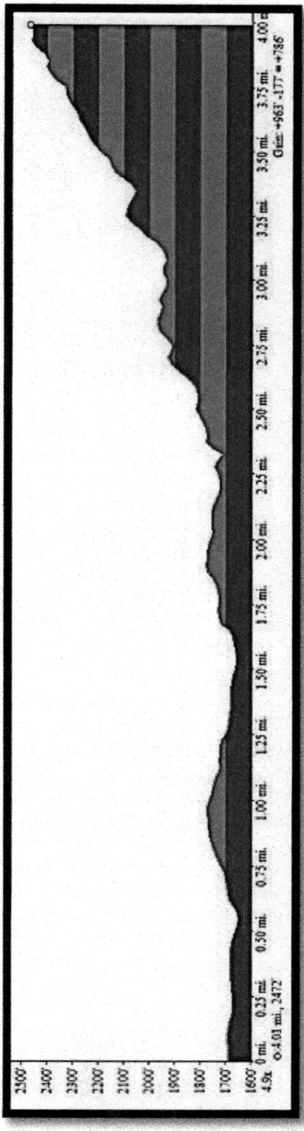

The miracle isn't that I finished. The miracle is that I had the courage to start.

John Bingham

Running in a counter-clockwise direction from the pavilion located just below the interpretive building you will start this loop. Follow the Yellow Trail disks with the snowshoe hare track. The beginning is rather flat and in a short distance you will come to the crossing of Jenkins Mountain Road. Cross here and continue to the base of a decent-sized hill. Atop the hill you will make a sharp left and slight descent to a high ridge. Following the rolling hills along the ridge you eventually come to a somewhat steep descent. At the base of the hill there is a viewing area to the right and a very sharp turn left. You will follow along the shore of the marsh near Barnum Pond and come to a 1600 foot long boardwalk.

This boardwalk goes through the marsh while protecting its fragile ecosystem from over use. Being a narrow boardwalk you will need to be cautious of others using it, not that this is an exception to the rule. Once out of the marsh, you come to an intersection with the Heron Marsh Trail. Follow right and work your way through an attractive forest. Pass by the Loggers Loop and continue following the Yellow

Snowshoe Hare Track Trail disks. You will cross Barnum Brook and immediately on the opposite side there is a left where the Boreal Life Trail breaks away. Follow along Barnum Brook and be sure to hang a left across the bridge over the brook. You will be running through more attractive forest and quickly come out to the Jenkins Mountain Trail just a few feet shy of the pavilion from which you started.

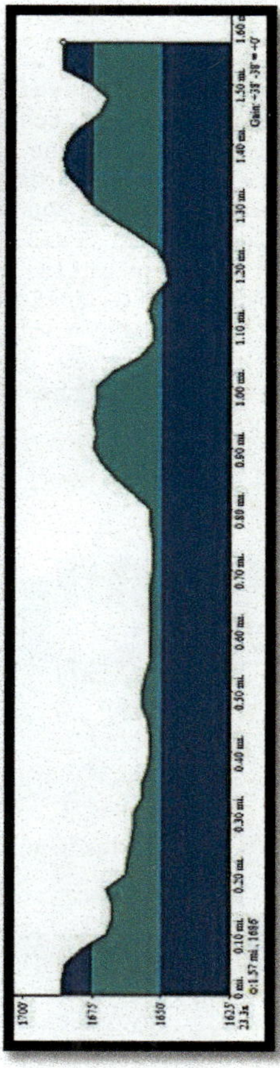

Heron Marsh Trail

This 3.0 mile trail starts and ends at the gazebo located to the right of the Interpretive Center. Be sure to follow the Orange Trail disks with the bobcat track.

Starting in a clockwise direction from the gazebo, turn left and downhill and run behind the Interpretive Center. There is a downhill to the shore of the marsh. You will follow along the marsh, passing two lean-tos and intersect a few of the other loops. At the bottom of a steep slope you will cross a bridge over a dam at Shingle Mill Falls. Past this point it is a series of rolling hills and many more intersections, just remember to follow the Orange Trail disks. There will be a 900-foot boardwalk through a peat bog with an amazing view of a pristine wetland. On the opposite side of the boardwalk you will run up a some-

what steep bluff to a hardwood forest with soft gentle turns and more rolling hills. Following a few turns at key intersections you will sweep your way back to the gazebo.

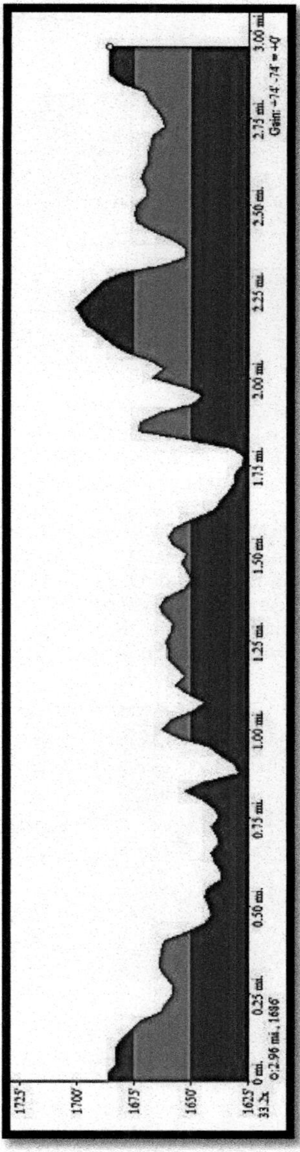

YOU CAN RUN WITH THE BIG DOGS OR YOU CAN SIT ON THE PORCH AND BARK.

Wallace Arnold

The Esker Trail is kind of an aggressive run for the VIC and is set up like no other. This is a lollipop loop. Meaning, the trail loops at the end and you will have to retrace your steps back to the VIC.

You will be following this trail out from behind the interpretive building and at the end following the modest loop in a clockwise direction. Be sure to follow the **Blue Bobcat Track Trail Markers.** You initially follow along with the Big Pines Trail for a very short distance before you break off to the left and run the trail through an attractive pine forest. As the trail meanders through the forest you will slowly descend and cross the Big Pines Trail. Dropping somewhat aggressively, you will cross the Heron Marsh Trail. With the aid of a bridge you should have no trouble staying dry however, but then again…

After you cross the floating bridge and take in the great views at 60-miles per hour you will exit at an intersection. Follow right and join the Heron Marsh Trail momentarily. Making a left off the Heron Marsh Trail you will soon come to a crossing of the yellow trail - three times. At the third crossing you will be joining it at the top of a modest hill near a viewing platform. This will be a momentary ménage à trois of trails. You will break free of this as the green trail exits on the left and the yellow trail exits on the right. Dropping nicely down to an old woods road you will hang a right and rejoin the exact three trails for a second round. After a short distance and slight descent you will be all alone on the solitary Esker Trail.

The Esker Trail from this point on is the start of the loop. Heading left you will start a decent climb to the height of land near the Esker. With several small switchbacks and a meandering trail that at times climbs more often than not; you may start to feel it in your legs. The trail never actually reaches the top of the eskar but circumnavigates it. After a couple more small climbs and one steep push you will start your descent back down and join the Woods and Waters Trail. You will continue to drop a ton of elevation as you join back up with the Loggers Loop and finish off the short Eskar Loop

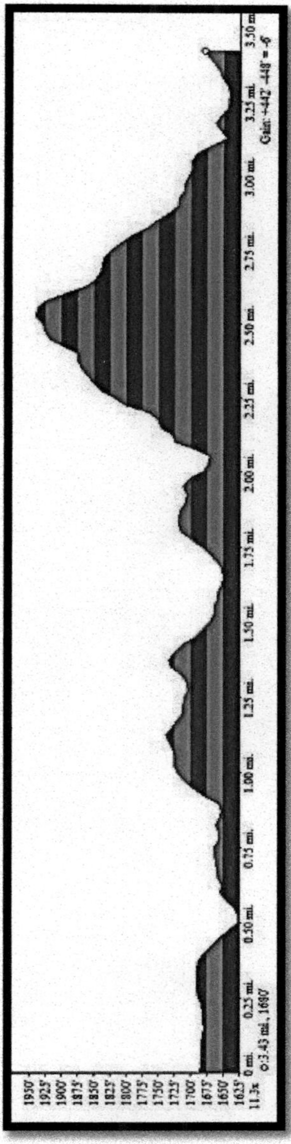

This trail starts just west of the Shingle Mill Falls Bridge and the dam located there. Be sure to follow the Yellow Heron Track Trail. Following in a clockwise figure-eight direction run along a mellow course, quickly you will come to an old woods road - an arrow on the trail marker points you left.

This road is very mellow and also includes a portion of the Loggers Loop. Running along this mellow terrain you will soon come to an intersection with this trail. I know this sounds odd, but the Silviculture Trail is a series of two loops that form a figure-eight pattern. You are at the center of the figure-eight.

Making a sharp left you will be at the base of a very steep hill. Atop this short hill the Silviculture trail again splits. Follow here to the right, toward a viewing platform. Pass the viewing platform and run over rolling hills and eventually to a new section of trail that follows a logging road. This newly developed trail is very wide and, being new, will be much softer under foot. This logging road has a couple nice steep hills that are very brief but offer a change in elevation. There is a steep down with a sharp left as you come to the intersection of the Eskar Trail, Woods and Waters Trail and the Loggers Loop.

Follow here to the left and continue on a woods road that is a little more developed than the previous. With smooth rolling hills you will quickly be back to the top of the hill near the platform you passed just a few minutes ago. Run down the short steep hill and head out straight at the next intersection. This small section of trail tends to be lightly marked and soon follows the Heron Marsh Trail for a bit, before it breaks off to the right and makes a smooth course back to the dam.

Loggers Loop Trail

The Loggers Loop incorporates many of the other loops in the center with only a couple short sections that are dedicated just to this loop. Some of the following descriptions may duplicate short portions of other loops. Doing this should ensure accuracy of the trail description as it currently exists at the VIC.

Start your run from behind the interpretive building next to the staff parking lot. The Loggers Loop follows the same course as the Big Pines Trail for the first portion. Heading in a clockwise direction begin your run. About 100 feet down the trail the **Green Heron Track Trail** will be a left. The trail follows the course of Route 30 for quite some time. The trail is rather mellow and uneventful. Aside from a small sweeping turn on a hill you can plan on a mellow run up to about half way. Just before you come to a decent downhill on a sharp left, the Big Pines Trail and Loggers Loop Trail splits. Follow the **Green Trail** marker straight ahead. The trail from here begins a slow descent ends on the shore of Heron Marsh.

Making a right you will follow the same course as the Heron Marsh Trail for a short distance. Crossing over the dam you run a bit on a flat to an old woods road at which time you need to take a left and join the Silviculture Trail. Running along a wide and well packed course you eventually cross the Eskar Trail and make a hard left and proceed to a moderate push up a steep slope. At the top of the slope there is a viewing platform to the right, turn here and run past. You are now having a threesome with three different colored trails (blue, yellow, and **green**). Stay on this course to a hard left; the **Green Trail** heads downhill and exits you onto another woods road and another section of the Silviculture Trail.

Follow here to the right, pass by a spur of the blue trail on the right. Then make a hard left as the yellow trail departs to the right. Passing the red trail on the left you make a hard right and coexist with the Eskar Trail again.

On a moderate uphill you will be working pretty hard before you break free from any other trail and are solely on the **Green Trail** again. You will descend slightly to a portion of the **Green Trail,** which follows the old Jenkins Mountain Road. Following here to the right you will remain on this old woods road as it raises and lowers in front of you and then kicks you out back behind the interpretive building.

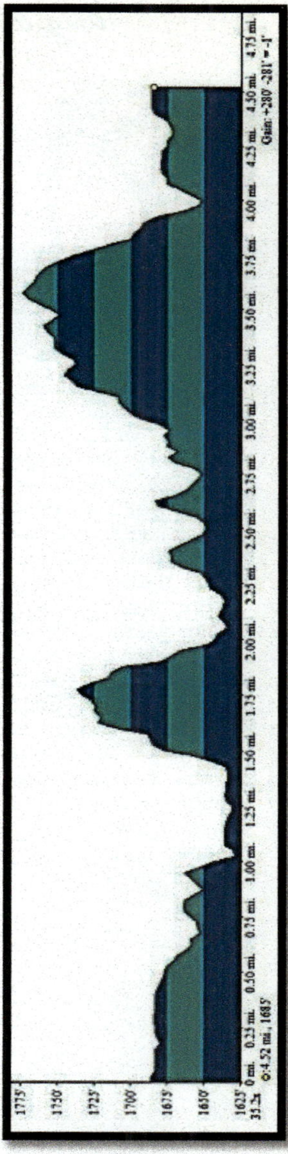

Big Pines Trail

This trail starts from behind the interpretive building next to the staff parking lot. Heading in a clockwise direction, begin your run. About 100 feet down the **Red Heron Track Trail** there will be a left. The trail follows the course of Route 30 for quite some time. The trail is rather mellow and uneventful. Aside from a small sweeping turn on a hill you can plan on a mellow run up to about halfway. The trail then drops to the shore of Heron Marsh and makes a hard right back toward the interpretive building. You will quickly come to and pass by the green trail on the right as you continue along Heron Marsh. The **Red Trail** leaves on the right and climbs rather steeply back up on an upper ridge. From this point the trail takes on a small downhill before again climbing slightly back to the start.

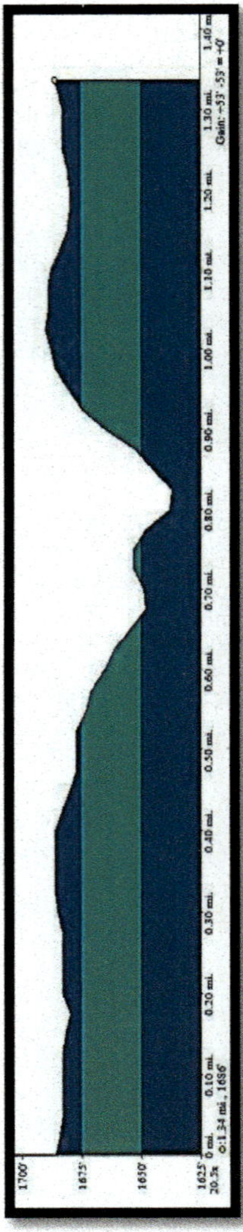

This trail was developed to connect the woods of the VIC to the waters that lie to the east. This trail does not start from the interpretive building but, rather, starts further in off the Eskar Trail. The Woods and Waters Trail starts from the base of a steep hill in a depression where the Eskar Trail, Silviculture Trail and the Loggers Loop come together. There is a sign at the start with a **Red Snowshoe Hare Trail** marker on the post. Running in a clockwise direction, begin your course.

The route is much narrower at this point. The branches of trees along this route overhang the trail. With little initial change in elevation the run is rather easy. You will soon have a small dip and roll through the trees and come out to a lean-to between Black and Little Black ponds. A trail goes around the lean-to and finishes off on Keese Mill Road, the trail you want drops down to water's edge and crosses a bridge. The bridge is only 20 or so feet in length and crosses the small outlet. The trail here is very narrow and seemingly very fast. The trail climbs very steeply on this side of Black Pond and the footing is a little tricky. The descent on the other side is also steep. You will descend down to an outlet of Long Pond, follow its shore and swing left over a bridge spanning a fish barrier dam. This bridge is very narrow and can be a bit slippery.

The opposite side of the bridge brings you to an intersection. Left leads back along Black Pond to Keese Mill Road; you want right. This route is very narrow and skirts a steep side hill. Footing can be very slippery and a tad bit on the difficult side. You will soon be at another lean-to. Behind the lean-to is the Jenkins Mountain Loop - right is also part of that trail but is also a continuation of the

Red Trail. This section is also very narrow but only last a short time before it exits onto the Jenkins Mountain Trail. Follow here to the right and run along an old woods road. You will be running here for a short distance before the Red Trail takes a hard right off the Jenkins Mountain Trail and onto an old logging road. This section of trail is relatively new and the footing can be a little more rugged than other trails in the VIC.

You will begin to climb here rather steep and steady to the height-of-land along this trail. The opposite side of the hill there is the descent. It is not quite as steep as the climb but it is all there.

With a few more rolling hills ahead of you will make your way around the Eskar on your right and pass by the Eskar Trail on a couple occasions. You will have one more decent down and come out to the Eskar Trail. Follow here to the left, back to the start of the Woods and Waters Trail.

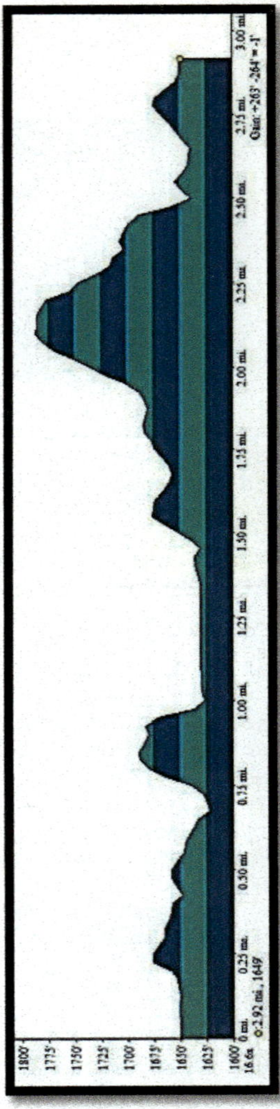

Grass Pond

Quad:

Saint Regis Mountain

Distances:

- **To Sheep Meadow Trail-0.4 miles**
- **To Lean-to 1.4 miles**
- **To east side of pond-0.2 miles**

Total distance 2.0 miles, one way

Directions to Trailhead:

From the intersection of Routes 86 and 30 in Paul Smiths, follow Route 30 north. Continue for 3.6 miles to the trailhead road for Hayes Brook on the right - this is also called Mountain Pond Road. Turn down this road and proceed to follow the old tarmac for 0.4 miles to the trailhead. There is a yellow gate on the left; park here.

Following an old woods road through some old growth forests you will be on a stable surface. At about 0.4 miles you will cross Osgood River and bear right. This right is unmarked and is a fork in the woods road. You will start out flat for a bit, but soon come to a decent sized uphill. While some small rolling hills exist along this stretch, you will be welcomed with smooth terrain. This area can be a wildlife haven - do not be surprised if you startle something off in the bush. At Grass Pond you will come to a lean-to a brilliant place to sit and relax. The grass-encircled pond is just down a small hill.

Being such a short run I highly recommend making a right on your way back out and running back to Sheep Meadows. See the trail description below.

1700'
1675'
1650'
1625'
1600'
1575'
18.5x
0 mi. 0.10 mi. 0.20 mi. 0.30 mi. 0.40 mi. 0.50 mi. 0.60 mi. 0.70 mi. 0.80 mi. 0.90 mi. 1.00 mi. 1.10 mi. 1.20 mi. 1.30 mi. 1.40 mi. 1.50 mi. 1.60 mi. 1.70 mi. 1.80 mi. 1.90 mi. 2.00 mi. 2.10 mi.
2.01 mi. 1649'
Gain: +181' -151' = +30'

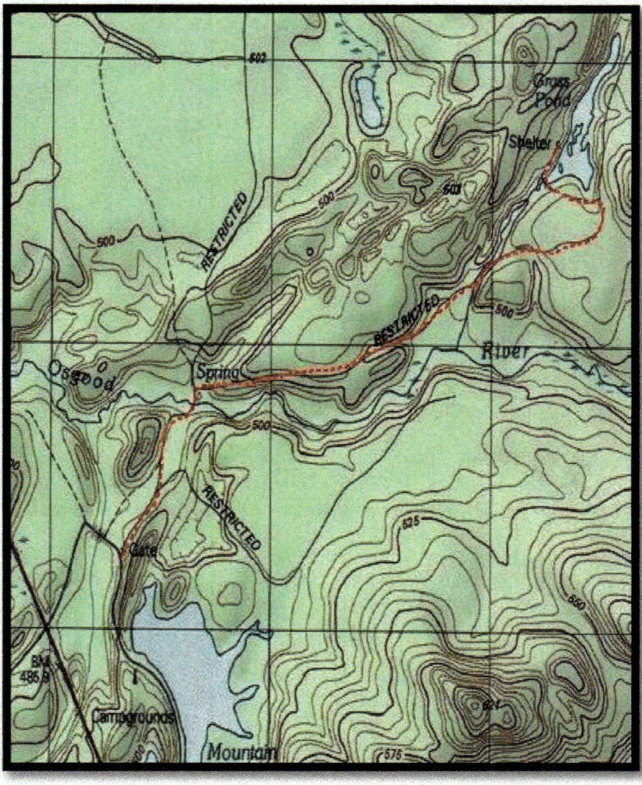

Grass Pond
Shelter
RESTRICTED
RESTRICTED
RESTRICTED
500
River
Osgood
Spring
Gate
BM
486.9
Campgrounds
Mountain
525
550
575

Sheep Meadow

Quad:

Saint Regis Mountain and Meacham Lake

Distances:

- **To the Grass Pond Trail-0.15 miles**
- **To the Osgood River-0.2 miles**
- **To Hayes Brook 1.1 miles**
- **To Sheep Meadow-1.8 miles**

Total distance 3.25 miles

Directions to Trailhead:

From the intersection of Routes 86 and 30 in Paul Smiths, follow Route 30 north. Continue for 3.6 miles to the trailhead road for Hayes Brook on the right - this also called Mountain Pond Road. Turn down this road and proceed to follow the old tarmac for 0.4 miles to the trailhead. There is a yellow gate on the left; park here.

Trail Conditions:

On the Hayes Brook Truck Trail, which is also a horse and biking trail, you will feel at home as you run through this quiet area toward two lean-tos nestled in a meadow.

So, why is this called Sheep Meadow? Well, this used to be grazing lands for sheep. I know, not the most exciting explanation - but I couldn't even come up with a wisecrack about this one.

At 0.4 miles along this route you will come to the Osgood River - a bridge spans the water flow. Immediately after the bridge the Grass Pond Trail comes in on the right. Bear left along the Hayes Brook Truck Trail. In less than 0.1 miles from this point the trail leaves the truck road and climb steeply into the forest. The much narrower trail now meanders it way through a darker forest of pines and eventually rejoins the truck trail just shy of Hayes Brook. Hayes Brook is then crossed as you make your way through a much brighter area. Not long after the crossing of Hayes Brook the trail begins to flatten

out. Old fields start to appear as you make your way to Sheep Meadow, and after 3.25 miles you are there. There are two lean-tos and a stable for horses. The area is totally surrounded by small mountains, offering a very unique backdrop.

The biggest mistake an athlete can make is to be afraid of making one.

L. Ron Hubbard

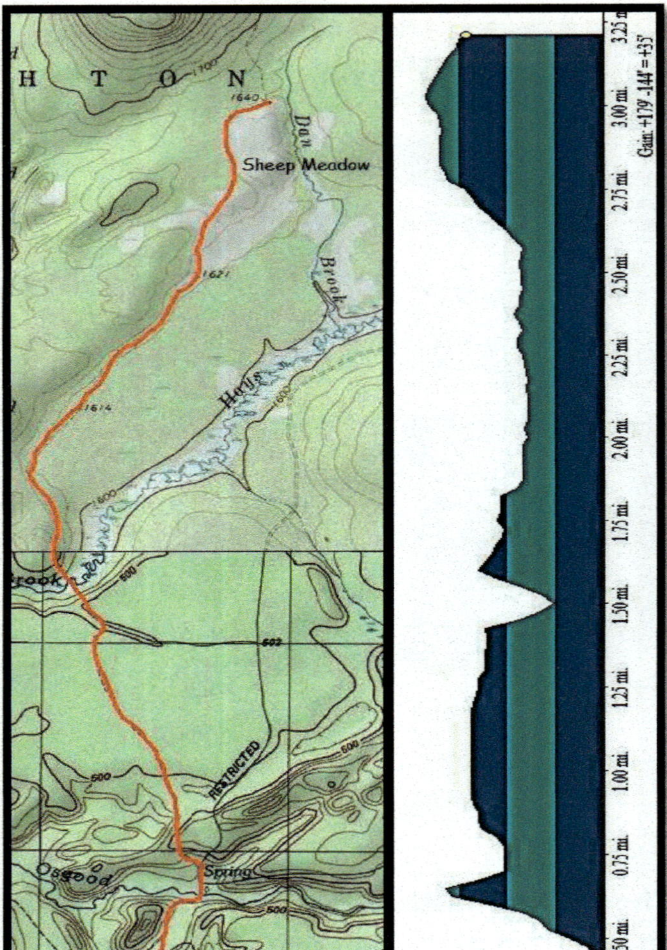
H T O N
Sheep Meadow
Dan
Brook
Hulls
Brook
Osgood
Spring
RESTRICTED
RESTRICTED
Gate
Campgrounds
Mountain
0 mi.
0.25 mi.
0.50 mi.
0.75 mi.
1.00 mi.
1.25 mi.
1.50 mi.
1.75 mi.
2.00 mi.
2.25 mi.
2.50 mi.
2.75 mi.
3.00 mi.
3.25 mi
Gain: +179' -144' = +35'
3.22 mi., 1646'
1675'
1650'
1625'
1600'
1575'
18.5x

Skiff Pond Loop

Quad:

Debar Mountain

Distances:

- **Parking to gate-0.3 miles**
- **To Skiff Pond-1.45 miles**
- **To snowmobile trail-0.75 miles**
- **To second gate-1.5 miles**
- **Back to parking-0.3 miles**

Total 4.3 miles, loop

Directions to Trailhead:

Follow County Route 26 (also seen as Route 99 on some maps) north out of the small village of Loon Lake, follow here for about 6.5 miles to Duck Pond on the left. Just past Duck Pond (about 0.75 miles) you will cross Hatch Brook and a dirt road will be on the left. This left is the road you need to use. Depending on the conditions you may need to park here to access the loop. If conditions are good you can drive this narrow but well graded dirt road. Follow the road for about 1.7 miles to a parking area of about 3-4 cars. There are state signs marking a snowmobile trail and signs prohibiting motor vehicles beyond this point; park here.

Trail Conditions:

95% of this trail is in prime trail running condition. There are hardly any rocks or roots to maneuver, and only a little water near the marshes at the end. This is a lightly used loop offering excellent footing and a carefree run.

From the parking location there are three trails that lead off. Right is where you will be coming out, center is a closed route that is not part of the loop and left is the start of the loop.

Following left you will be on an old woods road for 0.3 miles to the gate that is located before a culvert bridge that drains the wetland. Shortly beyond

you will cross another bridge, this time made of wood and which tends to be a little slippery when wet.

On the other side of the bridge the trail becomes more of a foot trail, but with signs of an old road still apparent. The grade is now slightly uphill. There is only one sort of steep section; the footing is so nice it can hardly be considered steep, but compared to the rest of the trail it's as steep as it gets.

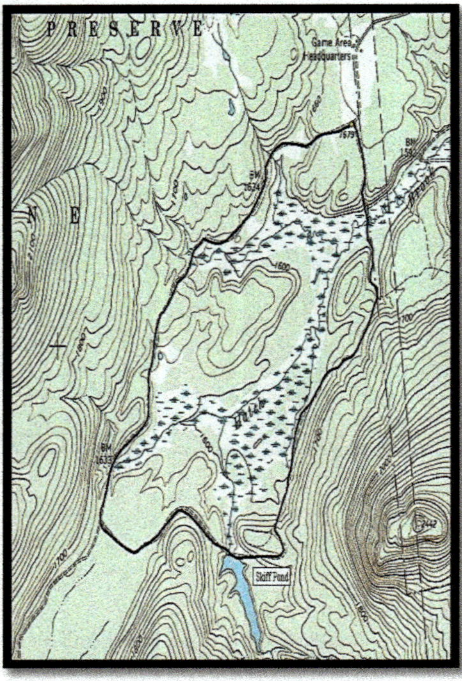

Once you crest the hill, which does last for a while, you will have a small down-hill and then an S-sweeping downhill with a sharp right at the bottom delivering you to the shore of Skiff Pond. There are a few nice camping spots along the shore and a small metal walkway out to a culvert dam.

Beyond this point it is a wide trail with the same excellent footing, but at this point it is quite flat. After 0.75 miles or so you will be at a T-intersection. This is a snowmobile trail, and you will need to hang a right here to head back to the parking location.

This right puts you back on a woods road that is wide and in excellent condition. However, after a short distance you will have to fight a slightly wet area near a marsh. Then in another 0.75 miles you will run through a wet section as you pass by a beaver dam. And lastly, you will navigate a large wet area near the end at the second gate.

At the second gate you will start to become high and dry again as you climb out of the marsh and finish the last leg back to the parking location.

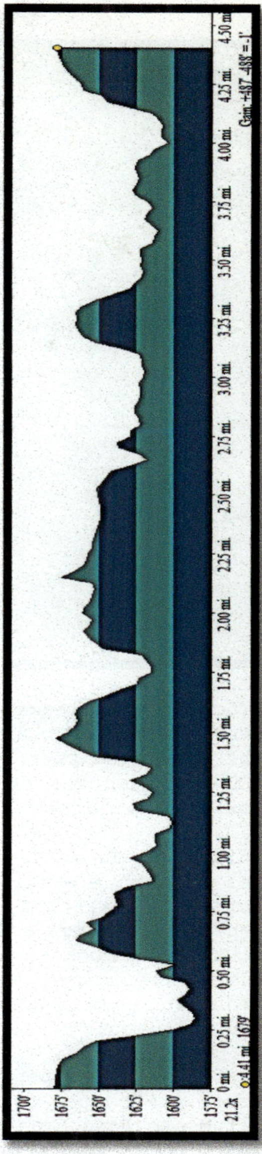

Moose Pond

Quad:

Saranac Lake and Bloomingdale

Distances:

- **Route 3 trailhead to pond-1.5 miles**

Directions to Trailhead:

From the intersection of Routes 3 and 86 in Saranac Lake follow Route 3 north toward Bloomingdale. Go around 4.25 miles and look for a small dirt road that passes closely by a farm house and an electric fence. The dirt road is a few hundred feet long and ends at the Saranac River. The trailhead is at the end of the road and will accommodate about four or five cars tightly.

Trail Conditions:

This trail is undoubtedly used more than one would think. With a much-hidden trailhead it looks to be lost from the public's eyes, at least to one driving through. The tread is very well packed, with no erosion and very little rock and roots to contend with. You can almost keep your eyes up on this out and back afternoon run.

From the trailhead cross the steel grated bridge over the Saranac River. Just across the bridge is the trail register; please sign in to help show the DEC how much the trail is being used and of course for your own safety.

This trail is an old woods road and at no point varies much in elevation. It starts out by circumnavigating a small hill that is seen behind the trail register. The trail then comes back around and stays south of a much larger unnamed mountain, the entire time remaining relatively flat. The forest is a beautiful open landscape with fascinating colors in the fall.

Just shy of the pond you will come to a fork in the trail. Left goes over to the state boat launch site off Moose Pond Road (this fork might not be feasible for a run, as it gets little use and tends to be grown in). The right drops a little in elevation but quickly regains a moderate to flat gradient. This fork will take you to a small rocky outcrop on Moose Pond with stellar views.

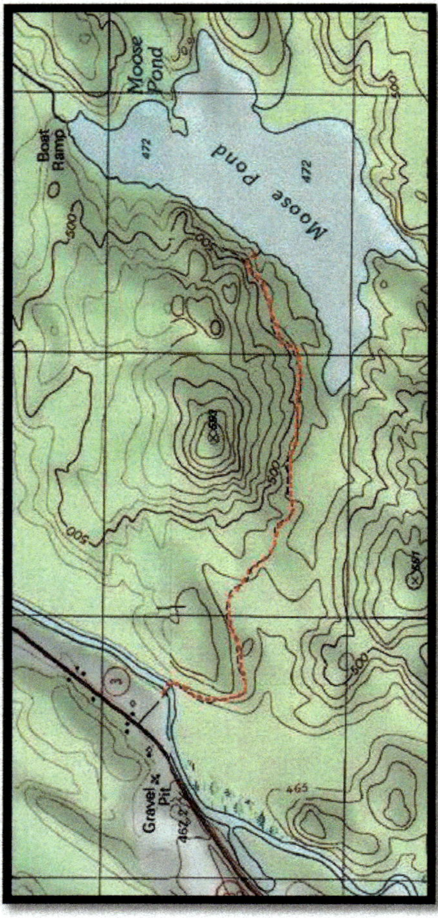
Moose Pond
Moose Pond
Boat Ramp
472
472
500
Gravel Pit
465

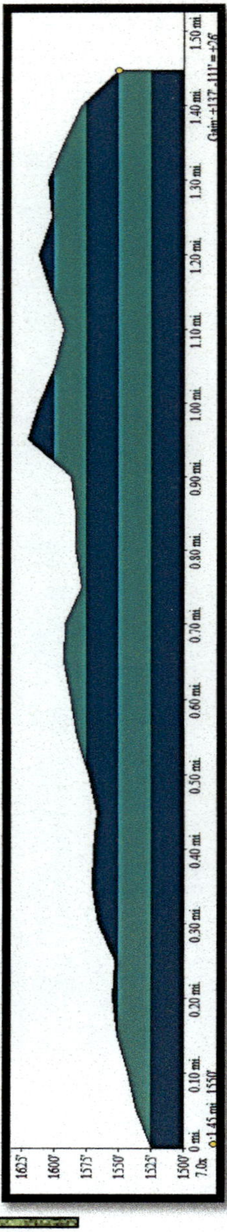
1625'
1600'
1575'
1550'
1525'
1500'
0 mi.
0.10 mi.
0.20 mi.
0.30 mi.
0.40 mi.
0.50 mi.
0.60 mi.
0.70 mi.
0.80 mi.
0.90 mi.
1.00 mi.
1.10 mi.
1.20 mi.
1.30 mi.
1.40 mi.
1.50 mi.

Bloomingdale Bog

Quad:

Bloomingdale

Distances:

- **Trailhead on Route 192 to start of bog-0.75 miles**
- **Through run to Route 86-3.8 miles**

Directions to Trailhead:

Bloomingdale Entrance

Follow Route 192 north from the four corners in Bloomingdale. After almost 2.0 miles you will see parking for an old railroad grade trail on both sides of the road. This is a popular trail for running, mountain biking, skiing and walking the dog. Follow the grade on the south side of the road.

Route 86 Entrance

From the intersection of Routes 3 and 86 in Saranac Lake follow Route 86 toward Paul Smiths. After around 3.5 miles there is a dirt road on the right follow this to the parking area for the bog. The run through is just under four miles.

Trail Conditions:

Seeing as how this is an old railroad grade the conditions you will find are nothing but perfect for running. Feels kind of like an old road of sorts. Just beware of the ravenous gray jays.

From the trailhead parking, begin following the flat and straight grade of an old railroad (flat and straight are relative of course). The railroad ties have been removed for the convenience of runners and mountain bikers.

The run starts through a wooded area but soon reaches the first signs of a bog at 0.75 miles. In another 0.1 miles you will cross a small bridge with nice views in both directions. Towbridge Brook passes beneath you. Continuing on you will see several different areas of the bog, and being one of the biggest bogs in the Adirondack Park there is plenty to see.

You have the option to turn around at any time or continue a through run out to Route 86, north of Saranac Lake. This trail, while very uneventful during most seasons, is a wonderful destination for a fall visit.

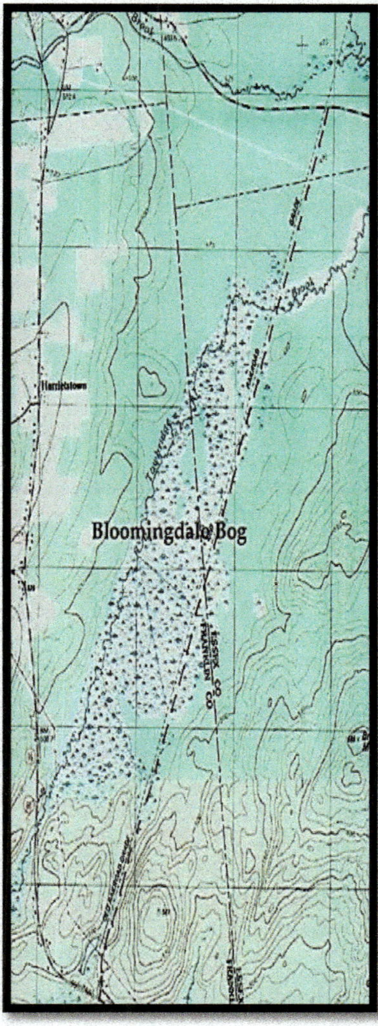
Bloomingdale Bog
Harrietstown

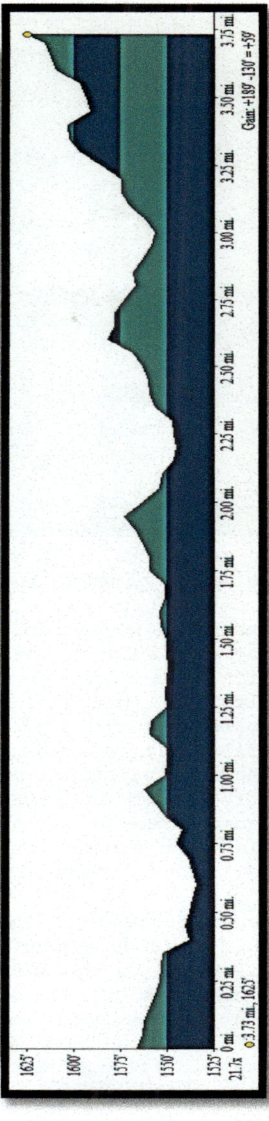
1625'
1600'
1575'
1550'
1525'
21.7x
0 mi.
0.25 mi.
0.50 mi.
0.75 mi.
1.00 mi.
1.25 mi.
1.50 mi.
1.75 mi.
2.00 mi.
2.25 mi.
2.50 mi.
2.75 mi.
3.00 mi.
3.25 mi.
3.50 mi.
3.75 mi.
3.73 mi, 1625'
Gain: +189' -130' = +59'

Rattlesnake Mountain

Quad:

Willsboro Bay

Distances:

Route 22 trailhead to summit-1.4 miles

Directions to Trailhead:

From exit 33 off I-87 head east to Route 9. Cross over Route 9 and follow Route 22 toward Willsboro. Continue for around 4.8 miles to Long Pond. Look for a small cabin with "Bears Den" on it. The unmarked trail is directly across the road. The parking area has room for three or four cars and as we mentioned is not marked.

Trail Conditions:

Trail follows an old woods road which at first is in excellent condition. Trail is rocky with heavy litter down low and steep, rocky terrain as you approach the top.

The old woods road enters the woods at the back of the small parking area. This trail is over private property but public easement has been set into place. The woods road starts out in excellent shape, wide and smooth. There is a slight downhill grade which soon switches over to a short uphill run. A half mile into the run logging will become quite apparent in the area. With the logging the route is still easy to follow but becomes littered with branches and pieces of wood. Among the litter is the introduction of rocks along a wash. Throughout the logged area the route continues a steady uphill climb and becomes steeper as you approach the foot trail for the summit.

The foot trail is found just below the top of the pass; a large wooden sign marks the location. From this point to the summit expect a steep ascent where running has turned to more of a fast hike. The terrain becomes very rocky with small cliffs and decent-sized boulders. Once upon the ridge there are a couple different herd paths, the one on the right leads along the top of the ridge with endless different views of Lake Champlain and Vermont's Green

Mountains. The summit is loaded with cherry trees and junipers; blueberries and wildflowers also cover a large portion of the ridge. The end of the ridge marks the summit as well as several rock cairns.

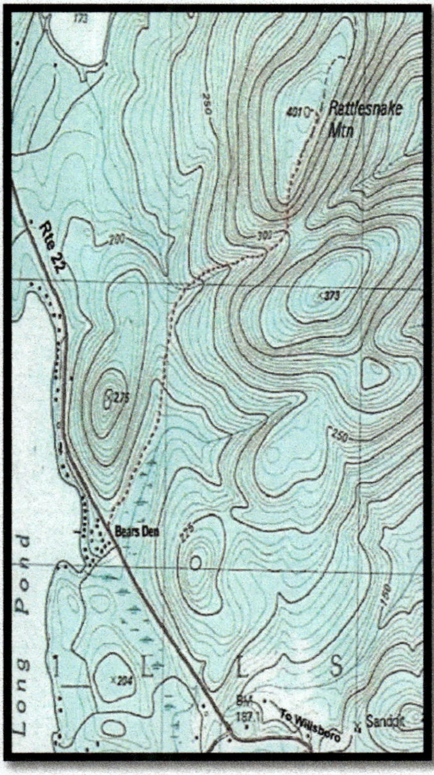

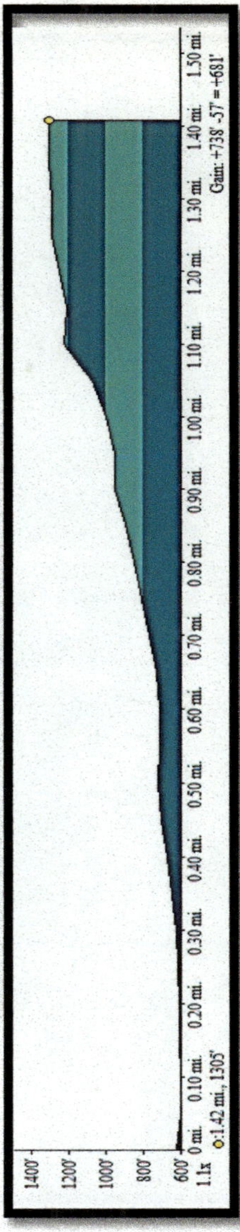

Taylor Pond Loop

Quad:

Wilmington

Distances:

- Forestdale Road to campground intersection-0.3 miles
- To Taylor Pond Lean-to #3-2.2 miles
- To beaver dam at west end of Taylor Pond-1.7 miles
- To Taylor Pond Lean-to #1-0.9 miles
- To Taylor Pond Lean-to #2-1.4 miles
- To Taylor Pond State Campground-3.1 miles
- To intersection with Forestdale Road Trail-0.1 miles
- To Forestdale Trailhead-0.5 miles

Total distance 10.2 miles, loop

Directions to Trailhead:

From the four corners in the town of Wilmington head west along the Whiteface Mountain Road for 2.9 miles to Franklin Falls Road on the right. Follow Franklin Falls Road for 3.0 miles to Roseman Lane on the right. Follow Roseman Lane for 0.85 miles to its end. Take a right onto Plank Road (which changes to Forestdale Road at the town line) for 6.7 miles to Nelson Road. Take a sharp left and follow for 0.8 miles to the trailhead on the left. There is room enough for two to three cars, packed like sardines, or you can park on the roadside.

Trail Conditions:

Conditions on this longer loop vary from point to point. Much of the tread is soft and unobstructed. However his trail seems to be one of the last ones worked on when trail maintenance is concerned.

There are several wet areas of concern and a beaver population that might require practice with walking on water.

This trail is designated as a snowmobile trail and gets little use from runners or hikers. The trail starts off from a small trailhead.

You will start this long loop following an old road, which is wide enough to pair up side by side. Over mostly flat terrain you will quickly be to the intersection with the Taylor Pond State Campground; continue left. From the trail you can see the pond through the trees but never really approach its shores. At 2.6 miles you will come to a lean-to on the shore of Taylor Pond. This lean-to sits in an amazing position, giving all who visit an excellent opportunity to relax as well as amazing scenery of the mountain over the north shore.

From the lean-to you again will be welcomed with various conditions. Downed trees along this loop seem to always slow progress a bit, but as a maintained trail these should frequently be removed. It's a fast and easy run to the west end of the pond where an inlet awaits your crossing. This inlet is somewhat of a crossing issue at times, especially if the weather has been unfriendly. Beavers have made this area a nightmare during wet months.

Crossing the inlet can kind of be a route-finding expedition. There are several different high points that are linked by either a log or small jump from Point A to Point B. Again, this should only pose a small issue if the stream itself is not overflowing and your balance and leaping skills are up to par; the ground and marshy areas around the stream should be of no concern.

Once across the inlet you will find yourself running near the western bay of the pond and then around yet another point of Taylor Pond. This section tends to be a little rougher and rockier underfoot. A little more care for footing is needed. Another lean-to is set off the trail on the west side of the pond. A faint herd path leads to it. As you round the west side of the pond to the north side you will be led away from the water to run on higher ground. You will cross several intersections as you run the north side; signs point you in the right direction.

A junction with a path to a third lean-to is approached roughly 1.45 miles from the second lean-to on the west side. Shortly after the lean-to there is an intersection to a trail that passes over the shoulder of Douglas Mountain and eventually reaches Silver Lake. Continue right as the trail leads you

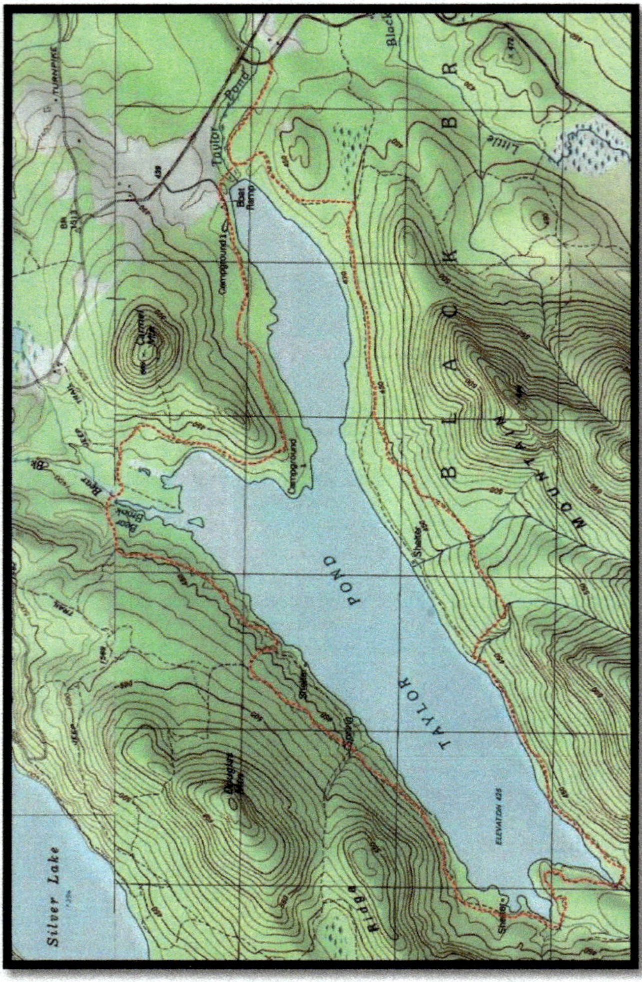

around the northern bay of Taylor Pond and over Bear Brook. Once around the bay you will head south around the shoulder of Carmel Mountain and again flat back to the Taylor Pond State Campground.

You will have to run the dirt road of the state campground back to the caretaker's cabin to reach the cutover trail back to Forestdale Road. The cutover trail is a simple 0.2 miles, and will connect you back to the trail 0.4 miles from your car.

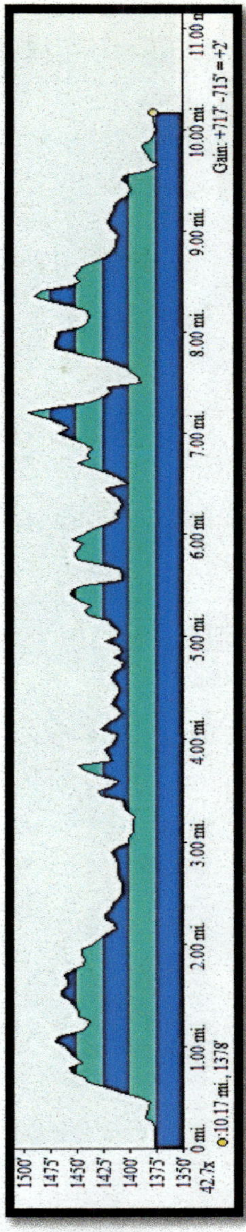

Western
Adirondacks

Ranger School Trails

The Ranger School in Wanakena is part of the State University of New York, Environmental Science and Forestry. This is a small college of 40-60 students pursuing degrees in Forest Technology, Surveying or Environmental and Natural Resources Conservation. The Ranger School is our Alma Mater and Forest Technology and our degrees.

The trails located on the Ranger School Property are part of the James F. Dubuar memorial forest and are open to the public for recreation. There are many trails located on the property that are open for exploring but below you will see descriptions for two routes that we have selected. Both trails start and end from the same location described below.

Quad:

Newton Falls

Directions to Trailhead:

From the intersection of Route 3 and CR-61 (Wanakena Road) follow Route 3 east for 0.7 miles to a gated road on the right. This is the start of the route.

Distances:

- Route 3 to first intersection-0.2 miles
- To second intersection-0.5 miles
- To Cathedral Rock fire tower-0.65 miles

Total distance 1.35 miles, one way

Trail Conditions:

This is a very dry run with solid footing, along a well-used woods road.

From Route 3 you will find yourself on a dirt woods road, referred to as the Hayes Brook Road, which will cross over Hayes Brook. Shortly beyond here you will be at an intersection. Follow here to the right along a nearly flat course. In another half-mile or so you will come to a second intersection, which is part of what is called the "Big Fish." At this intersection take a sharp left onto Cathedral Rock

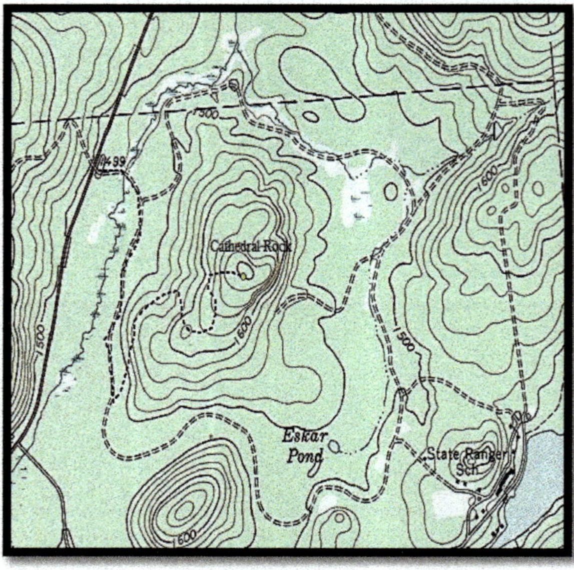

Road and approach your first hill. After 0.4 miles of climbing you will come to what is referred to as Tower Road on the left.

Tower Road is much steeper and more of a workout than what you previously were on. The fire tower will come quickly into view as you approach the end. The Cathedral Rock fire tower is now at home on the Ranger School property, but that wasn't always the case. It used to reside on Tooley Pond Mountain just northeast of this location. On a large boulder just below the fire tower you will see a plaque in honor of the New York State forest rangers. Be sure to take time to visit the fire tower's cab and soak in the excellent views.

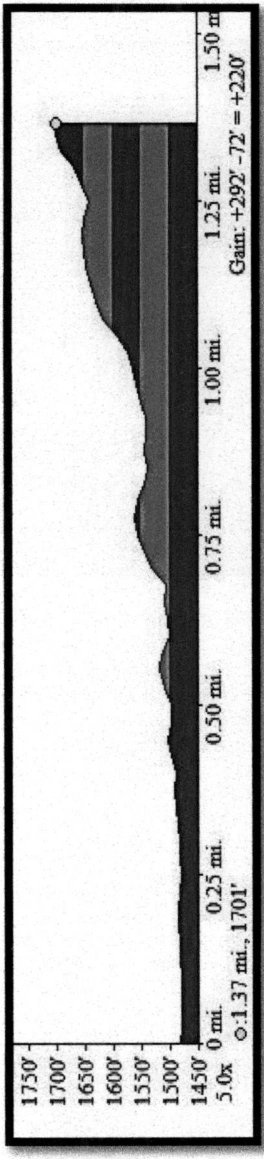

Big Fish Loop

Distances:

- Route 3 to first intersection-0.15 miles
- To second intersection-0.45 miles
- To Eskar Pond Trail-0.9 miles
- To third intersection-0.25 miles
- To fourth intersection-0.1 miles
- To fifth intersection-0.3 miles
- To Cathedral Rock Trail-0.3 miles
- To Tower Road-0.4 miles
- Back to second intersection-0.4 miles
- Back to Route 3-0.7 miles

Total distance 3.95 miles, loop

Trail Conditions:

Dry underfoot with even footing along a heavily used woods road.

From Route 3 you will find yourself on a dirt woods road, referred to as the Hayes Brook Road, which will cross over Hayes Brook. Shortly beyond here you will be at an intersection. Follow here to the right along a nearly flat course. In another half-mile or so you will come to a second intersection, which is part of what is called the "Big Fish." At this intersection take a right, which is more of a straight course than an actual turn; this portion of the route is referred to as Toboggan Hill Road.

Toboggan Hill Road is also a secondary dirt road whose course follows the low-lying lands on the Ranger School property. Toboggan Hill will be to your right as you pass through the area. In just under a mile you will pass by the Eskar Pond Trial on your left - this trail can be quite obscure in winter, if not looking for it. Briefly past this point is what is referred to as the Arboretum Road and leads to the parking area at the Ranger School; continue straight.

You are now on the Reservoir Road that leads past two additional side roads and a water reservoir for the Ranger School. The next left will be the road you want to follow - Cathedral Rock Road. Cathedral Rock Road is the section of the route that has the most elevation change along this loop. After 0.3 miles you will be at the Cathedral Rock foot trail, which comes in on the right. After another 0.4 miles will be the option for a side trip to an Adirondack fire tower. This is referred to as Tower Road and leads steeply up to the Cathedral Rock fire tower. The Cathedral Rock fire tower was moved here, piece by piece and reassembled by Ranger School Students. A plaque in honor of the New York State Forest Rangers sits just below the fire tower on a sizable erratic.

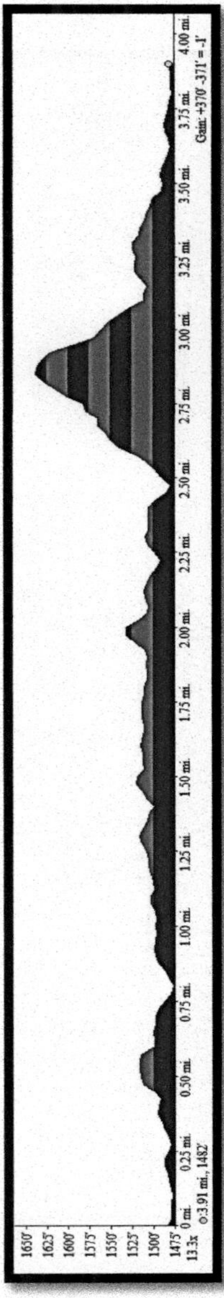

From the intersection with Tower Road you will continue somewhat flat for a short distance before you begin a nice descent back down to Toboggan Road. You will need to make a sharp right at the intersection to head back to your vehicle on Route 3.

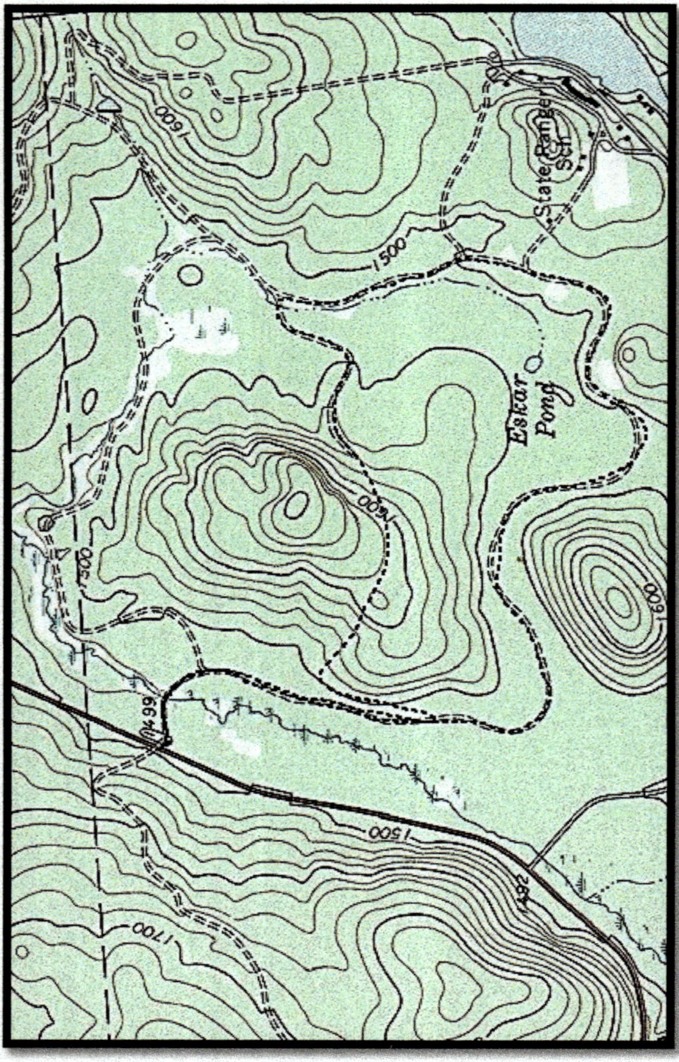
Eskar Pond
State Ranger Stn
1500
1600
1700
1499
1492

Peavine Swamp Loop

Quad:

Cranberry Lake and Newton Falls

Distances:

- Route 3 to first intersection-0.4 miles
- To second intersection-0.8 miles
- To third intersection-0.4 miles
- To fourth intersection-1.5 miles
- To fifth intersection 0.9 miles
- To Lean-to on Cranberry Lake and back to intersection-0.4 miles
- Back to third intersection-2.2 miles
- Back to second intersection 0.3 miles
- Back to first intersection using the Balanced Rock Loop-2.3 miles
- Back to Route 3-0.4 miles

Total distance 9.6 miles, loop

Directions to Trailhead:

From the intersection of Route 3 and CR-61 (Wanakena Road) follow Route 3 east for 4.9 miles to the Peavine Swamp ski trail on the right.

Trail Conditions:

Conditions vary but are mostly very soft underfoot. Wet sections do occur during rainy seasons. This is a low impact trail, that gets very little runner and hiker use.

From the trailhead you will begin a run along a section of short rolling hills as you quickly come to the first intersection. Passing by here you continue in the same fashion and pass by a second intersection of another loop.

The third intersection is a very short distance away; you will return to all three of these intersections on your return trip. Past the third intersection you will have a short distance of flatter terrain before the rolling hills get a little more serious. The fourth intersection you will be passing is 1.5 miles away, also on the left.

Not far past the fourth intersection will be an access trail on the right that leads to the SUNY ESF Ranger School. Unless you want to learn how to identify trees by their buds and the scientific name for chicken of the woods avoid this access trail. In about 0.2 miles you will be at a spur trail that leads to Cranberry Lake and an amazing lean-to located right above the shore.

After you visit the lean-to, if you decide to do so, you need to backtrack to the end of the spur trail and hang a right along the upper portion of the Peavine Swamp Trail. So, I say upper portion - well, that's because after you run along for a while at just above the level of the lake you will be on a steady uphill climb for quite some time. The uphill in parts feels fairly rigorous and as well it should; you will climb almost 300 feet in elevation, which is much more elevation change than before. Along this section you will pass by an intersection which is the other end of the fourth intersection you passed on the way in - wow, that was a mouth full. Then you begin a slow descent back to the trail you came in on at the third intersection.

Once you reach the third intersection, follow the trail to the right for 0.3 miles to the next intersection and hang a right; this was the second intersection you passed on the way in. This would be a perfect time to bail out back to your car if you are feeling overwhelmed or if time is not on your side. It's just over a mile back to the trailhead if you go straight or almost 3.0 miles if you do the last loop.

If you decide to do the last loop you will need to climb again, but this time there is less than 200' in elevation gain to the height of land. There are a few rolling hills over some hogbacks after this and you can look forward to a nice ending with a decent little downhill back to the trail you came in on. This time you pop out at the first intersection, 0.4 miles from the trailhead - to your right.

STATE FOREST PRESERVE
Ridge
Gravel Pit
Peavine Creek
STATE FOREST
PRESERVE
FLOW
Flatiron Point
Shelter
Janacks

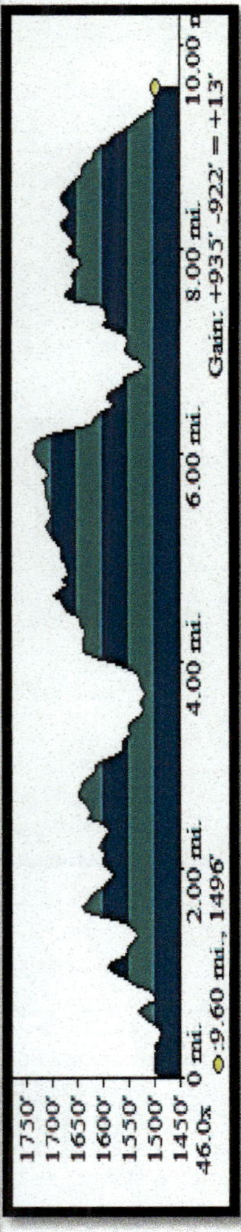
1750'
1700'
1650'
1600'
1550'
1500'
1450'
46.0x
0 mi.
2.00 mi.
4.00 mi.
6.00 mi.
8.00 mi.
10.00 mi
9.60 mi., 1496'
Gain: +935' -922' = +13'

High Falls Loop

Quad:

Newton Falls and Five Ponds

Distances:

- **Trailhead to High Rock-3.5 miles**
- **To Five Ponds Trail-3.75 miles**
- **To High Falls Spur Trail-1.0 miles**
- **To High Falls and back-1.3 miles**
- **To Cat Mountain Trail-2.3 miles**
- **To Janacks Landing-0.8 miles**
- **To South Shore Road-2.8 miles**
- **Back to starting trailhead-0.5 miles**

Total distance 15.95 miles, loop

Directions to Trailhead:

From the intersection of Route 3 and CR. 16 (Wanakena Road) follow CR.16 for 0.75 miles to Main Street on the right; follow Main Street. Continue for 0.5 miles to the trailhead on the right at the corner of South Shore Road. The trailhead has a DEC trail sign with parking in a field.

Trail Conditions:

This loop is not only long, but can be very wet with settled water up to a foot deep in spots. Be prepared to be wet and consider carrying dry socks or use non-waterproof running shoes.

Side note

Portions of this trail can be very wet from increased beaver activity.

A large portion of this loop follows an old woods road, before turning into a trail, before turning into an old railroad grade, before turning into a county route road. Well, you get the drift; here's a little more detail.

Start off along the old woods road on a very low-key and flat course. During the initial section you will cross what is named Skate Creek and then a secondary tributary of Skate Creek shortly beyond. The route follows the truck trail for the entire route to the falls. While this new route is not as exciting of a run as the old trail, it is still very pleasing to the eye and the mind.

At 3.5 miles you will be to a very short spur trail that leads to High Rock. High Rock is a large erratic outcropping that overlooks the Oswegatchie River. But what an amazing location this is. There are expansive views out over the oxbows of the river as well as a perfect place to take a break - if the notion persuades you.

Continuing on you will find yourself running along a very level trail, returning to the riverside for some brief views of the low-level rapids. At 7.2 miles from the trailhead you will come to a bridge over the Oswegatchie River and the Five Ponds Trails to the right. Continue straight for another 1.0 miles into what is called "The Plains" to the spur trail for High Falls.

Be sure to visit High Falls, it is only 1.3 miles round trip and well worth the little added effort - after all, that's what this loop is all about. Located off this spur trail is a rather impressive piece of history - if you are interested in logging in the area you will see exactly what we are talking about.

Once back at the intersection you will make a right and continue on through your 16-mile day loop. This next section of trail flows along some rolling hills at the base of Threemile Mountain for what will seem like an eternity; actually about three miles to be more exact - odd coincidence? After 3.2 miles you will come to the Cat Mountain Trail intersection on the right also known as the Cowhorn Junction Trail - continue left.

From here you will begin a slow descent through a ravine and in less than a mile, come to another intersection. This intersection is a short spur trail to the Janacks Landing lean-to. Follow left again to finish the loop.

Following left you will run around the southern end of Dead Creek Flow, which is essentially an arm or bay of Cranberry Lake. As the trail follows the flow and makes its way back toward Wanakena you will find yourself on a trail that was built over a railroad grade. This section is very level and in wet conditions certain areas can be flooded.

You will end this trail on South Shore Road and it is a 0.5 miles walk/run along a paved road back to the start of the loop.

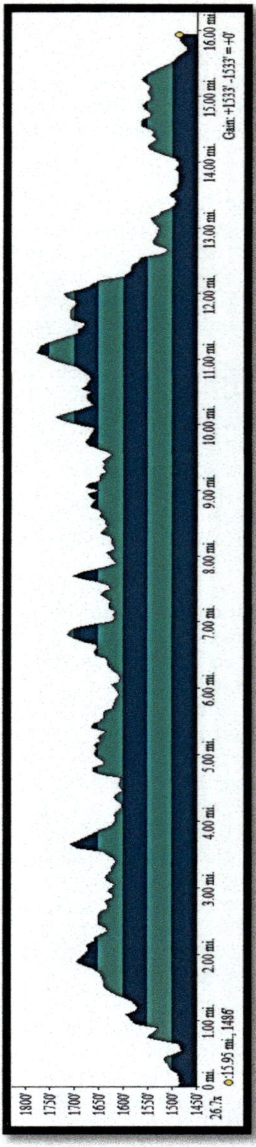

FOREST PRESERVE
FINE
CLIFTON
RONDACK STATE PARK
DEAD CREEK FLOW

Cascade Lake Loop

Quad:

Eagle Bay

Distances:

- **Big Moose Road to Loop Intersection-0.85 miles**
- **To inlet crossing on west side-1.8 miles**
- **To Link Trail-1.55 miles**
- **Back to Loop intersection-0.3 miles**
- **Back to Trailhead-0.85 miles**

Total distance 5.35 miles, loop

Directions to Trailhead:

From the intersection of Route 28 and Big Moose Road in the Hamlet of Eagle Bay, follow Big Moose Road. Continue for 1.2 miles to the Cascade Lake Trailhead on the right.

Trail Conditions:

More of the trail is wet than not. The trail on the south side of Cascade Lake is much dryer than the north side trail. There is also a nice waterfall for the runner's viewing pleasure.

Side note

This trail has the tendency to be very wet around the eastern side of the lake. Be prepared for less than friendly conditions.

This route is described in a counter-clockwise direction - because sometimes it's just more fun to go against the grain.

From the trailhead you will enter the woods and follow along Big Moose Road for a bit before it turns left and comes to a somewhat steep downhill. At the base of the hill is an old woods road intersection. Right leads to the old trailhead and left is the direction you want. Continue to follow this wide course on a slight uphill grade to a shoulder of Cascade Mountain. Shortly after you crest the shoulder you will descend to the intersection for the loop at around 1.0 miles. This woods road section had a rather modest scattering of rocks loose stones, but is relatively dry. From here, head right on a slight uphill to start the counter-clockwise loop.

At the top of the small hill the course flattens out as Cascade Lake sits well below you. As small rolling hills work your legs you will be running through an area where wet conditions can easily exist in the wet months of spring. You will then descend slightly to the shore of Cascade Lake and follow along the main inlet of the lake, which looks a bit like a wetland.

As you come to the crossing of the inlet be sure to watch for wild-life - not because you might have a collision but it might be kind of cool to see something in its natural habitat. Runners don't usually get that luxury because we are moving so fast and usually making quite a bit more noise than hikers.

Once at the inlet, if you head upstream slightly you will come to the cascade from which the lake gets its name. The crossing of the wetland at times is a chore and wet areas are inevitable Start to look for a re-routed trail in this section. It has been flagged to bring visitors up on the side hill to avoid the muck. The trail remains wet even after the re-route, but in many cases it can be skirted. If you can't avoid it or don't want to, suck it up and run through it, it's not that deep.

The trail will dry as you sweep through a very quiet hardwood forest with the steep slopes of an unnamed ridge to your right. You will run through some open fields and then through history - so to speak. You will notice remnants of an old camp on both sides of the trail. Cascade Lake remains fairly close to your left. At around 4.25 miles you will come to an intersection with the Link Trail on your right, which will bring you to Queer Lake as well as many other destinations in the Pigeon Lake Wilderness Area.

At 0.15 miles past this intersection is the crossing of Cascade Lake's major outlet, there's a bridge here - thank God. In another 0.2 miles you will come to a slight uphill to the intersection for the loop. This remaining distance is the same 0.85 miles you ran in on and will bring you back to the trailhead, exactly the place where you started - we hope.

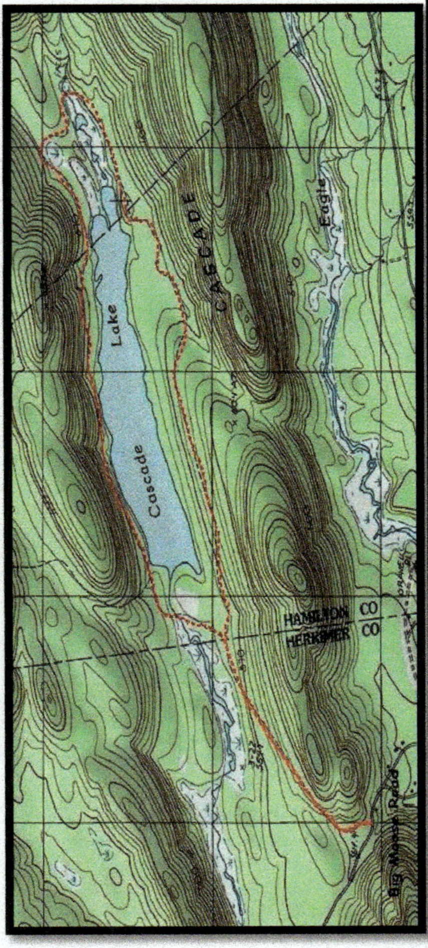
Lake
Cascade
CASCADE
Eagle
HAMILTON CO
HERKIMER CO
Big Moose Road

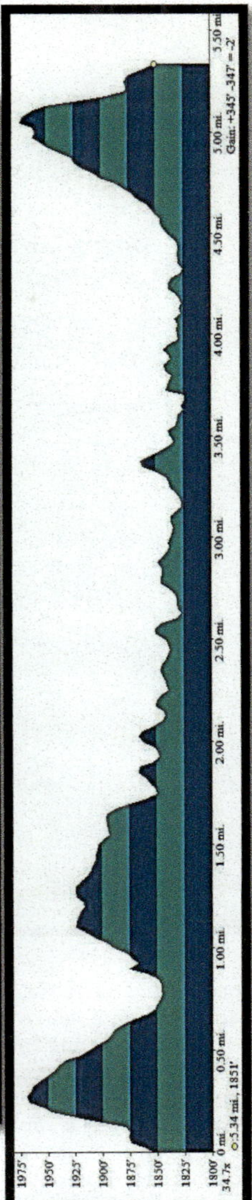
1975'
1950'
1925'
1900'
1875'
1850'
1825'
1800'
34.7x
0 mi.
0.50 mi.
1.00 mi.
1.50 mi.
2.00 mi.
2.50 mi.
3.00 mi.
3.50 mi.
4.00 mi.
4.50 mi.
5.00 mi.
5.50 mi.
○:5.34 mi, 1851'
Gain: +345' -347' = -2'

Quad:

Eagle Bay

Distances:

- Higby Road Trailhead to Hermitage Trail-0.55 miles
- To the Queer Lake Trail-1.25 miles
- To the Chain Ponds Trail-0.4 miles
- To the Mays Pond Trail-0.3 miles
- To the Chub Pond Trail-2.3 miles
- Back to the Constable Pond Trail-0.3 miles
- To the North end of the Mays Pond Trail-1.2 miles
- Back to the Hermitage Trail-0.8 miles
- Back to the trailhead-0.55 miles

Total distance 7.65 miles, loop

Directions to Trailhead:

From the intersection of Route 28 and Big Moose Road in the Hamlet of Eagle Bay, follow Big Moose Road. Continue for 3.75 miles to Higby Road on the right. Continue here for 1.3 miles to the Heritage Trail and Judson Road on the right. Judson Road was not signed last time we were there - it is a gated dirt road from which the trail starts.

Trail Conditions:

There are few sections of wet terrain but overall the conditions are quite good for running.

From the official trailhead which follows Judson Road for 0.2 miles; you will be running on a hard-packed dirt surface. After which you will come to the DEC trail register and begin a truer trail run. Running along Constable Brook now for a short distance you will soon come to the Hermitage Trail on your right - make this right to run in a counter-clockwise direction for this loop. Following south you will climb slightly to the side of an unnamed peak high above Mays Pond and the marshy area surrounding it. You will then descend to an area of rolling hills before you come to a wet area at 1.1 miles from the Constable Pond Trail. In a little over 0.1 miles from this crossing is the intersection with the Queer Lake Trail. The Hermitage Trail has now officially ended.

Following left or south - whichever you prefer - along the Queer Lake Trail, you will make a kind of odd roundabout dogleg. The trail dips you south further and then sharply north to go around the very southern tip of private land. In doing this, you will have to push yourself up a ridge and coast yourself back down. After a short wet area you will find yourself at yet another trail intersection - this one is the Chain Ponds Trail. Remain on the Queer Lake Trail.

In only a couple hundred feet you will be near what is considered a bay of Queer Lake - which at most seems more like a separate pond. Be it as it may, it's water and it's very nice to look at. As you run along the bay you will begin to climb and eventually come to the south end of the Mays Brook Trail. From this intersection, which is at the height of land along this circuit, you begin a somewhat steep descent back to the shore of Queer Lake. Climbing again you will make your way through the contours of an unmanned little bump and run your way around the eastern side of it.

As you make the sweeping turns you will soon be able to see Chub Pond to your right and pass by a very short spur trail that leads to its shore. In 0.3 miles you will be back to the Constable Pond Trail and the Queer Lake Trail ends. Following left again in a short time you will be able to see Constable Pond to your right - there are short herd-paths that will bring you to the shore. This trail follows Constable Brook and at several times crosses the flow. Other small, wet sections are usually encountered and the wetter the previous days are, the worse the wet sections will become. The crossings are generally not an issue however, but high water as you know changes course. On the run back to the trailhead you will pass the north end of the Mays Pond Trail on your left and the Hermitage Trail, also on your left. Aside from your typical rolling hills this section of trail is very moderate.

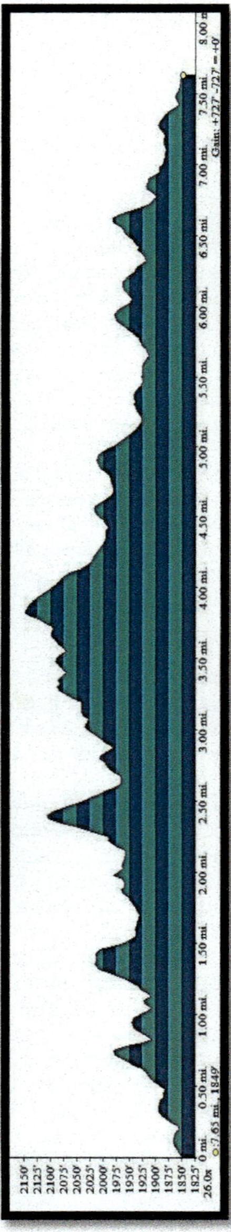

Sis, Bubb and Moss Pond Loop

Quad:

Eagle Bay

Distances:

- **Route 28 to Bubb Lake-0.45 miles**
- **To Sis Lake-0.35 miles**
- **To Moss Pond Trail-1.3 miles**
- **Around Moss Lake-2.4 miles**
- **Back to trailhead-2.2 miles**

Total distance 6.7 miles, loop

Directions to Trailhead:

This trailhead is located off Route 28, roughly 1.5 miles outside the Town of Eagle Bay. The trailhead is on the right and can hold a decent number of cars.

Trail Conditions:

There's not much to talk about when it comes to this loop. The trails are in nice condition - we don't recall a speck of mud on the trail that wasn't easily avoidable and it was raining the last time we were there. It's a little rocky on the initial uphill from the trailhead, but heck, if that's the only drawback.

From the trailhead you will immediately start an uphill run over a somewhat bumpy course. You will gain a couple hundred feet in elevation to the high point before dropping down slightly near the shore line of Bubb Lake. The trail continues, then hooks left slightly and follows a side hill and then crosses an inlet to Bubb Lake and slowly moves its way back around north to the outlet of Sis Lake, which just so happens to be an inlet of Bubb Lake. The trail doesn't give great views of Sis Lake, so a little exploring might be warranted for a better view.

The trail then moves along to the north edge of Bubb Lake and follows the shoreline somewhat closely at times. Once you cross the outlet of Bubb Lake at the north end the trail starts to head slightly downhill to the Moss Lake trail.

The Moss Lake trail is a simple trail built nicely for running, but for great lake vistas, it falls a little short. You will get to see the lake on a few different accounts but the trail veers to and from, and it seemed more often to be from. Moss Lake does have a little history and it can be read about at the park off Big Moose Road. You will be passing through it on the run. The Moss Lake Trail goes all the way around the lake in about 2.4 miles. Once around start to look for the Sis and Bubb Trail and follow this route back to the parking on Route 28.

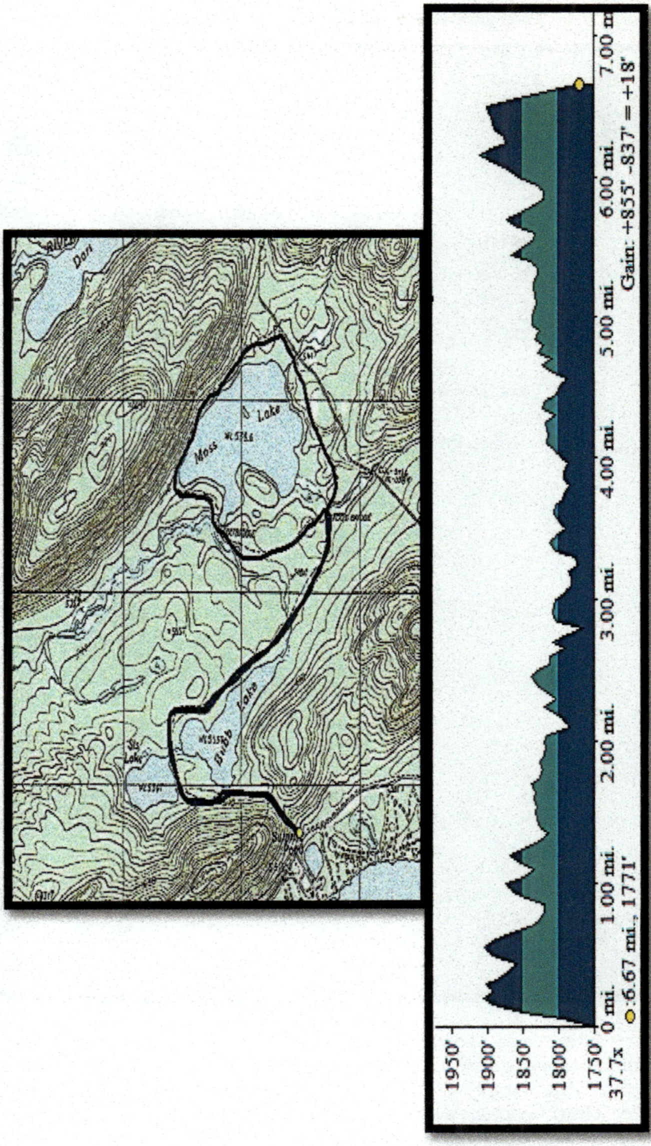
Moss Lake
Bubb Lake
Sis Lake
1950'
1900'
1850'
1800'
1750'
37.7x
0 mi.
1.00 mi.
2.00 mi.
3.00 mi.
4.00 mi.
5.00 mi.
6.00 mi.
7.00 mi.
:6.67 mi., 1771'
Gain: +855' -837' = +18'

Nelson Lake Loop

Quad:

Thendara

Distances:

- **Trailhead to railroad tracks-0.4 miles**
- **To bridge over the Moose River-0.3**
- **To Nelson Lake intersection-0.3 miles**
- **To Nick Lakes Intersection-3.8 miles**
- **To Tooker Mountain Intersection 2.8 miles**
- **Back to Nelson Lake Intersection-1.5 miles**
- **Back to trailhead-1.05 miles**

Total distance 10.15 miles, loop

Directions to Trailhead:

Head south along Route 28 from the town of Old Forge; after you go through the underpass of the railroad continue for 5.75 miles or so to the Nelson Lake Trailhead on the left. This trailhead is marked with a brown DEC sign. The trailhead is 0.1 miles down this dirt road; ending at a gate.

Trail Conditions:

This extended outing has one downfall; there is no bridge over the Moose River so you will have to utilize a railroad and a herd path to get back to the trail. This isn't really a big deal unless of course you have a train phobia; if that is the case this might not be the run for you, trains do run these tracks. The loop does involve the use of the railroad tracks and the herd path - twice.

The tread is in nice shape. Much of the route is an old road which has good drainage and a wide track to run in pairs if you'd like.

From the gate follow the old woods road as it descends away from the trailhead and toward the Moose River. The descent is gentle but ends up being much more than you realize. After a quick 0.4 miles you will be at the railroad tracks.

On some maps they show this road crossing the railroad tracks, which it does, but also crossing the river, which it doesn't. At one time, there was a bridge here - it has either been dismantled or has unwillingly moved down stream by rushing water. Your only option is a short run along the railroad tracks. Run north along the tracks for 0.3 miles to a bridge over the Moose River, and cross the bridge.

Once across the river you can follow along the shore; this will lead you back to the trail. A herd path has developed here. This herd path, while very narrow, doesn't really aide travel much as the forest is open and the route is quite obvious. You will pass by some very scenic waterfalls and rapids along this short herd path.

Now that you are back on the trail, you should be at or near the Nelson Lake Intersection. Either way you should follow the trail left. The trail at this point is a snowmobile trail and quite wide.

Following this wide path you will encounter numerous small, mellow, rolling hills and mini hogbacks. The trail goes around the west side of Jones Mountain;

the mountain's steep slopes will be apparent. As you run around the west side and start to loop to the north you will notice a river to your left. This is the Middle Branch of the Moose River. The trail will follow along the shores for quite some distance. At this point the grade is almost flat and the views of the river are amazing. The trail eventually starts to lean away from the river and begins a mild ascent up a shoulder of Little Roundtop.

The trail then descends slightly and crosses a marshy area, which should be easy to get through. It's a little soggy at times, but you can cool your feet a little. After a flat half-mile you will be to the Nicks Lake Intersection. Head right at the intersection and start a nice mellow run back toward Nelson Lake. There are some nice short sections of downhill, but there is also a modest climb involved.

The highest point on this trip is just less than 1900 feet in elevation; this is coming up very soon. A small climb will be involved but the payoff is nice. This high point is in a valley between two small, unnamed knolls. From the high point, it's almost all downhill to Nelson Lake.

From the base of the hill at Nelson Lake it's a very straightforward, easy, mostly flat, jaunt around. The trail never really approaches the lake's edge, but the woods are open enough to approach via a little bushwhack if you wish. The trail eventually leads away from the lake and you will quickly find yourself at the Nelson Lake Intersection. Look for the herd path you followed on the way in and follow this route back to the railroad track, then back to the trail, then to a cold beer.

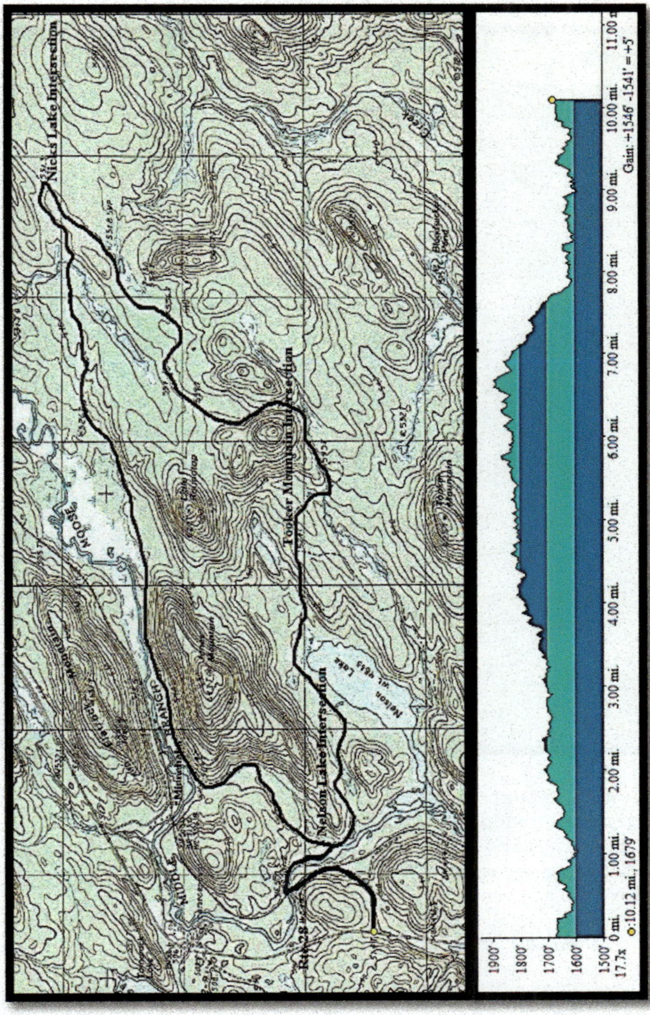
Nicks Lake Intersection
Tooker Mountain Intersection
Nelson Lake Intersection
Rte 28
Nelson Lake
MOOSE
RANGE
MIDDLE
0 mi.
1.00 mi.
2.00 mi.
3.00 mi.
4.00 mi.
5.00 mi.
6.00 mi.
7.00 mi.
8.00 mi.
9.00 mi.
10.00 mi.
11.00 mi
1900'
1800'
1700'
1600'
1500'
17.7x
:10.12 mi.; 1679'
Gain: +1546' -1541' = +5'

Woodhull Mountain

Quad:

McKeever and Honnedaga Lake

Distances:

- **McKeever Road to railroad tracks-0.2 miles**
- **To trailhead-0.3 miles**
- **To Bear Lake Trail intersction-1.1 miles**
- **To Remsen Falls Trail intersection-1.8 miles**
- **To start of foot trail-2.4 miles**
- **To summit of Woodhull Mountain-1.9 miles**

Total distance 7.7 miles, one way

Directions to Trailhead:

From the intersection of Route 28 and McKeever Road follow McKeever road for just over 0.1 miles to a dirt road on the left. There is a house just to the right of the dirt road. If you are winter running, you may need to park here. Under other conditions drive the dirt road, cross over the railroad tracks and park at the trailhead - this is roughly 0.3 miles from McKeever Road.

Trail Conditions:

This route mostly follows an old woods road before finishing on a foot trail. There is a long flat section with a modest ascent at the end.

You will start running along an old woods road with a gentle grade. Heck, a gentle grade would be an added benefit to the woods road. The woods road, aside from a couple small depressions in the way, is a very flat run.

At 0.7 miles you will come to an intersection with the Bear Lake Trail on your right. Continue straight for another 1.9 to a cross roads with Remsen Falls Trail. At 5.8 miles you will finally be to the end of the woods road and base of the foot trail.

After crossing a small stream you will start a moderate ascent of Woodhull Mountain. The trail is a little narrow in areas with a scattering of sharp turns.

At around 7.0 miles from where you parked the terrain gets a little steeper and steadier. Once the steep ends you will be at the firetower on the summit of Woodhull Mountain. The views from the tower are quite nice. If you want to seek out the summit surveyor disk, it's located on the top of the boulder next to the firetower.

I do not seek to follow in the footsteps of the men of old; I seek the things they sought.

~~Basho

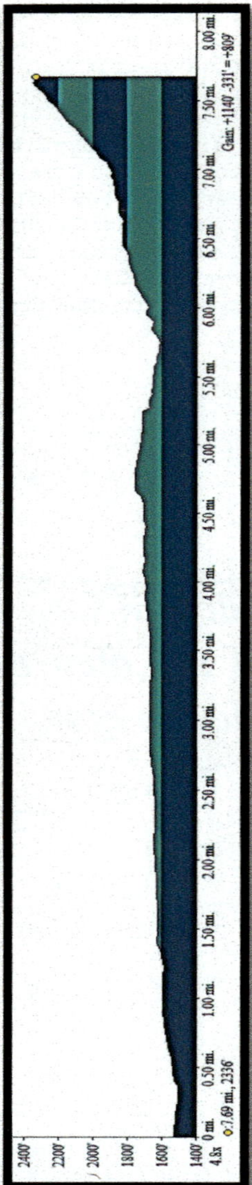
2400'
2200'
2000'
1800'
1600'
1400'
4.8x
0 mi.
0.50 mi.
1.00 mi.
1.50 mi.
2.00 mi.
2.50 mi.
3.00 mi.
3.50 mi.
4.00 mi.
4.50 mi.
5.00 mi.
5.50 mi.
6.00 mi.
6.50 mi.
7.00 mi.
7.50 mi.
8.00 mi.
7.69 mi., 2336'
Gain: +1140' -331' = +809'

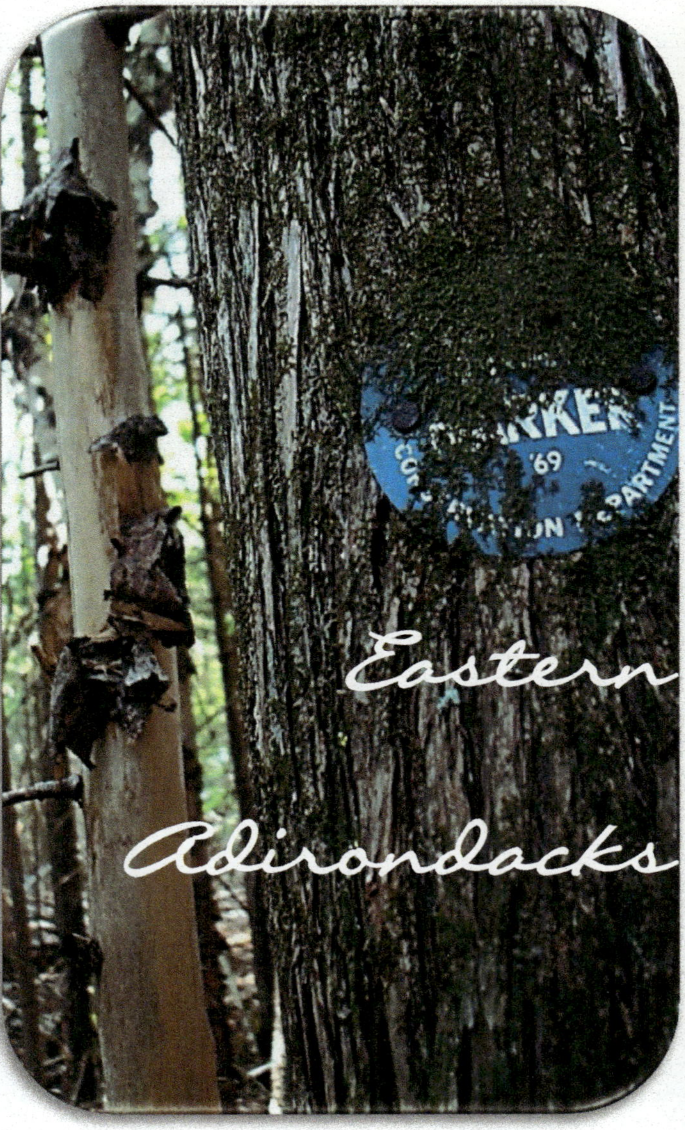
Eastern
Adirondacks
'69

Side note

These are designated Bike Trails and the probability of encountering a mountain biker is pretty high. Be sure to give right-of-way to them.

The Beaver Brook Tract Trail Network and the Wilmington Flume Trail System are two separate mazes of trails. Beaver Brook is around 3.6 miles of trails in total and The Flume Trails are around 8.0 miles in total. You will be discovering both in the following pages.

These trails are a multi-purpose landmark for the DEC. They are open to mountain biking, hiking, trail running, skiing, snowshoeing, and pretty much whatever else you can do without the use of a motor vehicle.

These trails were developed by the International Mountain Bicycling Association and the DEC. This development gives mountain bikers essential trails to use without the conflicts of other outdoor enthusiasts or land management practices. Mountain biking has been kept to a minimum in the Adirondack Park to preserve Wilderness areas - that makes these trails very important to the biking community. So, interaction with mountain bikers should be planned for. Be aware of their high probability of being on the same trail as you, and each party should be willing to respect each other's being there. The only trails closed to mountain bikes in these networks are the Flume Trail and Bear Den Trail, both of which are in the Wilmington Flume Area - all other trails are open to everyone.

Below you can read about the 16 different trails that make up the Flume Trail System and the 6 trails that make up the Beaver Brook Tract. However, only 12 of the Flume trails will be described in detail for running. There are two smaller trails located within the Flume Trail network named Delta Cut-off, they are only a couple hundred feet and provide nothing more than a cut over to a different trail. These can be considered uneventful but highly useful trails. There is also a trail that leaves the Whiteface Upper Connector trail (19) that leads to Bear Den Mountain (12) and is considered a foot trail only, and is not in very good condition for running and at times very hard to navigate. The Flume Knob Trail (11) is considered a hiking trail only and is very steep in sections, not making it a very good trail running destination - but feel free to give it a try. Another trail leaves from the ridge trail (10) and is a continuation of the Marble Mountain Trail (8). This trail eventually connects with the Whiteface Mountain Trail that starts at the Reservoir Road in Wilmington - this upper portion of the trail could be run, but is not included in the map or in the descriptions.

All of the trails described below also have an elevation profile chart which is somewhat accurate, but in very small scale due to shortness of terrain and minor elevation changes over that course. Use the profiles as a guide but not a "be all to end all."

The maps included on the following pages are the network maps developed by the DEC. Then, on the following page after the map, is their trail names with mileage set up in accordance to the numbered trails on the previous map.

The difficulty ratings on the maps are color coded and developed by the DEC and the International Mountain Bicycling Association with mountain biking in mind and not trail running, but you may find that they are of similar usefulness.

The numbers next to the trail name in the following descriptions are in reference to the DEC maps and the trail information page.

The mileages for the trails are for the individual segments of trails and are not a reflection of any combination of trails or loops.

Both of these trail networks are under constant construction and new trails are added each year. Be sure to keep up to date on the progress by visiting the DEC web pages.

Beaver Brook Tract

Quad:

Lake Placid

Directions to Trailhead:

From the intersection of Routes 86 and 431 (Whiteface Memorial Highway), follow Route 86 toward Jay. Continue for just under 2.1 miles to Hardy Road on the right. Follow here for around 2.2 miles to the Wilmington Wild Forest, Beaver Brook Tract Trail System on your left.

Trail Conditions:

Most of the trails can be expected to be dry, but in the spring and after heavy rainfall they can be wet and muddy since the local soils tend to get saturated very fast. Under conditions like these the DEC asks users to avoid these trails. There are a few sections of consistently wet terrain, but they are brief at most; these brief areas are in typically hazardous areas and are a cause for caution.

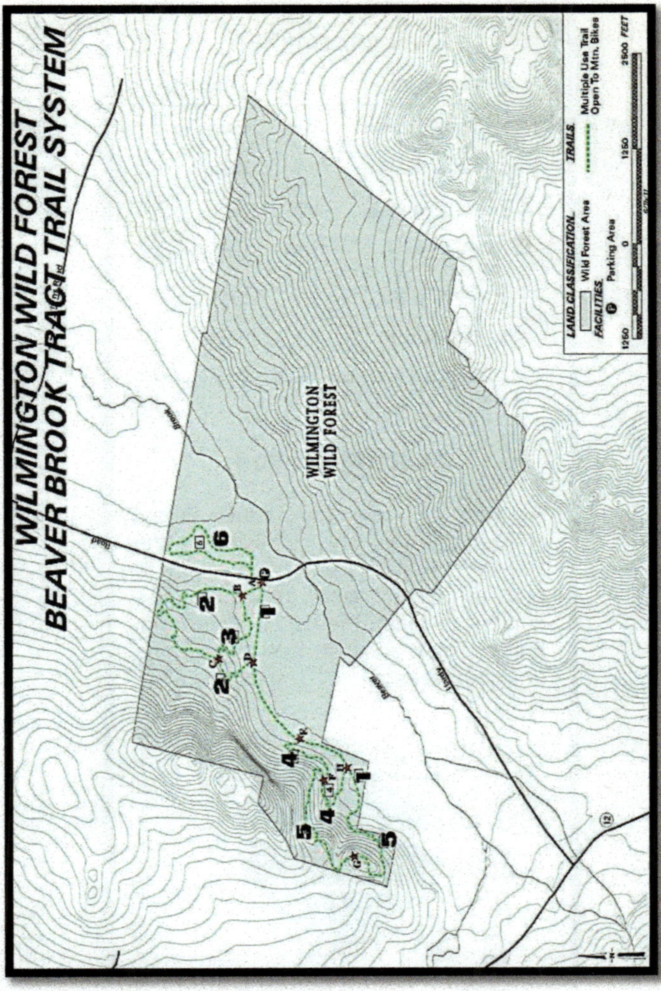

Map produced By DEC

Trail Information

Number/Name		Mileage	Difficulty
1	Double Time	0.6	Easy
2	Make Believe	0.8	Easy
3	Twisted Pine	0.3	Hard
4	Safe Bet	0.4	Moderate
5	Good Luck	0.9	Hard
6	Coniferous	0.6	Easy

Hunting Season

As with all New York State Forest Preserve lands, the lands within the Wilmington Wild Forest are open to hunting (subject to all applicable laws and regulations). Please be aware that hunting may occur in this area during any open season

DEPARTMENT OF ENVIRONMENTAL CONSERVATION • NEW YORK STATE •

Trail information from DEC produced trail map

Double Time (1)

This trail could also be called a corridor trail, as it is the link to four of the other trails. Double Time is located across the road from the parking area; this is where you will start. About 20 feet up the trail is the intersection with Make Believe (2) on the right. Continuing straight you will run along an old road on a very wide trail. The footing is very good through here.

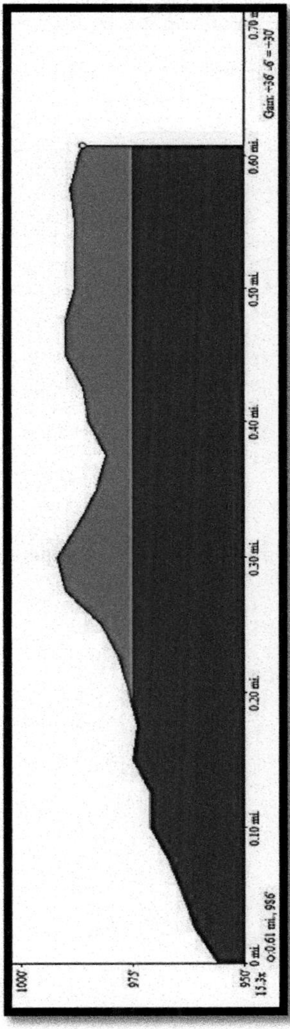

Your next intersection is on the right and that will be for Safe Bet (4). Past here, continue for another 0.2 miles to the end of the trail and the start of Good Luck (5) and Safe Bet (4).

Make Believe (2)

From Double Time (1) start your run on a moderate uphill in a counter-clockwise direction. In 0.1 miles you will pass by the Twisted Pine (3) intersection on your left. Continuing on you will climb gradually with a couple small dips and a few sharp turns. You cross over two old rock wall property lines in route to the height of land.

After a few more switchbacks and a slight descent you will climb again to the height-of-land. Running on mostly flat terrain for a bit you will come to the top end of Twisted Pine (3). Beyond this point you drop off the ridge and along a very narrow section; weave through the trees to a more open trail near the end. You will exit on Double Time (1).

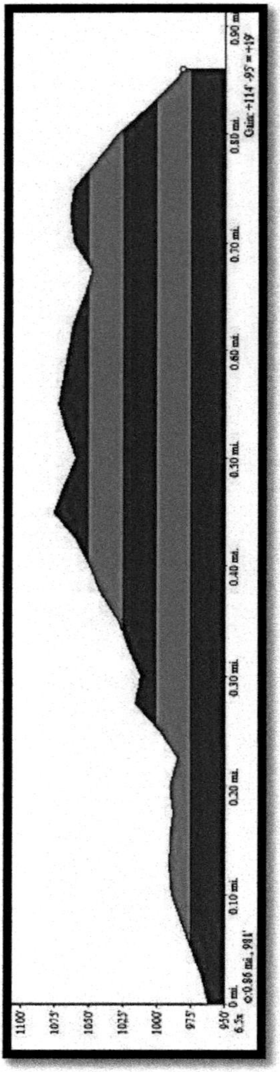

Twisted Pine (3)

Starting on the south end of the trail off Make Believe (2) you run a mostly flat course in the beginning. You will be running through a pine plantation, with perfect rows of conifers to welcome you. Weaving through the rows you quickly come to the hill at the end. This hill is a serious gain in elevation but is broken up with some of the sharpest, sickest, switchbacks we have ever had the pleasure of running. Mind you, your heart might still want to jump

out of your chest, but at least it's not a straight B-line for the top. You will end the trail and exit onto the top side of Make Believe (2).

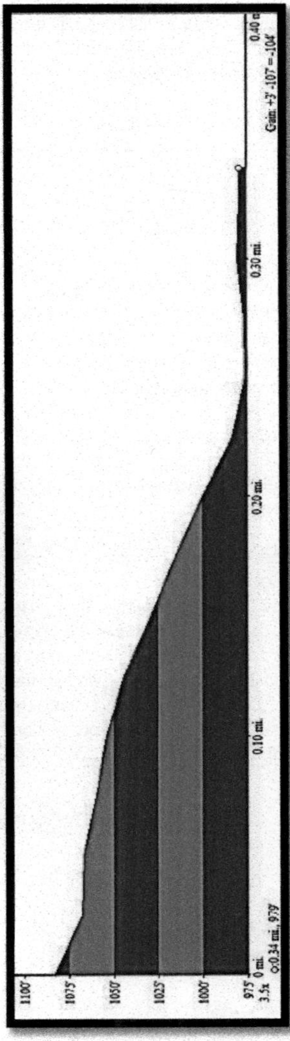

Safe Bet (4)

Starting from the end of Double Time (1) and going in a clockwise direction you make a hard right and start a moderate uphill run toward the base of an impressive cliff that we have aptly names Good Luck Cliffs, after the trail of the same name.

Nearing the top of the hill you will have to fight a bit of a wet area from ground seepage and then make a sharp right and run along the base of the cliffs with numerous boulders littering the side. Along this side hill you come to the intersection with the end of Good Luck (5). From here you will drop slightly and run on a trail with not the best footing and more slippery terrain. After a slight uphill push you will make a final sweeping descent back down and exit onto Double Time (1).

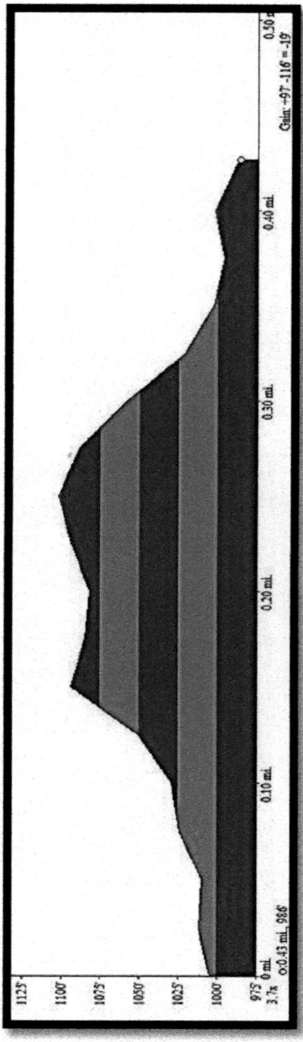

Good Luck (5)

This trail is a very aggressive run and in early winter it is a riot. Starting from the end of Double Time (1) and running in a clockwise direction, Good Luck is straight ahead. You almost immediately cross over a series of boardwalks on a stagger - the boardwalks are staggered, you shouldn't be.

Almost immediately the trail begins to climb, only moderate at first and then quite steep. It will swing back to the left as you approach the base of the ridge and offer a view through the trees. As you begin to approach the ridge you will start to see junipers lining the trail and more views creeping out over the horizon. The trail brings you behind the ridge at first and behind a rather impressive rock wall before it swings you back toward the ridge.

Along the ridge there is a short unmarked trail to your right that leads you to a very nice overlook with killer views. You may also notice that at the intersection there is also a horseshoe tied to a tree with a yellow ribbon - possibly the good luck you have been looking for, but leave it there for the next maniac.

You will drop slightly off this section of the ridge on some tough footing and climb again to a second amazing view off in the same direction - this will be your height-of-land for the trail. After a couple small switchbacks over more difficult footing you will be on a steady downhill. With a final heavy sweep to your right you will exit onto Safe Bet (4).

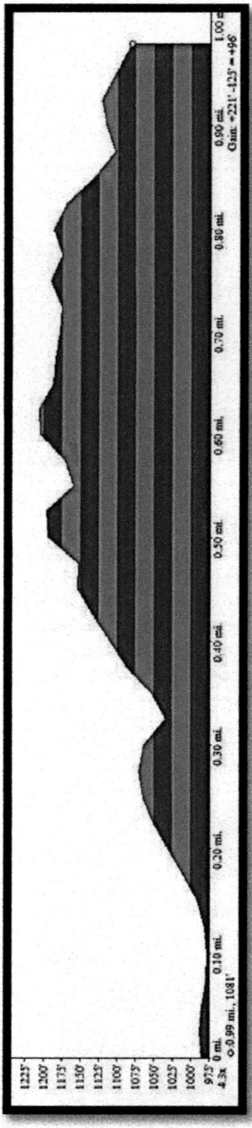

Coniferous (6)

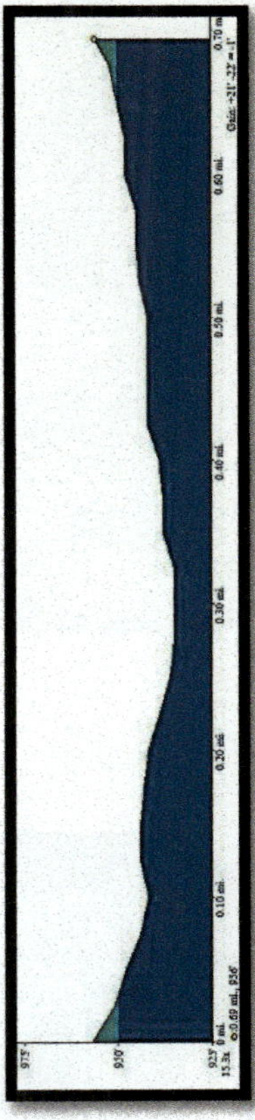

The trail is not connected at all to the first five trails. This trail is on the same side of the road as the parking area. This area looks to be under further development and more trails on this side of the road will most likely be open in the near future. Roughly 30 feet north of the parking area along Hardy Road is the start of the trail, it is hard to see from the parking area, but it's along the north side of the overgrown field.

Follow the loop trail in a counter-clockwise direction; be sure to pass by the first intersection and go to the second. The second intersection is one with an unmarked trail that drops down over a small hill. This is a possible future trail, not yet fully developed. Taking a left at this intersection you will be running through a very attractive mixed conifer forest. The first half of this loop is flat with narrow trails and sharp turns. As you near the end and make the turn back toward the parking lot you will come across a small, subtle hogback that you will need to run up. Of course what goes up must come down, and that would be you. The closer you get to the end you will notice Hardy Road on your right through the trees and then exit back on the trail itself only feet from the road.

Quad:

Lake Placid and Wilmington

Directions to Trailhead:

From the intersection of Routes 86 and 431 (Whiteface Memorial Highway), follow Route 86 toward Lake Placid. Continue for just under 2.0 miles to the Wilmington Wild Forest Flume Trail System Trailhead on your right.

Trail Conditions:

Most all of the trails can be expected to be dry. There are a few sections of wet terrain, but are quite brief at most. Bridges and boardwalks have been built and developed to alleviate any wet issues for the users. Any small wet areas contribute to a couple small runoffs and wet seasonal conditions.

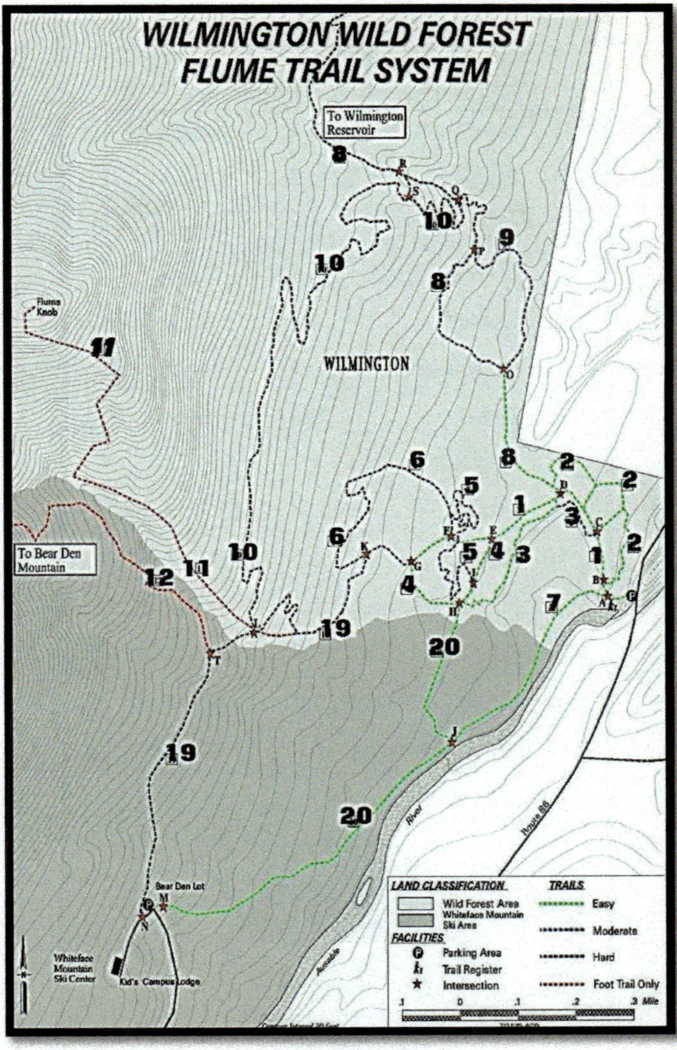

Map produced By DEC

Trail Information

Number/Name		Mileage	Difficulty
1	Corridor	0.3	Easy
2	Delta	0.4	Easy
3	Bluff	0.4	Moderate
4	Corridor Loop	0.4	Easy
5	Cedar	0.4	Moderate
6	Rock Garden	0.5	Hard
7	River	0.4	Easy
8	Marble Mountain	1.5	Hard
9	Erratic	0.3	Moderate
10	Ridge	1.5	Hard
11	Flume Knob♣	1.0	
12	Bear Den Mtn.♣	1.2	
19	Upper Connector	1.0	Hard
20	Lower Connector	0.9	Easy

♣ Foot Trail Only.

DEPARTMENT OF ENVIRONMENTAL CONSERVATION • NEW YORK STATE •

Trail information from DEC produced trail map

Corridor (1)

This trail starts from the trail register and makes a hard right on a decent up-hill clip, not the best warm-up for cold legs. The hill is rather short but definitely not pleasant as it starts right from the car. Atop the hill there is a small campsite on the right, and the Delta Trail (2). A quick clip further is the Bluff Trail (3) on the left and the Delta Cut-off Trail 1 on the right. A short distance beyond that is the Delta Cut-off Trail 2.

Running on a mostly flat surface you soon come to the Marble Mountain Trail (8) on the right. Still on a level grade, you come to the end of the Corridor Trail and the start of the Corridor Loop Trail (4).

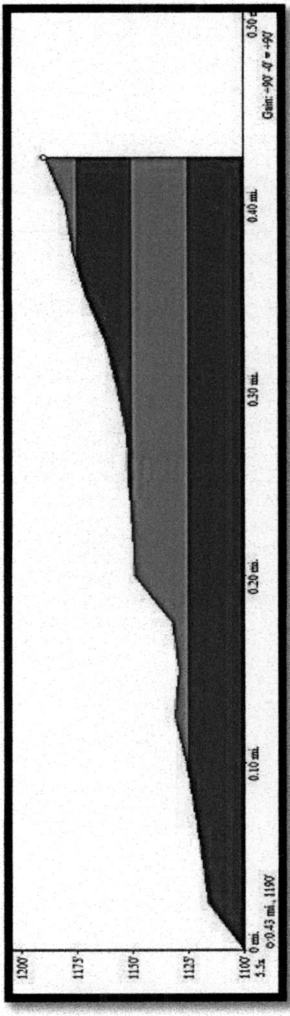

Delta (2)

This is a mostly flat section of trail that initially follows high above Route 86 within earshot of the cars traveling by at 90 mph to get no place. From the top of the hill off the Corridor Trail (1) you enter the woods on a very narrow trail that weaves very hard at times through the trees. There are two side trails off to the main trail that will be on your left. Both of these are called Delta Cutoff. Both of them lead directly back to the Corridor Trail (1). Use these to change up a loop on a following day, or whenever you want to bail on the Delta Trail. The Delta Trail ends a short distance up on the Marble Mountain Trail (8).

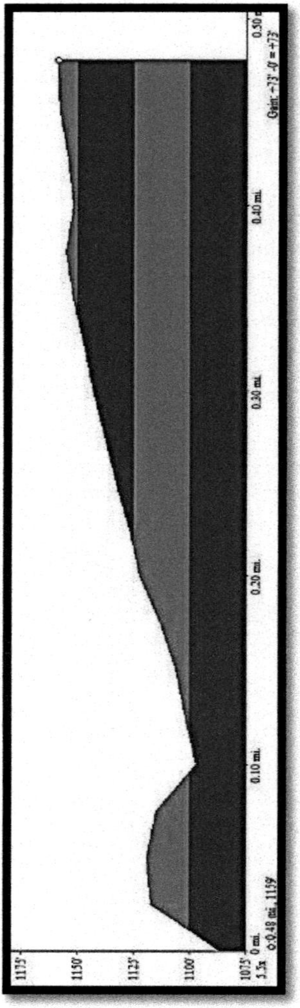

Bluff (3)

While quite short, this fun and exciting trail will put twitch in your pants. You will leave Corridor (1) on the left a very short distance from the top of the short hill. You immediately start a run along a very narrow trail at the top of a bluff above a beaver pond, pictured above. The trail, while not only narrow, is loaded with sharp turns and drastic drops. Out over the pond you will see an osprey's nest high in a tree, and when you turn back to the trail you will quickly see the tree you are about to run into. This trail ends at an intersection with the Corridor Loop Trail (4) and Whiteface Lower Connector (20).

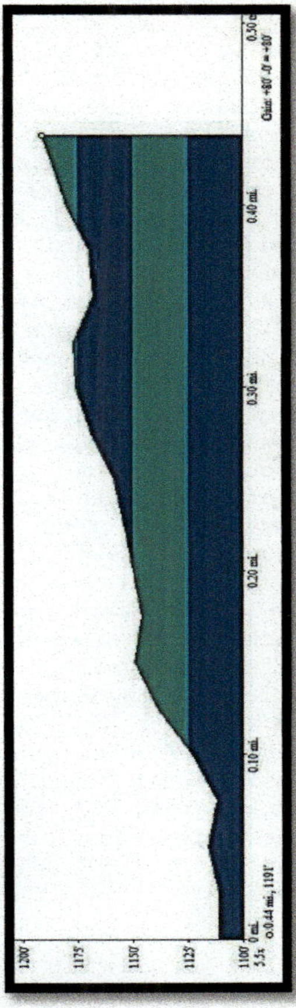

This short 0.4-mile trail will soon be a favorite of yours and surely be one you revisit again and again.

Corridor Loop (4)

Starting from the end of Corridor (1) at 0.3 miles you will start this small loop. Going in a counter-clockwise direction, you immediately start a southern route on a flat route. You quickly come to the southern end of Cedar (5) on your right. Briefly beyond this is the intersection of Bluff (3) and Whiteface Lower Connector (20). Actually, this is not a true intersection, as Whiteface Lower Connector (20) is about 100 feet beyond Bluff (3). A sharp right, and on a strong ascent you will remain on Corridor Loop. At the height-of-land you will pass by Rock Garden (6) on your left. Then you will start a long, slow descent back to Corridor (1). On your way back down you will pass by the other end of Rock Garden (6) and then the crossroads of Cedar (5).

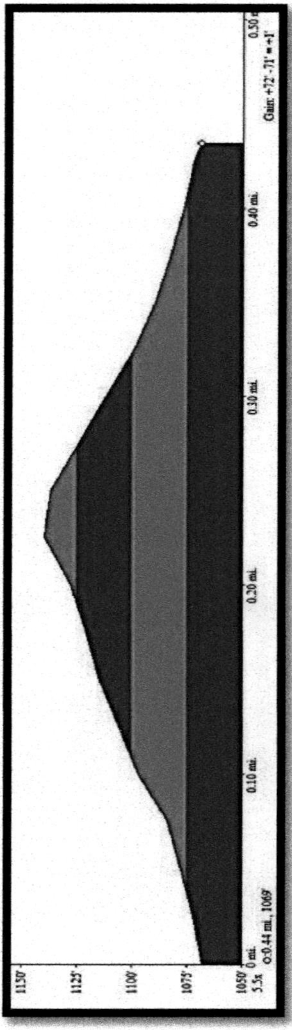

Cedar (5)

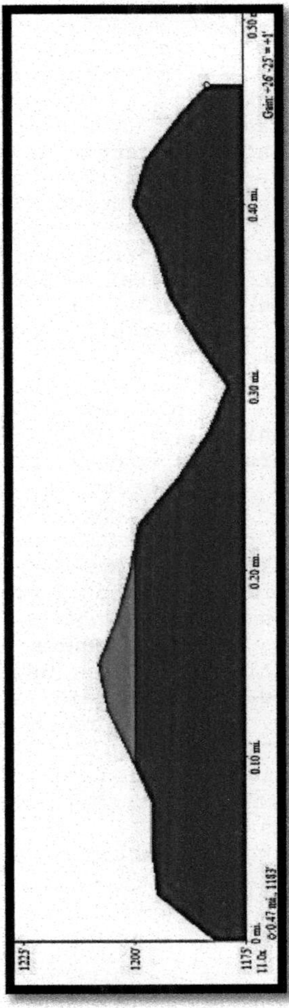

Starting off from Corridor Loop (4) you will be entering a trail course that has more turns per square mile than Lake Placid has tourist traps.

The first section of trail brings you along narrow trails with a huge sweeping turn that brings you to within a few feet of Corridor Loop (4) again. From this point you will climb slightly, with more switchbacks. You may start to notice what are called ground cedars - hence the origin behind the trail's name. Ground cedars are not part of the cedar family but are part of the club moss family.

OK, enough dendrology for today - back to the trails. In a short distance you will cross the north section of Corridor Loop (4) and regain the trail on the opposite side. Be sure to look both ways; bikes will be cruising through here and you don't want to be road kill.

The northern end of this trail is a continuation of switchbacks that literally almost come back around to meet you. You will exit Cedar slightly up off Rock Garden (6).

Rock Garden (6)

This is an interesting name for a trail, not sure exactly where it came from, but I'm thinking if from the rocks that have been planted in certain areas to add to the difficulty of the bike trail. This is a loop trail that is described below in a counter-clockwise direction. From Corridor Loop (4) you will start immediately on a slight uphill grade, before turning sharply north and running on an easy course. A couple sweeping turns bring you up to the height-of-land before a moderate downhill with some tricky footing takes over. Along this downhill you can see areas where obstacles have been developed for mountain biking. As you approach the end along a flat you will pass by Cedar (5) on the right. The trail ends shortly beyond, back on Corridor Loop (5).

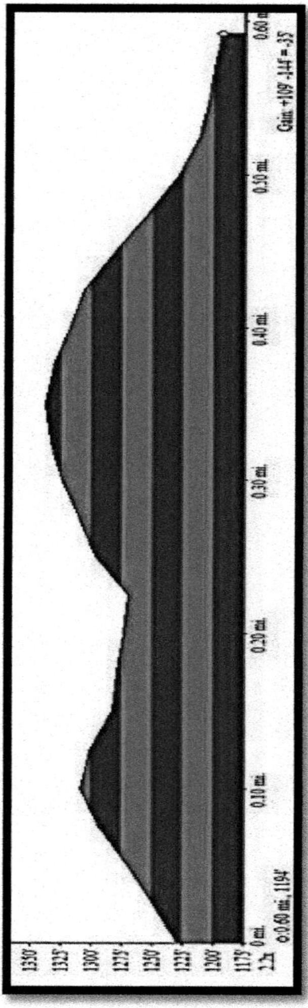

River (7)

River is just that, a trail following the course of the Ausable River. From the trail register head straight and drop down slightly to the shore of a beaver pond. There is a beaver dam on the right side of the trail and in many spots makes the trail rather moist and near impossible for a runner to stay dry. While running on this trail you will see the toll that Hurricane Irene in 2011 really took its toll. The trail is washed out in areas, driftwood on the opposite side with debris six feet up a tree. River is mostly flat, with only the slightest of dips ends along Whiteface Lower Connector (20).

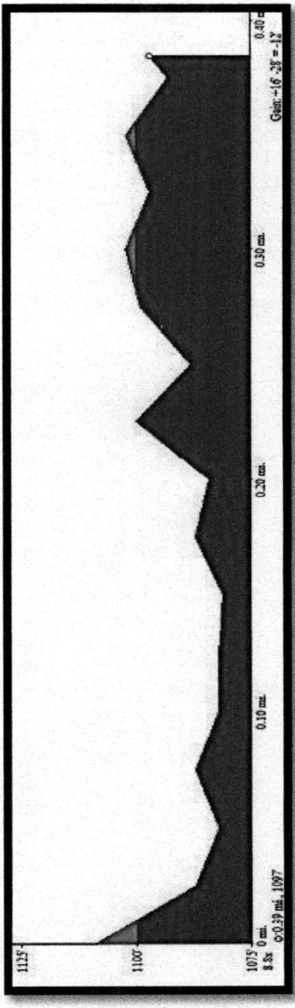

Marble Mountain (8)

This trail will be described in part - from Corridor (1) to Ridge (10). It continues past this point to join the Whiteface Mountain Trail from Reservoir Road.

Starting at Corridor (1) this trail is rather wide, especially in the beginning. In a short distance you will pass by the Delta Trail on the right as the trail climbs higher in elevation. The trail is rather easy up to the southern end of the Erratic Trail (9), which is on your right. Continuing to the left you will start a more moderate uphill climb, opposed to a downhill climb, which, really doesn't exist. As you sweep through the trail you will ra-

ther quickly come to the northern end of Erratic (9), again on your right. Shortly beyond this intersection there are some heavy switchbacks before you come to Ridge (10) - the end of the described section for the Marble Mountain Trail. The Marble Mountain Trail continues straight ahead and disappears into the forest.

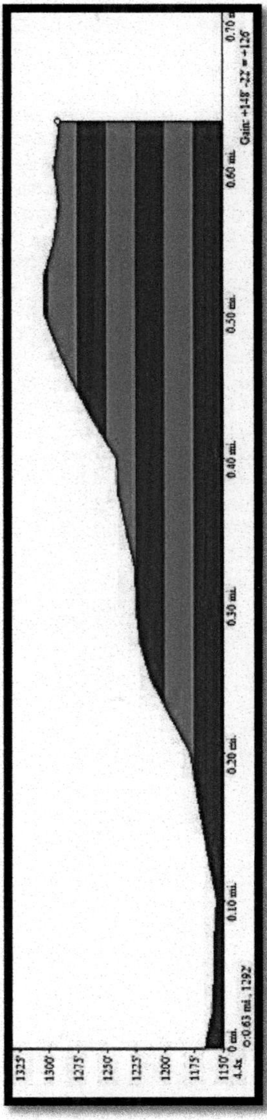

Erratic (9)

Erratic is simply a spur trail that adds a loop option with The Marble Mountain Trail (8). It does its job really well. Starting from the southern end along the Marble Mountain Trail (8) you will continue rather flat for about half the distance of the trail before the climb starts. Along the climb you will pass by an erratic or two, giving the trail its name. You will end this short spur trail along the Marble Mountain Trail (8) just below the end of Ridge (10).

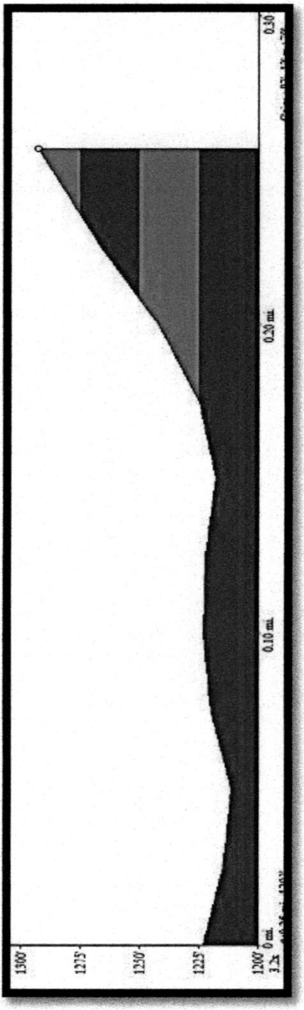

Ridge (10)

Ridge is one of the more exciting trails in the Flume Trail System. Starting from the intersection of Whiteface Upper Connector (19) and the Flume Knob Trail (11) you will climb slightly before the trail levels off for a moment and sweeps hard left. As you switch back you will climb a few contours before the trail moderates and follows along a few key contour lines on the slopes of Flume Knob. This section is littered with rocky terrain and wet areas from seeping groundwater and run-off. After climbing only slightly to the height-of-land, you will hit a couple more switchbacks under rough footing as you descend somewhat steeply. The trail stays on a slight downhill course for a while longer before it turns sharply west and uphill. After doing a nearly 180 degree turn you will head downhill again and encounter several more hard switchbacks. Along this switchback course you will pass a Marble Mountain Trail cut-off on the left. The trail ends after the switchbacks along the Marble Mountain Trail (8).

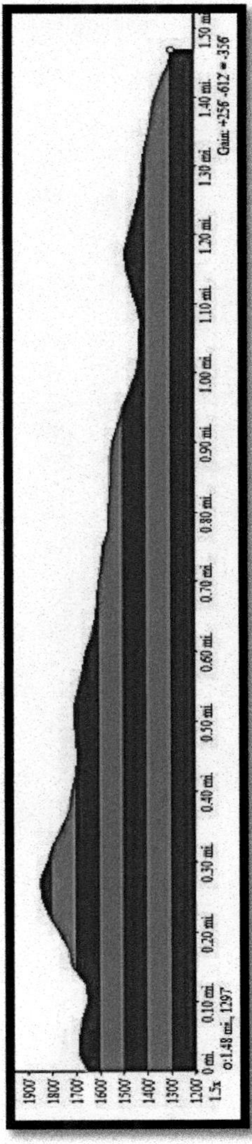

Whiteface Upper Connector (19)

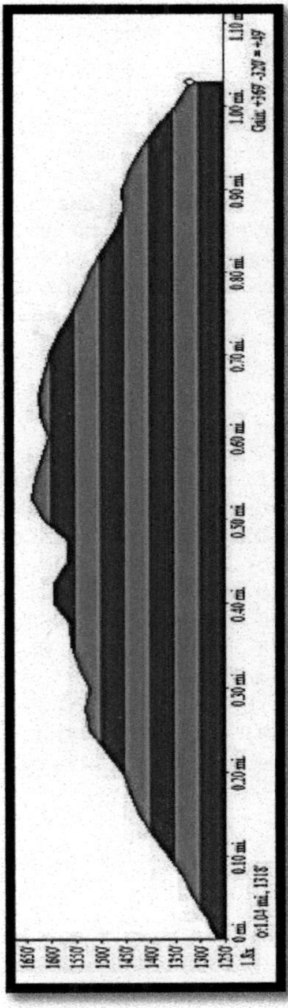

This trail starts from the Bear Den Lot at the Whiteface Mountain Ski Area. You can find the Bear Den Lot by entering the Whiteface Ski Center. This lot is at the end point of Whiteface Lower Connector (20). This trail is a rather difficult run. The terrain is very rough, mostly uphill, wet and slightly eroded.

From the Bear Den Lot, make your way up the steep roadside at a trail register. The trail register is for people using this as a starting point for their day or their destination is Bear Den Mountain - use it if you are. You will be running on a consistent uphill with only a couple small breaks and a couple very slight downs. Eventually you will come to the Bear Den Mountain Trail (12) on your left. You will notice right off that it is a rather recent development and possibly still under final construction. A sharp right drops you through the woods, crossing a brook and crossing the Flume Knob Trail (11). This crossing is also the start of Ridge (10), which heads uphill and to the left. You want to run slightly straight and right to continue along this trail. A few switchbacks bring you downhill to the start of the Flume Knob Trail (11). Head left, still on a constant downhill course, and sweep to the north and end this trail at Rock Garden (6).

Whiteface Lower Connector (20)

Starting from Corridor Loop (4) you will drop in elevation along and at times wet footing. The drop is rather slight and will bring you down to the Ausable riverside at the end of River (7). Hanging a sharp right and running parallel to the Ausable River for a short distance, you again will see remnants of 2011's Hurricane Irene. As you move away from the Ausable River you will start a moderate climb. The terrain is not too steep but the footing is rather difficult and unstable in spots, with loose stones and debris. You will exit the trail at the Bear Den Lot for the Whiteface Mountain Ski Center. Whiteface Upper Connector (19) is down and across the lot to the left.

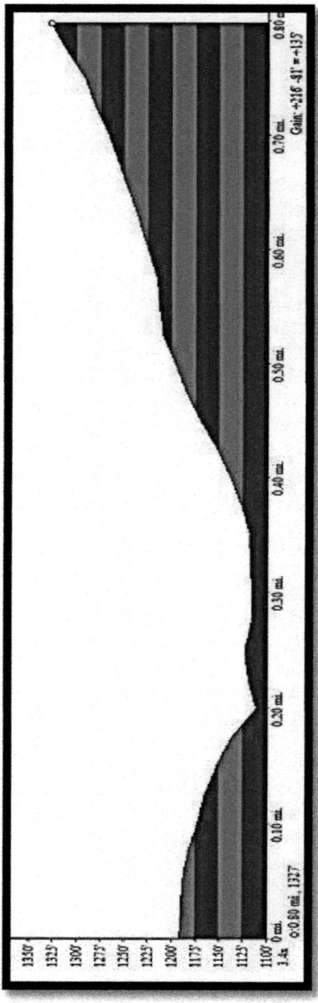

McKenzie Mountain Pass

Quad:

Saranac Lake

Distances:

- **McKenzie Pond Road to ball field-0.1 miles**
- **To power line-0.1 miles**
- **To McKenzie Pond Spur Trail-1.4 miles**
- **To McKenzie Mountain Trail-1.8 miles**
- **To Whiteface Club Road-1.9 miles**

Total distance 5.3 miles

Directions to Trailhead:

McKenzie Pond Road

From Ray Brook, less than 0.1 miles from the DEC office is McKenzie Pond Road on the right. Follow here for 1.5 miles or so to the trailhead on the right. The sign for the trailhead is small and light blue; it can be easily missed.

Whiteface Club Road

From the intersection of Routes 73 and 86 in Lake Placid drive toward the village on Route 86 and pass through heading toward Saranac Lake. On the outskirts of town look for the Whiteface Lodge on the right; Whiteface Club Road is just before it. Follow Whiteface Club Road for 1.4 miles or so to the trailhead for the Jackrabbit Trail/McKenzie Mountain. There is no obvious trail sign, so you will need to be focused on locating it.

Trail Conditions:

This trail is mostly dry with several small elevation changes. There is one large ascent and descent which is referred to as McKenzie Mountain Pass, starting from the McKenzie Pond Road Trailhead. This is a one-way run; two cars will be needed to complete this, unless of course you want to do an out and back, which is just crazy talk!

Starting at McKenzie Pond Road you will come to a hill almost immediately. This will exit you just feet from the parking area for a local ball field.

The trail enters the woods to the left along the forest edge. This is a short steep downhill through a narrow passage of trees to a powerline. At this point it is a mellow run along rolling hills to the trail register. From here enjoy some nice small ups and downs for a while.

At about 0.75 miles from the road will be a short, very steep pitch. At the bottom is a brook, with a bridge over it. From this bridge you will climb slightly to a long flat section and eventually to the spur trail for McKenzie Pond on the left.

Past McKenzie Pond is a long uphill climb, also known as McKenzie Pond Hill. Once atop this hill you will be in the col between Haystack and McKenzie mountains with a nice downhill in front of you to the McKenzie Mountain Trail Junction at 3.4 miles. The downhill section is a little rocky and littered with loose stones.

First is a low key downhill, almost flat to the Lake Placid Lean-to. It will be somewhat flat for a little bit of time before the long downhill that leads

you to the trail register at the Whiteface Club Road.

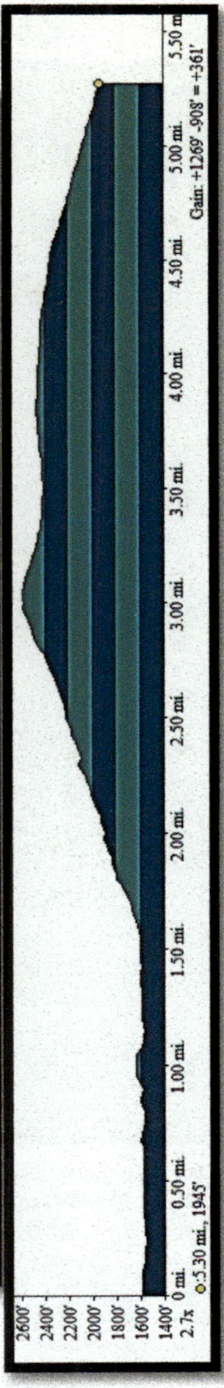

Old Mountain Road

Quad:

Lake Placid and Keene Valley

Distances:

- **Trailhead to 1st beaver pond-0.7 miles**
- **To 2nd beaver pond-0.85 miles**
- **To Alstead Hill Road-1.65 miles**

Total distance 3.2 miles, one way

Directions to Trailhead:

Old Mountain Road parking

From the intersection of Routes 86 and 73 in Lake Placid follow Route 73 toward Keene. Continue for 5.5 miles or so and start looking for Old Mountain Road on the left, located in a depression on Route 73 on a tight corner. Drive the 1.0 miles down Old Mountain Road for the start of the run.

Alstead Hill Road Parking

From the intersection of Routes 86 and 73 in Lake Placid follow Route 73 toward Keene. Continue for a little under 14 miles to Alstead Hill Road on the left. This is on a sharp corner most of the way down Keene Valley Hill. Follow Alstead Hill Road to its end, a little over 3.5 miles from Route 73.

Trail Conditions:

This trail has some issues but most will be overcome rather quickly. Aside from a few wetter sections there is one beaver flow that has taken over the trail; you will have to follow a faint herd path to get around it. The majority is a well-graded and fast run. This is a one-way run where a second car will need to be spotted, or, the run could be turned into an out and back.

From the trailhead off Old Mountain Road it is mostly flat, passing by several boulders along the way. A beaver-flooded area will be met at 0.7 miles and you will have to follow a herd path around it. Your first glance of the cliffs on Pitchoff will come soon, over a wet area on the right.

Once past here you will start a slow ascent before eventually coming to the base of the climb to the notch. This climb is rather steep, but short. From here you will enjoy a long downhill stretch which ends crossing a small marshy area. You will continue on a moderate downhill and eventually cross a second small marshy area before hitting the flats and running out to the parking lot.

Rock and River Guide Service
Alstead Hill Road
Old Mountain Road
Rte 73
2400'
2200'
2000'
1800'
1600'
3.2x
0 mi. 0.25 mi. 0.50 mi. 0.75 mi. 1.00 mi. 1.25 mi. 1.50 mi. 1.75 mi. 2.00 mi. 2.25 mi. 2.50 mi. 2.75 mi. 3.00 mi. 3.25 mi. 3.50 mi. 3.75 mi. 4.00 mi. 4.25 mi. 4.50 mi.
4.32 mi., 1693'
Gain: +732' -1061' = -329'

Sentinel Ponds Loop

Quad:

Lake Placid

Distances:

- **To Owen Pond-0.55 miles**
- **To Winch Pond Intersection-0.65 miles**
- **To 2nd Winch Pond Intersection-0.25 miles**
- **To 3rd Winch Pond Intersection-0.2 miles**
- **To Winch Pond and Back-0.5 miles**
- **To Copperas Pond-0.15 miles**
- **Back to trailhead-1.2 miles**

Total distance 3.5 miles, loop

Directions to Trailhead:

From the intersection of Routes 73 and 86 in Lake Placid follow Route 86 toward Wilmington. Go for 5.0 miles to the southern trailhead which is on the right.

Trail Conditions:

Expect mixed conditions for most of the year. Very wet in the spring, more so than most. Great trail for winter running - it's somewhat heavily used, which develops a strong and solid base. A large portion of the trail has slippery rock - proper footwork and footwear is highly needed.

From the southern trailhead for Owen Pond start your run over a moderate course on the newly rerouted initial 0.2 miles. The new portion has been in use for a while but there are still some very soft areas. You will quickly come to the original trail and run alongside a brook in an area that is notorious for being wet and slippery. As you pass by an erratic on your right, you will begin to slowly move away from the brook and climb slightly before dropping again to the brookside and eventually Owen Pond.

Past Owen Pond you will find the trail to be slightly more moderate than most of the other sections of this trail. Before hardly any time at all you will see Copperas Pond with the sweet views of Whiteface Mountain over the far side. Passing through a camping area and over a long boardwalk you will come to an intersection. Right heads to Winch Pond and left goes along Copperas Pond and meets up with the northern trail approach to the region. For this loop follow left along Copperas Pond.

The tread here is narrow in spots and quickly comes to a trail sign pointing right. Go right, left is the lean-to trail - a deadend. From here you will be in a wet area again, rock-hopping on an uphill slope. The trail now sweeps and goes over a few small hog-backs before it reaches another intersection. Follow here to the right; left will bring you steeply down to Route 86.

This short section of trail is all but perfect for running, but it makes the loop interesting and challenging. For the next 0.25 miles or so, you will be fighting serious mud, rocks and slippery root systems. There are some old corduroy along the trail, but they act as more of a false hope than anything. Pick and choose you steps carefully, or not, it's just mud and they say mud is good for the complexion.

Your next intersection will bring you to the Winch Pond Spur Trail. Following it left for 0.25 miles to the shore of Winch Pond, take in its hidden beauty, turn around and high step it back to the intersection. Once back, take the left toward Copperas Pond. This section has a short re-route around a mud pit, which we recommend using. Getting back to Copperas Pond is a flash; once back, you should recognize the intersection near the boardwalk. Take the left and follow the trail back to your car. This last stretch is the same trail you were on for the first portion of the day.

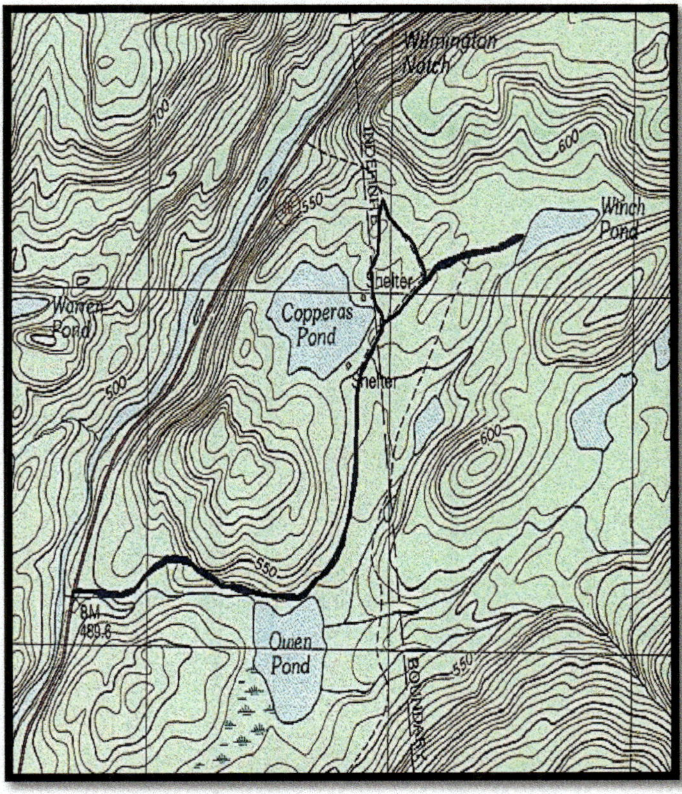

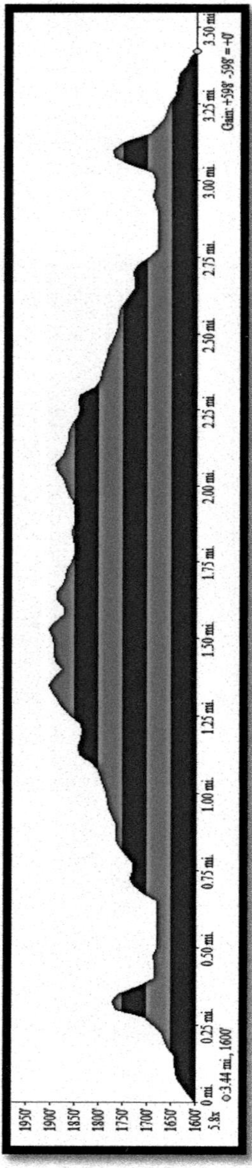
1950'
1900'
1850'
1800'
1750'
1700'
1650'
1600'
5.8x
0 mi.
0.25 mi.
0.50 mi.
0.75 mi.
1.00 mi.
1.25 mi.
1.50 mi.
1.75 mi.
2.00 mi.
2.25 mi.
2.50 mi.
2.75 mi.
3.00 mi.
3.25 mi.
3.50 mi.
3.44 mi., 1600'
Gain: +598' -598' = +0'

Whiteface Landing

Quad:

Lake Placid

Distances:

To Whiteface Landing-2.5 miles

Directions to Trailhead:

The trailhead is located off Route 86 at the end of the Connery Pond Road. From the intersection for Routes 86 and 73 follow Route 86 out of Lake Placid toward Wilmington for 2.9 miles; Connery Pond Road is a dirt road on the left that offers hiking into Whiteface Landing and Whiteface Mountain. If winter running is your game, the gate at Route 86 might be closed for the winter season. If this is the case you will need to park just up Route 86 at the parking areas. If it is open and conditions warrant, you can drive for the 0.8 miles to the summer parking lot.

Trail Conditions:

This run is along an old woods road now turned trail. The terrain is much like an old woods road, with wet sections, rubble and nice stretches of well-packed earth.

Side note

The gate shown on most maps is actually the second gate along the trail. There is an initial gate just after the marked trail to Connery Ponds and at the start of the Whiteface Mountain/Whiteface Landing Trail.

Starting from the gate you will be running on a soft track, which is a private woods road leading to state land. This portion of the road is still used by private vehicles. Please stay on the road and do not go on private land.

As you are running around Connery Pond you will soon come to the state land gate which is roughly 0.4 miles from the gate at which you parked. From here the trail is more like a foot trail, but still fairly wide, following the route of an old woods road.

The initial climb starts at about 1.0 miles and lasts for about 0.5 miles before becoming much more of a moderate run.

Many spots along this trail are littered with loose stone and rubble; be very careful to not turn an ankle on the rough terrain.

Just before Whiteface Landing on Lake Placid there is a major intersection. Right heads toward Whiteface Mountain, straight is an old trail around Lake Placid and left is a short trail to Whiteface Landing on Lake Placid. There is a nice dock here to relax at and take a dip.

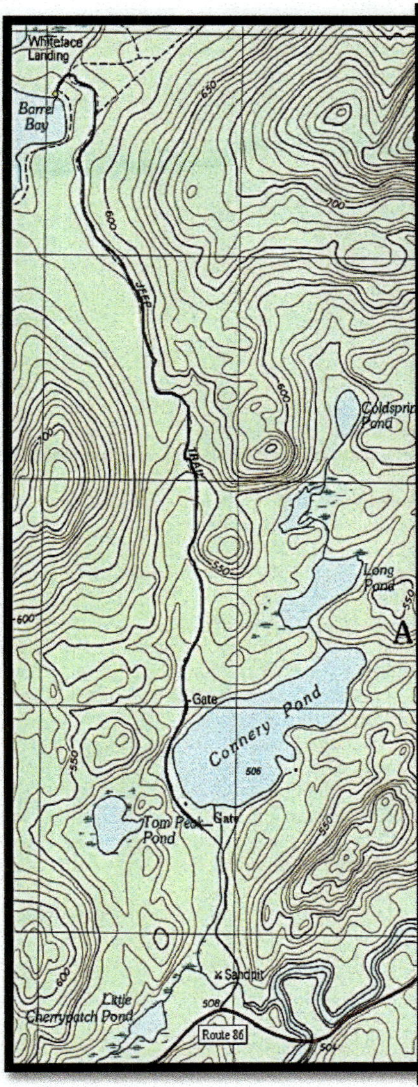
Whiteface Landing
Barrel Bay
650
700
600
JEEP
TRAIL
550
Pond
Long Pond
A
Gate
Connery Pond
506
Tom Peck Pond
Gate
Sandpit
Little Cherrypatch Pond
508
Route 86
504

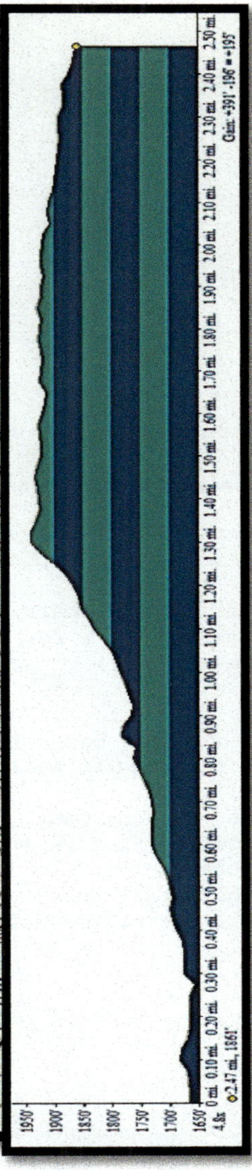
Gain: +391' -196' = +195'
2.47 mi, 1861'
4.8x
1950'
1900'
1850'
1800'
1750'
1700'
1650'

Crowfoot Pond

Quad:

Witherbee

Distances:

- **To Crowfoot Pond-2.4 miles**

Directions to Trailhead:

From I-87, Exit 30; head south along Route 9 for 0.15 miles to Tracy Road on the left. Follow Tracy Road for about 1.7 miles to the Crowfoot Pond Trail-head on the right. The trailhead is actually down a steep dirt side road in about 400 feet - it can be driven.

Trail Conditions:

Mostly dry, and apart from a couple wet crossings this run is a nice afternoon jaunt.

From the parking area you can easily see a bridge over Crowfoot Brook. This is the start of the run.

For the most part, you will follow Crowfoot Brook, crossing it a few times en route to Crowfoot Pond. The steep rocky slopes of Stiles Hill on your left come down to meet the trail as you approach closer to the pond. While the slopes are rocky, the trail is not too bad; the footing for a large percentage of this run is mellow and comfortable.

You can continue along the trail to the north of Crowfoot Pond, which will bring you closer along its shore offering many different views. Eventually the public portion of the trail ends and a private park will begin. You will need to return the way you came in.

Crowfoot Pond
Stiles Hill
Brook
Newport
Crowfoot
Little Howard Pond
Howard Hill
Moriah Pond
TRACY

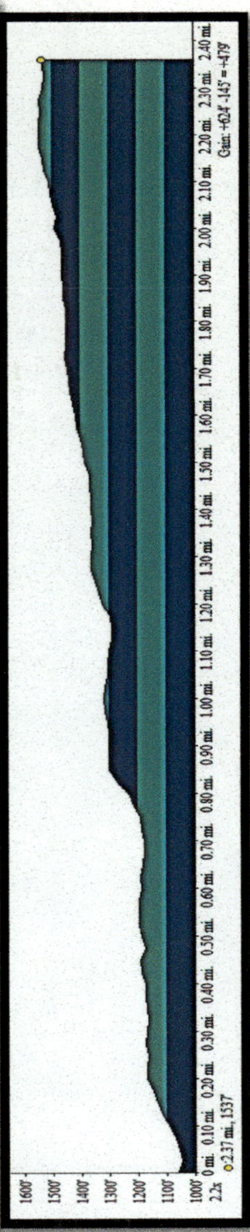
Gain: +624' -145' = +479'
2.37 mi, 1537
2.2x

Upper Works Loop

Quad:

Santanoni Peak, Ampersand Mountain

Distances:

- **Upper Works Trailhead to Northern Henderson Lake-1.7 miles**
- **To Upper Preston Pond-1.9 miles**
- **To Hunter Pond-0.4 miles**
- **To Lower Preston Pond-1.1 miles**
- **To Duck Hole-0.5 miles**
- **To Northville/Placid Trail-0.3 miles**
- **To Bradley Pond Trail-0.4 miles**
- **To Bradley Pond-3.65 miles**
- **To Easement Road-2.45 miles**
- **To Santanoni Mountains Trailhead-1.8 miles**
- **Back to Upper Works-1.5**

Total 15.7 miles, loop

Directions to Trailhead:

From I-87, Exit 29 head toward Newcomb along Blue Ridge Road. Continue for around 18 miles to the Tahawus Road. Follow Tahawus Road for just under 10 miles to Upper Works. Bear left at the two intersections.

The Santanoni Trailhead is 1.5 miles before Upper Works on the same road.

Trail Conditions:

This trail has a mixture of the good, the bad, and the ugly. Not only do you gain and lose over 2,000 feet in this loop, you also have to compete with serious mud and some slippery water crossings. But it's not all that bad; the scenery is spectacular and there are some nice dry sections of trail where you can move along very well.

Starting from Upper Works you will find yourself on a gravel road that leads to the southern approaches of a number of the High Peaks. The road soon crosses an outlet of Henderson Lake before coming to an intersection. The right intersection leads to Calamity Pond and Flowed Lands where high peaks like Colden, Cliff, Marshall, and many others can be climbed. Continue left along an older section, not as well maintained as the other trail. The trail will begin to climb through some wet and muddy sections; you will need to step carefully through some of these and use the corduroy that has been laid out to keep your feet dry. Soon you will start to see a marsh to your left; don't mistake this for Henderson Lake. The trail will then descend moderately for around 0.5 miles before flattening out at another intersection. Straight leads into Indian Pass, and left drops down to a bridge, go left.

The run continues by following the north shore of Henderson Lake before breaking away at the site of a new lean-to. From here the trail just rolls along, with small ups and downs. At about 3.6 miles from Upper Works you will come to a small trail intersection with a handmade wooden sign on a tree (which may or may not still be around). Left will take you on a short spur trail to the shore of Upper Preston Pond; Hunter Pond is a very short distance away.

The terrain is now quite nice, lightly used, and soft under foot. There are small rocky sections to run through but nothing that will slow you down too much. The continuous, year-round muddy sections you will encounter are another story.

There is a brook crossing near Lower Preston Ponds that can be quite tricky, but if you need to, go upstream a little ways and a tree over the inlet can be used as a catwalk. Again this feature is a temporary one and can be missing. A little further upstream there is a small beaver flow you can jump. But that could all change over time as well; that's part of the fun. You will get your first glimpse of Duck Hole from the east near an inlet. The tough brook crossing is the one over Roaring Brook. During high water this will be impossible to rock hop; wading will be your only choice. So carry a towel just in case the water has submerged the rocks.

Once across the brook you will notice the trail goes in two directions; this is the NPT. Left goes to the Duck Hole Camps and the Ward Brook region; follow here to the camps.

Along the next 0.5 miles you will have several opportunities to approach the shore of Duck Hole. The unfortunate thing is Hurricane Irene in 2011 and the fury of the water that it developed managed to destroy the dam. With the dam no longer there, the water has drained and Duck Hole is left as a future wetland and meadow. There is another intersection near the camps where the NPT splits off to head west. Continue south and in this case also known as left, this will lead toward Bradley Pond.

This section of trail to the Bradley Pond Lean-to is hit or miss in terms of conditions. It tends to be a very wet trail most times of the year due to the fact that it skirts marshes, crosses streams, follows streams and just gets muddy from overuse.

Once at the lean-to, the mud really starts to get deep. There are small walkways, logs, bridges and a couple missing bodies through here - use them at your own risk. There is a short herd path to Bradley Pond on the south side of a beaver marsh - this is the herd path that leads to Times Square in the Santanoni Range.

The trail from the Bradley Pond herd path to the easement road is mostly downhill. The initial part is very wet and water tends to run down sections of it. But as you get further out of the area the trail dries up and the running is rather pleasant.

You will have to cross two bridges as you near the end of the foot trail. The first one you come to is very strong and well built. The second has been cocked by the rushing waters of Hurricane Irene - yet another fatality from the year of the floods.

As you exit the foot trail you will come to an easement road that has to be run out to the trailhead for just under 2.0 miles. Follow this to the left.

A second car would be a great idea for this run, one for Upper Works and a second at this trailhead. If a second car isn't available it is a run of 1.5 miles along the Tahawus Road back to Upper Works.

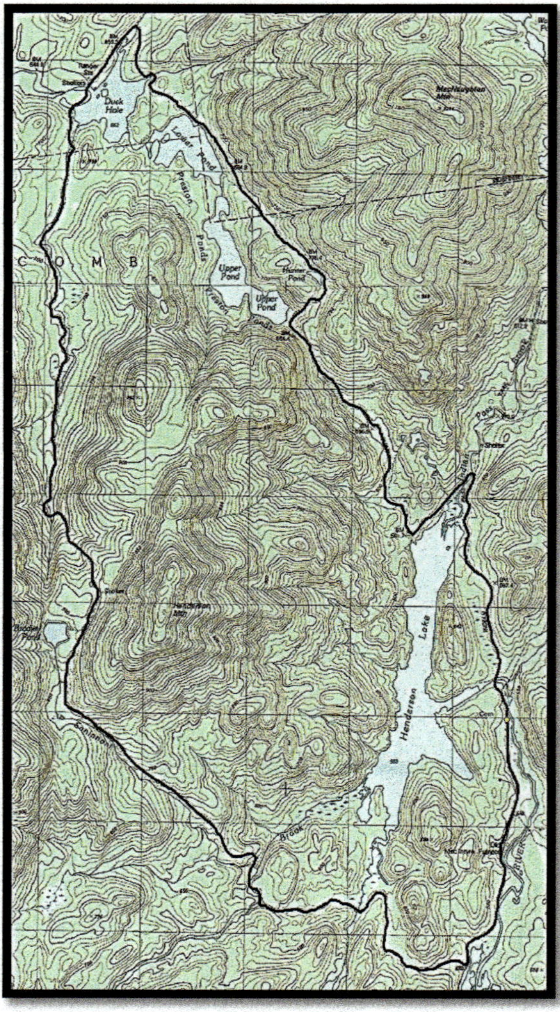
Duck Hole
Lower Pond
Preston Ponds
C O M B
Upper Pond
Upper Pond
Henderson Lake
Brook

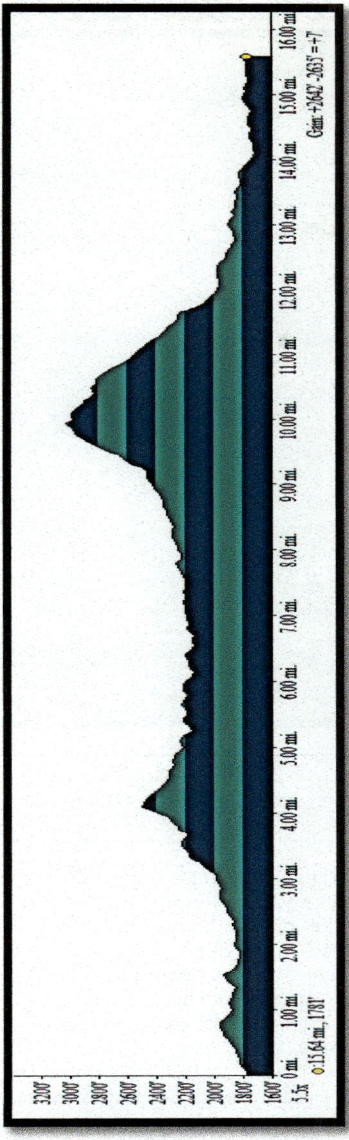
3200'
3000'
2800'
2600'
2400'
2200'
2000'
1800'
1600'
5.5x
0 mi.
1.00 mi.
2.00 mi.
3.00 mi.
4.00 mi.
5.00 mi.
6.00 mi.
7.00 mi.
8.00 mi.
9.00 mi.
10.00 mi.
11.00 mi.
12.00 mi.
13.00 mi.
14.00 mi.
15.00 mi.
16.00 mi.
15.64 mi., 1781'
Gain: +2642' -2635' = +7'

Scott and Wallface Ponds

Quad:

Keene Valley and Ampersand Lake

Distances:

- **Adirondack Loj Parking to 1st Rocky Falls intersection-1.90 miles**
- **To 2nd Rocky Falls intersection-0.2 miles**
- **To Scott Clearing-1.7 miles**
- **To Scott Pond-1.2 miles**
- **To Wallface Pond-0.85 miles**

Total milage-5.85 miles, one way

Directions to Trailhead:

From the intersection of Routes 73 and 86 in Lake Placid follow Route 73 toward Keene. At 3.25 miles is Adirondack Loj Road on the right. Follow this road to its end. You will need to park in the hiker parking lot and cross the road back by the toll booth. The trail is at the back of a small turnaround.

Trail Conditions:

There is only one serious wet section along this trail, between Scott and Wallface Ponds; however this one section is rather memorable.

Side note

There is paid parking at the Adirondack Loj with reduced rates for ADK members

---

This route starts from the Adirondack Loj, and follows the trail toward Rocky Falls and Indian Pass. The trail starts on the opposite side of the road as the Loj parking and heads toward Heart Lake. The trail initially follows along a gravel walkway and comes to a T-intersection. Follow right here and enter onto a rocky but dry course. The rocks are rather sizeable along this section to the trail register. Past the trail register, be sure to follow to the left. There is one more intersection which will be reached rather quickly and that is the one for the Heart Lake Loop. For the most part it is gradual from here with only a couple small climbs to the first junction with the Rocky Falls Trail. Shortly beyond this is the second intersection for Rocky Falls.

Up to this point the trail is usually dry except for one muddy crossing just before the Scott Lean-to. After the lean-to there is a wide brook crossing which in most cases is not an issue. From this point to Scott Clearing is a very fast-paced run; the old dam will be on your right. The Wallface Ponds Trail is to the right of the dam and again over a decent-sized brook crossing, this one slightly trickier to cross.

The trail from here is a little over 2.0 miles to Wallface Ponds. The trail climbs almost immediately to the height of land before moderating out for a short period of time. This is where most all of the elevation is gained. Some of the ascent is quite rocky and can be a little tough on the descent. At 1.2 miles you will be at the site of the old dam for Scott Pond. Up to Scott Pond the trail has been pretty dry with only a few exceptions, but be prepared for anything.

The trail from here gets pretty sloppy and wet, crossing streams and old corduroy, before you eventually reach Wallface Pond. This section may be skipped as a run and become more of a fast-paced hike, in some parts. If you decide to skip this portion and stop at Scott Pond, no one would think any less of you. Running seems almost impossible.

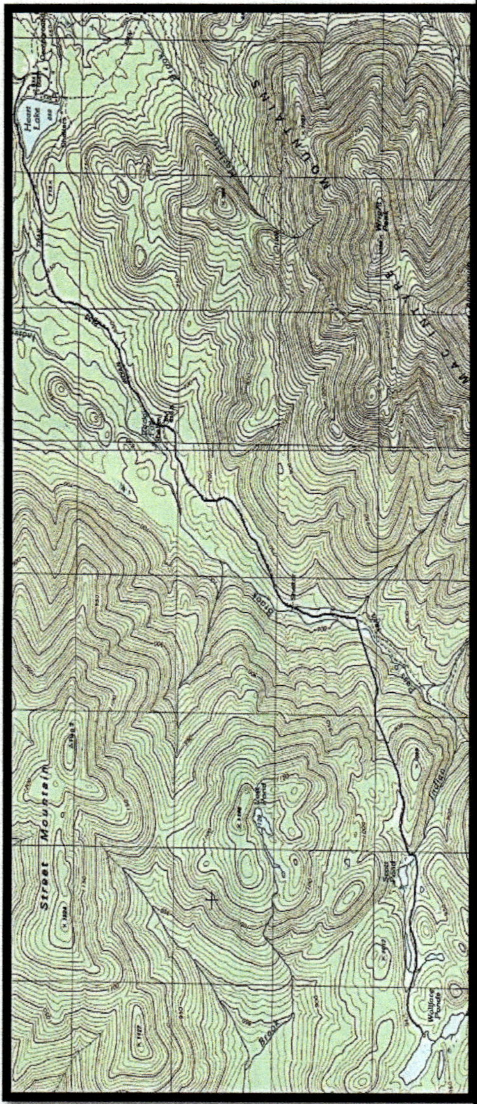
Heart Lake
MacINTYRE MOUNTAINS
Street Mountain
Wallface Ponds
Indian

3200'
3000'
2800'
2600'
2400'
2200'
2000'
2.9x
0 mi 0.25 mi 0.50 mi 0.75 mi 1.00 mi 1.25 mi 1.50 mi 1.75 mi 2.00 mi 2.25 mi 2.50 mi 2.75 mi 3.00 mi 3.25 mi 3.50 mi 3.75 mi 4.00 mi 4.25 mi 4.50 mi 4.75 mi 5.00 mi 5.25 mi 5.50 mi 5.75 mi 6.00 mi
5.86 mi 3127'
Gain: +1809' -880' = +929'

Moose Mountain Pond

Quad:

Paradox Lake

Distances:

- From Ensign Pond Road to intersection-1.4 miles
- To Bass Lake-0.6 miles
- Back to intersection-0.6 miles
- To Moose Mountain Pond-2.0 miles

Total distance 4.6 miles, one way

Directions to Trailhead:

From I-87, take Exit 29, head east 0.35 miles to Route 9. Follow Route 9 north for 2.45 miles to Caza Turn on the right. Go 0.3 miles to North Hudson/Moriah Road (Ensign Pond Road), follow here for 2.75 miles to the trailhead for Hammond Pond and Bass Lake.

Trail Conditions:

This trail is lightly used during most seasons. Soft underfoot, but wet in sections. Some sections can be easily missed, especially when moving at a higher rate of speed.

This route is seldom run by visitors, but for locals it can be a gem of a run. The trail is an amazing place for quiet recreation of all types.

The trail follows Berrymill Brook for the first section, and along this section the trail is mostly flat. You will have to make a small uphill climb to get on the hillside above Berrymill Brook, but after that it's very gentle. At about 0.8 miles the trail will swoop down toward and follow the brook, then climb back up to the ridge. One last descent will bring you to the intersection with Moose Mountain Pond.

Berrymill Pond is seen from the intersection and looks simply like a widening of Berrymill Brook, which essentially, I suppose, it is.

The trail crosses a bridge over the flow and follows the shoreline and after about 0.4 miles the trail heads away from the shore and into the forest. The trail follows an old tote road for a while through a large stand of softwoods. After a short, steep climb the trail moderates again and visits a couple beaver ponds, also known as flooded areas. Shortly beyond is the shore of Moose Mountain Pond.

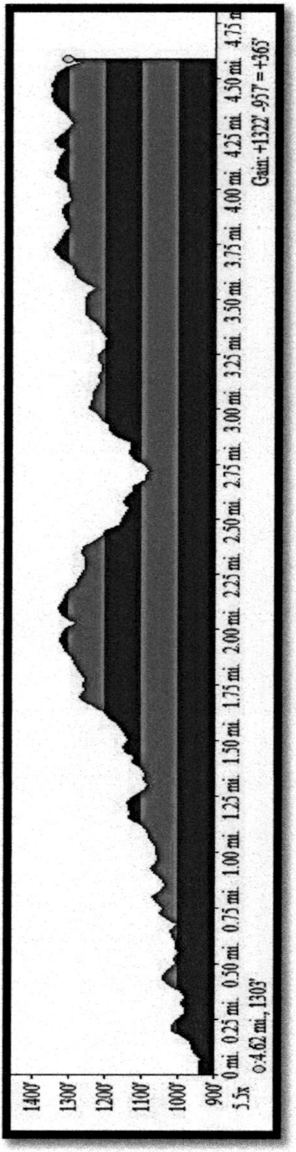

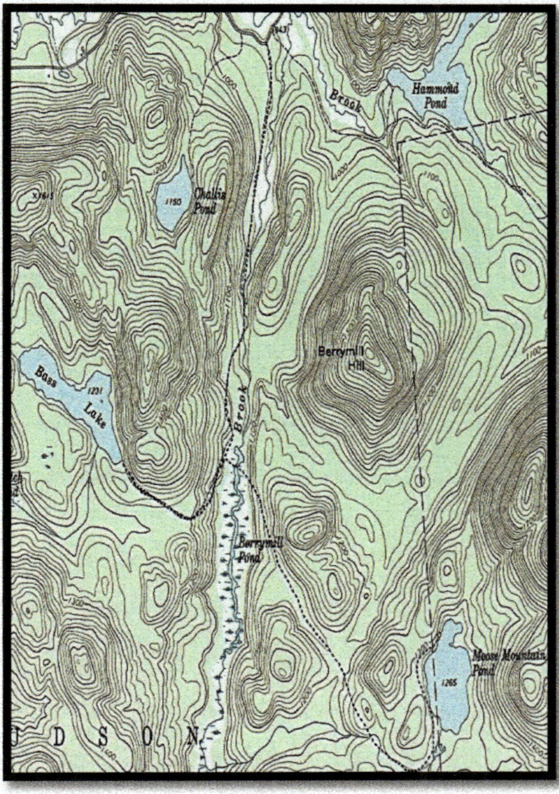
Hammond Pond
Brook
Challis Pond
1150
Berrymill Hill
Bass Lake
1231
Brook
Berrymill Pond
Moose Mountain Pond
1265
U D S O N

Trail Run (Formally known as West Black Pond)

Quad:

Paradox Lake

Distances:

- **To trail intersection-0.8 miles**
- **To Bloody Pond Trail-0.9 miles**
- **To West Black Pond-0.2 miles**

Total distance 1.9 miles, one way

Directions to Trailhead:

From I87, exit 29 head east 0.35 miles to Route 9. Follow Route 9 north for 2.45 miles to Caza Turn on the right. Go 0.3 miles to North Hudson/Moriah Road (Ensign Pond Road); follow this road for 2.75 miles to the trailhead for Hammond Pond and Bass Lake.

Trail Conditions:

This is a dry trail with no water issues and very little mud. This is a lightly traveled trail with soft landings and follows an old woods road for a large portion.

Side note

This unusual and politically incorrect name for a trail was baked-up by yours truly. West Black Pond is simply a pond on the west side of Black Ponds, and with that, has become more of a grass land than an actual body of water.

This trailhead is the start to many different destinations, such as Bloody Pond, Bass Lake, Moose Pond, and Berrymill Pond. The trail you want is the one at the top of the steps to the left. It may be unsigned but it is marked.

This trail soon joins a woods road as it approached a bridge over Berrymill Brook. The woods road drops down slightly to cross the brook downstream on a foot bridge. On the other side of the bridge you rejoin the woods road and run through a pine forest on a mostly flat trail. At 0.75 miles from the trailhead the trail splits; right is Bloody and Black Ponds, left is a short trail to Hammond Pond and a dam at the end of the pond.

Follow the trail right and slightly uphill, still on an old woods road. The south side of Hammond Pond comes into view as you run above the shore. At 0.7 miles from the Hammond Pond Trail you will cross a stream near a broken and unusable bridge. Then shortly after the bridge is another stream, this one an outlet of Bloody Pond. The unmaintained trail to Bloody Pond is shortly after this crossing; a small rock cairn marks the trail as well as a yellow paint blaze, which has become much harder to see. This trail to Bloody Pond is not recommended for a run, but is recommended as a hike. There is talk of reopening this trail for hikers and making it more suitable for travel. If this becomes the case, it would be an excellent spur trail to run.

Continue straight along the trail for another easy but slightly uphill run to West Black Brook Pond. We named this West Black Pond because; two other Black ponds lie further east, but along a private trail. You can visit only this Black Pond, which over time has become more of a dried-up field of grass and debris, but in wet conditions after snow melt it may hold water for a short period of time. Swimming not recommended.

Two roads diverged in a wood, and I--
I took the one less traveled by,
And that has made all the difference.
--Robert Frost

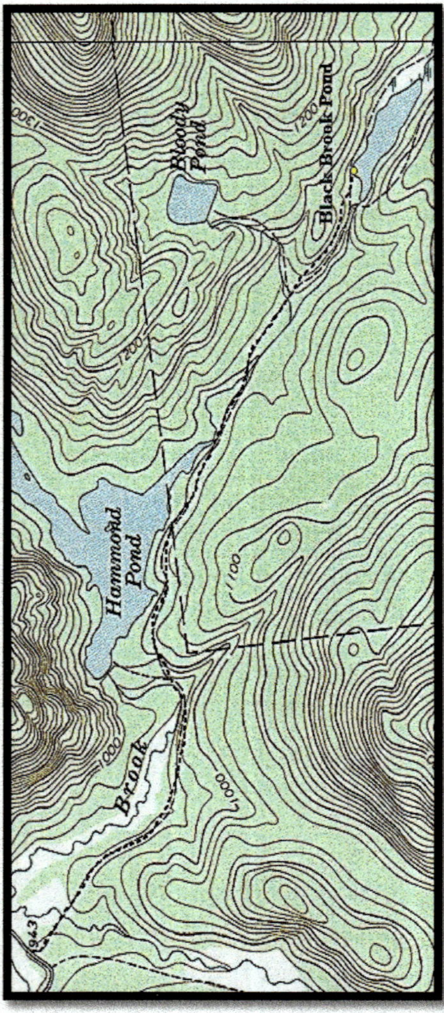
Hammond Pond
Bloody Pond
Black Brook Pond
Brook
1300
1200
1200
1100
1000
1000
943

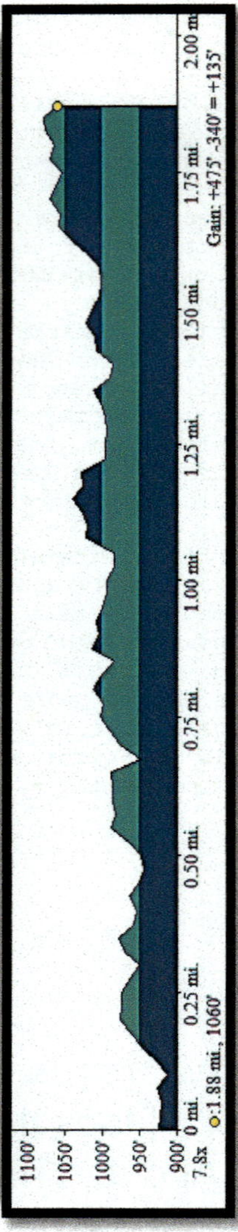
1100'
1050'
1000'
950'
900'
7.8x
0 mi.
0.25 mi.
0.50 mi.
0.75 mi.
1.00 mi.
1.25 mi.
1.50 mi.
1.75 mi.
2.00 mi
:1.88 mi., 1060'
Gain: +475' -340' = +135'

Cheney Pond and Lester Flow

Quad:

Blue Ridge

Distances:

- **From Blue Ridge Road to Cheney Pond 0.55 miles**
- **To Lester Flow Trail-0.15 miles**
- **To Lester Flow-2.15 miles**

Total distance 2.85 miles, one way

Directions to Trailhead:

From I-87, get off Exit 29, head west on the Blue Ridge Road. Once you cross the Boreas River about 10 minutes from I-87, start looking for the trailhead on the left side of the road. The trailhead is about 1.75 miles from the river crossing - a DEC sign marks it.

Trail Conditions:

This trail has a variety of conditions but mostly dry. The initial run will be a downhill adventure along an eroded woods road. The foot trail/snowmobile trail is a little grown up in spots but in excellent shape for a run.

The Lester Flow Trail is located 0.35 miles down a dirt road that leads to Cheney Pond. This dirt road is the official start of the trail. In summer it can be carefully driven to the Lester Flow Trail and Cheney Pond.

From the Blue Ridge Road you will immediately start a downhill run along a wide woods road. This is also a designated snowmobile trail. You will lose about 150 feet in this initial descent to the shore of Cheney Pond. You should have noticed the trail for Lester Flow on the right as you came through. It is a short uphill run to the trail from Cheney Pond; just retrace your steps.

This foot trail is also a snowmobile trail, and is gated. The trail register is located next to the yellow gate. It is a pleasant run through old-and new-growth forests. The grade is very shallow with only short ups and downs. The trail starts at 1790′ and only climbs to a maximum elevation of 1840′. But Lester Flow is actually lower than the trailhead at 1710′. So, in short, the longest climb is on the return to the car and that's, only 130′ over a 0.8 mile section, hardly noticeable.

Just 0.1 miles shy of the flow there is a nice little tamarack marsh at the site of an old beaver dam. Only feet from the dam there is a right fork, then in a few more feet a left fork. This is a carry for boaters to get around the rapids where the dam once was. There is a nice camping spot just feet up the left fork. Straight ahead is the site of the old Lester Dam, where only remnants remain. This is also the crossing for the snowmobile trail that eventually exits in the Township of Minerva, 11 miles from the trailhead.

Blue Ridge Road
CAMPSITE
Cheney Pond
WL 1519T
SNOWMOBILE
Lester Flow
River
Boreas
Lester Dam
RAPIDS
0 mi.
0.50 mi.
1.00 mi.
1.50 mi.
2.00 mi.
2.50 mi.
3.00 mi.
2.83 mi., 1711'
Gain: +190' -368' = -178'
1900'
1850'
1800'
1750'
1700'
15.6x

Barn Rock Bay

Quad:

Westport

Distances:

- **Trailhead to Ridge Trail intersection-0.3 miles**
- **To Barn Rock Trail-0.75 miles**
- **To Loop Trail-1.1 miles**
- **To Barn Rock Bay-0.35 miles**

Total distance 2.5 miles, one way

Directions to Trailhead:

From the town of Westport follow Route 22 just past the Westport boat launch site. Turn right on Lake Shore Road and follow here for roughly 4.5 miles to a DEC trailhead for Split Rock Wilderness. There is parking for a dozen cars or more.

Trail Conditions:

This is a snowmobile trail in parts; however there is a little bit of wet areas scattered throughout, but nothing substantial in any one spot. Footing is a little difficult in one section but mostly well graded.

This is a gated foot trail used for snowmobiling in the winter but makes for a great run as well. Located in the Split Rock Preserve this is just one run available from here.

Almost immediately the trail begins to climb (avoid the Elbow Trail on the right) and soon reaches an intersection with the ridge trail over Split Rock Mountain. Take this right and run on a mostly flat route, then to a slight downhill. There will be another intersection that comes in on the right. This is the other end of the Elbow Trail - the next right is the Barn Rock Trail.

The Barn Rock Trail is a foot trail now; it is no longer designated a snowmobile trail, but does get modest traffic. Follow here as it climbs uphill for a short section and passes by an old culvert. Soon the trail will begin to slowly descend. Eventually you will find yourself running steadily downhill along some water drainages. Soon the sides of the trail begin to rise into small cliffs on either side. You will notice several spots that look not so natural. These are parts of old rock walls and foundations of old-time dwellings.

As you approach Lake Champlain you will run by a 10 foot rock retention wall, and to your left is Barn Rock Bay. You will begin to see parts of Barn Rock Bay as you continue down to the bay. To reach the bay, follow the steep herd paths.

LAKE
SHORE
SPLIT ROCK
Barn Rock
Barn Rock Bay
Rock Harbor
2.52 mi., 95'
Gain: +505' -732' = -227'

Quad:

Keene Valley, Mount Marcy, Santanoni Peak

Distances:

- **Adirondack Loj to Marcy Dam-2.1 miles**
- **To Avalanche Camps-0.8 miles**
- **To Avalanche Lake-1 miles**
- **To Lake Colden-1.2 mile**
- **To Flowed Lands-1.65 miles**
- **To Calamity Pond-0.35 miles**
- **To Upper Works Trailhead-3.7 miles**

Total distance 10.9 miles, one way

Directions to Trailhead:

Adirondack Loj Trailhead

From the intersection of Routes 73 and 86 in Lake Placid follow Route 73 toward Keene Valley. Drive 3.5 miles to the Adirondack Loj Road on the right. Follow here to its end at the Heart Lake Trailheads.

Upper Works Trailhead

From I-87 take Exit 29 and head toward Newcomb along the Blue Ridge Road. Continue for around 18 miles to the Tahawus Road. Follow here for just under 10 miles to Upper Works. Bear left at the two intersections.

Trail Conditions:

This route is a high traffic area which has created a large amount of erosion in certain areas; accompanied by mud, rocks, roots and very unstable footing. You may also need to be aware of numerous hikers along this route, which could slow the pace a little. Ladders, catwalks and boulders exist along Avalanche Lake with may require a short section of hiking rather than running. Not all is muddy and in bad shape, but be prepared for long sections of below par terrain.

Side notes

There is paid parking at the Adirondack Loj with reduced rates for ADK members

A car spot is needed to complete this course

After Hurricane Irene in 2011 a re-route was developed to avoid river crossings on the Upper Works side of this run. This re-route has not been delineated on most maps, but has been laid out for you on ours

This particular run is one of the most popular hikes in the High Peaks Region. This run also encompasses the use of three Adirondack quads, two cars, and a bunch of ambition. You also have the choice to do it from either direction by starting at Upper Works or from the Adirondack Loj; no one direction is better than the other, but for the purposes of this guide it will be from the Adirondack Loj to Upper Works.

From the trailhead at the Adirondack Loj follow the well-used and stomped trail to Marcy Dam. This 2.1-mile section of trail is one of the most popular trails, if not the most popular trail in the Adirondack Park. The popularity doesn't come as much from its beauty but its location. It is the gateway to the High Peaks Region, so it is used as an approach by a great many hikers visiting the region.

The trail starts out flat before descending and crossing MacIntyre Brook on a long catwalk type bridge. The trail then climbs somewhat steep for a short period of time up the opposite slope. There are several small rolling hills before intersecting with the Algonquin Trail at 0.9 miles. Hang a left at this intersection, Marcy Dam is 1.3 miles away. The trail from this point is more rolling hills through an open hardwoods forest. Along this course there is a major reroute. Just shy of Marcy Dam the trail was rerouted to drop across Marcy Brook. The trail then meets up with the Marcy Dam Truck Trail and continues to Marcy Dam. The reroute was developed because Marcy Dam Bridge was destroyed along with the dam during Hurricane Irene and it cannot be crossed.

There is a plan in motion that will reopen the Marcy Dam Bridge - upon completion of a rebuild, this route will change slightly. If this happens you will remain on the original trail rather than drop down to cross the brook. You will be running uphill and begin a slow descent to the bridge on the left.

At Marcy Dam you will be able to take in excellent views through Avalanche Pass, with Avalanche Mountain and Mount Colden in the foreground. The Angel Slide and the new 2011 Marcy Dam Slide is to the back right of the former location of Marcy Dam Pond. The pond exist now only as a stream course through a wetland.

Angel Slide and 2011 Marcy Dam Slide

From here follow the trail that leads to Avalanche Pass - this will be a right at the next trail intersection. The next 0.8 miles brings you to what is referred to as Avalanche Camps. It has a slight incline for a slope; while the incline is relatively low your pace should still be fairly high. At the intersection at Avalanche Camps, left leads toward Lake Arnold and Feldspar Lean-to. Right leads toward Avalanche Pass and is also referred to as Misery Mile. It really is not that bad, but this is the point where you will start to really gain some elevation. Near the top of Avalanche Pass you will be below the site of the Stein Slide in Avalanche Pass, Slide on Mount Colden.

Shortly beyond this point you will drop through the pass in a dark forest. The base of a second slide will be on your left. This was created during Hurricane Irene as well. It was actually more of a widening of a former dike. Large boulders, cool air, thick moss, and steep cliffs line the trail as you run through. Slowly you will descend to the shore of Avalanche Lake, where the breathtaking views of the cliffs of Avalanche Mountain and Mount Colden can be seen disappearing into the lake itself.

Now you will enter the boulder field, where scrambling, ladders and catwalks are put out for you to use. This 0.75-mile section might be best used as a hike rather than a run; you know your abilities, but remember, you are a long way in to get out on a broken appendage. After you leave Avalanche Lake you will start a downhill run toward Lake Colden. Be sure to take the trail to the right around the west side of the lake. You will be running through one of the Adirondacks' premiere camping destinations, where a high volume of hikers may be encountered. The run now goes along the west shore of Lake Colden where periodic views can be had. At the southern end of the lake is Lake Colden Dam; do not cross the dam. This next section trail that ends at Flowed Lands is a very tricky run. Aside from steep rolling terrain the footing is rough.

At Flowed Lands Camp follow the Calamity Pond Trail as it slowly descends through a small valley between Mount Marshall and Calamity Mountain. After a quick and easy 0.3 miles you will be to the shore of Calamity Pond. The Henderson Monument stands out in the pond just off-shore. David Henderson was accidentally shot and died on this very spot while scouting for a water source for the blast furnaces at the Tahawus Iron Works. Other stories say he was hunting at the time of the accident. This was the "Calamity" that happened that gave the pond and the mountain their names.

Beyond this point, toward Upper Works you will continue a slow descent - but with periodic short ups for which at times seem very steep. Passing by Calamity Mountain on your left, the slopes drop slightly to the right. Most of the trail is a moderate push with scenic qualities. After a very long and somewhat steep downhill with a particularly interesting dog leg left you will have Calamity Brook on your left. After a bit of running along the brook you may notice the remnants of an old bridge. This bridge was taken downstream - no not by rangers but by Hurricane Irene. This is where the reroute begins. This reroute follows the Duck Hole Cross-over Trail for a bit to a bridge

crossing. After the bridge it is a hard left. You will drop to the shore of a marshy area and run along what looks to be an old woods road. The brook will be to your left and a small pond to your right. You will remain on old logging roads for over a mile as you run through the rolling hills that eventually lead you to the Upper Works Parking Area.

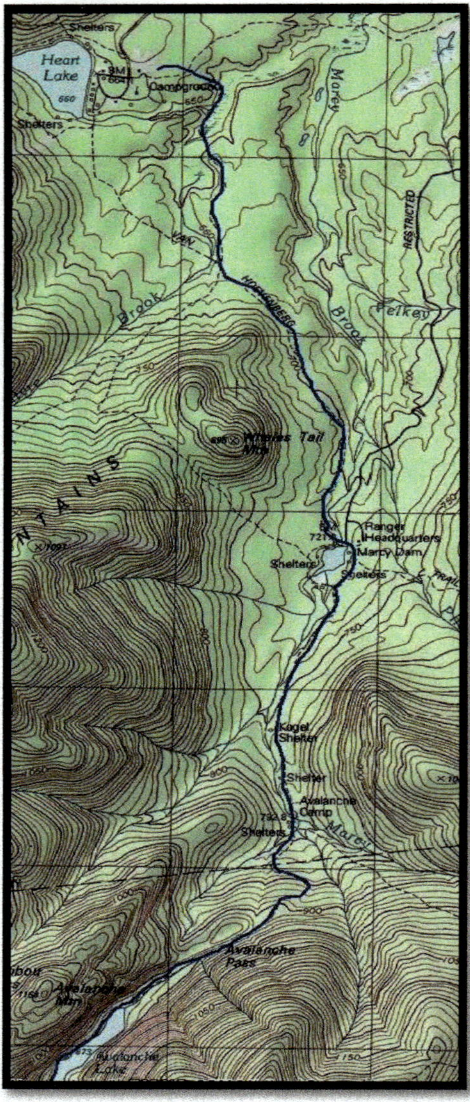

Northern Portion

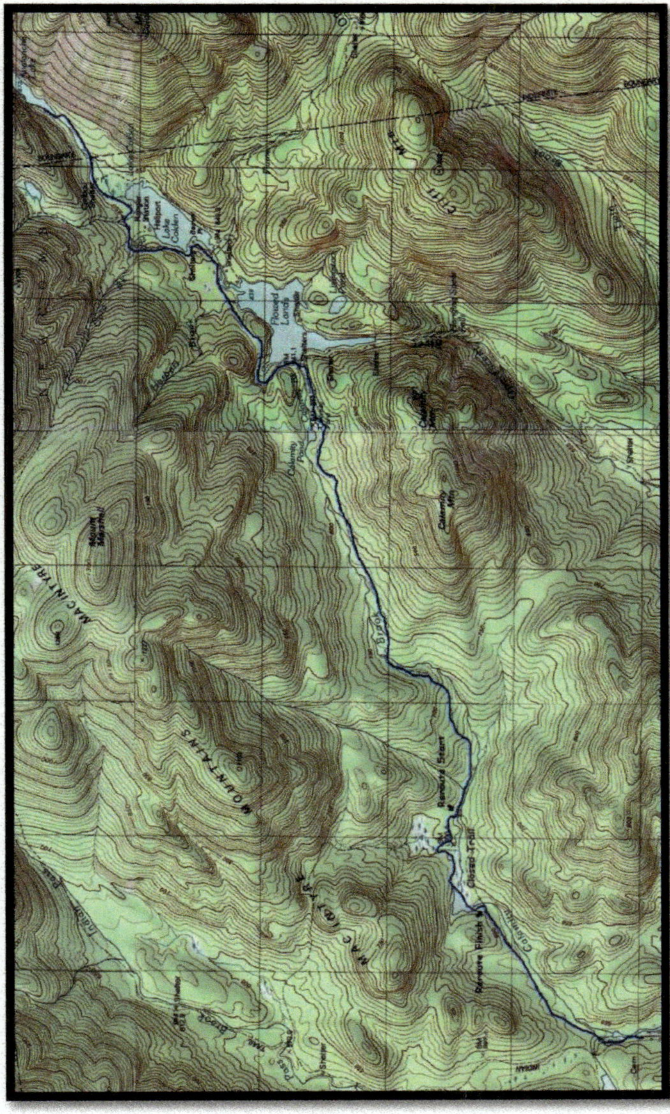

Southern Portion

Lower Ausable Lake

Quad:

Keene Valley, Mount Marcy

Distances:

- **Trailhead Parking to gate-0.8 miles**
- **To Lower Ausable Lake-3.3 miles**

Total distance 4.1 miles, one way

Directions to Trailhead:

From I-87 take Exit 30 head west along Route 73 toward Keene Valley. Follow for 7.4 miles to the trailhead parking in St. Huberts on the left. The Roaring Brook Falls Trailhead to Giant is directly across Route 73. The trailhead is 0.8 miles further down this road; it will need to be hiked, no vehicle parking at the gate.

Trail Conditions:

This is a woods road run; conditions are dry as a bone. The only downfall is the initial run on tarmac.

From the trailhead parking you will be running a dirt road to a paved road which accesses the trails into the High Peaks Area. Along the road take a left after the tennis courts and downhill to the gate at 0.8 miles. At the gate there is a small ranger hut and a trail register. This is the point for which the best part of the run begins.

The remaining 3.4 miles will be a 700′ climb along what is referred to as Lake Road. The Lake Road is used very heavily by hikers and members, so the road is very hard under-foot. This is also a private road for public hiker easement - respect the owner's rules and regulation, which are posted at the gate.

Along the Lake Road there are several intersections, none of which you will need to follow, but do offer alternatives if you are in the mood to explore. First are the intersection of the Ladies Mile on the right and then a second intersection of the Ladies Mile.

The Dial and Nippletop trail comes in on the right after an uphill climb. At about 1.2 miles you will come to a flume near the road; this is a short loop over, to and from, be sure to check this little gem out. The next inter-section is a crossover trail for Gothics and Beaver Meadow Falls on the right. Shortly after that on the left is the Gill Brook Trail. Less than a half-mile past this is the Gill Brook Cut-off Trail on the left.

Just beyond the Gill Brook Cut-off the road begins to descend. On the left you will pass the trail to Indian Head. Just down over the hill is Lower Ausable Lake. The dam is over the hill to the right - this is the best viewpoint.

Since Lower Ausable Lake is private, swimming is not permitted in the lake. The run out is mostly downhill and much faster.

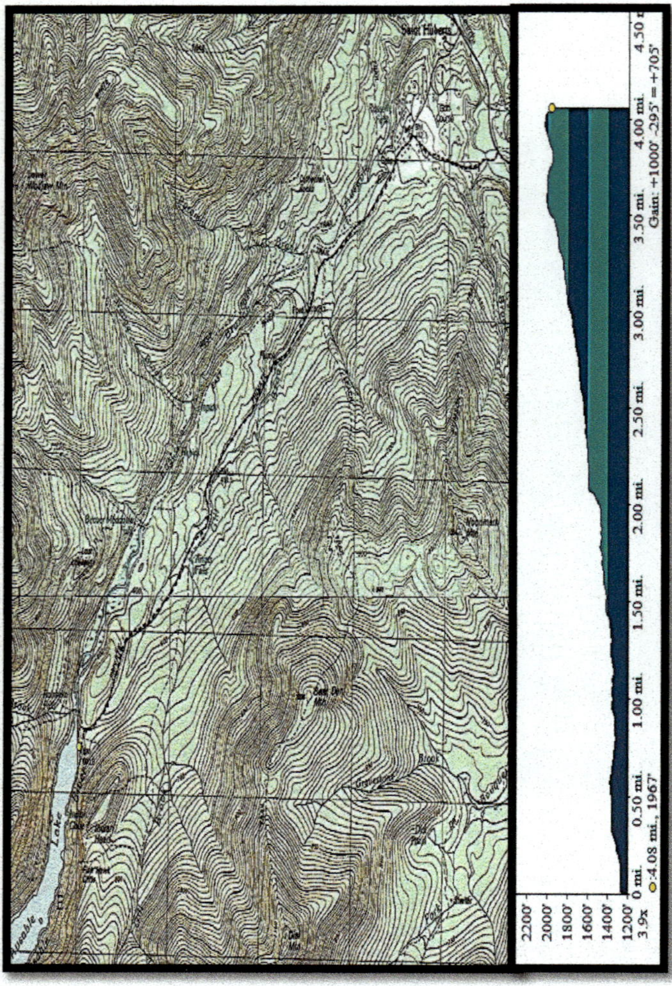

Quad:

Blue Ridge and Mount Marcy

Distances:

- **Clear Pond to Elk Lake Trailhead-1.9 miles**
- **Elk Lake Trailhead to Slide Brook Lean-to-2.1 miles**
- **To Lillian Brook Lean-to-1.2 miles**
- **To Dix Pond-0.45 miles**
- **To Hunter Pass-1.9 miles**
- **To Round Pond/Dix Trail-0.5 miles**
- **To Dial Pond outlet-2.1 miles**
- **To AMR-3.7 miles**
- **To AMR Parking-0.3 miles**

Total distance 14.15 miles, one way

Directions to Trailhead:

For the southern trailhead

Off I-87 take Exit 29 - follow the Blue Ridge Road toward Newcomb. Go 3.9 miles to the Elk Lake Road. Follow the Elk Lake Road to its end and park in the hiker parking lot.

For the northern trailhead

Off I-87 take Exit 30 - drive toward Keene Valley on Route 73. Follow Route 73 for 7.5 miles to the entrance for the AMR the Giant Mountain/Roaring Brook Falls Trailhead is directly across the road.

Trail Conditions:

This trail is a mix of conditions. The beginning starts off dry but turns very wet and remains wet for quite some time. There are some sections of flat, mostly found at the end. Very steep sections and large boulders make the pass itself a serious challenge.

The trailhead is one of the most popular in the High Peaks Region. The trail starts out on a slight uphill, first passing a couple private Elk Lake Lodge trails, then joining an old tote road. There are a few small ups and downs along the route with several stream crossings. At 2.25 miles you will be at the Slide Brook Lean-to area. You may notice a rock cairn on the right that marks the herd path for Macomb Mountain. Continue to follow the DEC-marked Trail. The first portion of this run along the old road tends to be very wet with quite odd footing.

From Slide Brook the trail dips a little to cross another brook before climbing slightly. You will then find yourself with a gentle downhill slope that will bring you to the Lillian Brook Lean-to. After an additional short climb and a short, steep descent you will find yourself on a hillside above Dix Pond. You will stay above Dix Pond with several small ups and downs before you eventually descend to the shore. Many short herd paths lead you to different viewpoints on the pond.

Approximately 0.15 miles after you have passed the pond you will come to an intersection with the Beckhorn Trail to the right. Hunter Pass is straight ahead and the route you want to follow. This pass can be a wind catcher and very cold even when surrounding areas are mild.

Climbing up to Hunter Pass is one of much scenery, seclusion and ruggedness. This next section starts off immediately by crossing East Inlet and on a moderate to flat course opens up several different views of the west side of Dix Mountain. As you get closer and start nearing the top of the pass the trail gets narrower and steeper in short sections. Then at one point the trail passes beneath tall cliffs coming off from Nipple Top Mountain. There are a few false tops, luring you to the idea that you are there, but guess what.

From the top of the pass you can see Dix Pond below and the cliff faces of Dix. Continuing on from here it will be more of a high paced hike as the terrain is quite steep.

From the top of Hunter Pass the trail take a hard right crossing several large boulders and begins a steep and arduous climb up the shoulder of Dix. The next 0.5 miles to the intersection with the Round Pond/Dix Trail is relentless and climbs 1,000 feet in elevation is this to be considered an easy traverse. Once at the intersection you have the choice of continuing up the shoulder of Dix to the summit, which at this point is very moderate in comparison, or hang a left and descend down and out of the mountains toward Keene Valley.

On the descent you will begin a very steep course - this is not for the newbie runner. If you feel uncomfortable on narrow, rocky, eroded and steep terrain, hike at a modest pace until you get to the Dix Slide. This is one of the steepest sections of trail found in the Adirondack Park. At the end of the steep descent you will find yourself at the base of the north face slides on Dix.

From the base of the slide you will be on a much more moderate downhill trail, but still with an occasional steep spot. Crossing several small brooks on the way, you eventually level out and cross the Bouquet to the lean-to. This brook can be more like a river at times and may require you to wade.

In another 0.55 miles you will cross two forks of Gravestone Brook. In 1.2 miles from Gravestone Brook you will come to a large intersection with the Noonmark Mountain Trail and the Round Pond Trail. Continue straight along the Dix Trail. This trail passes you between Noonmark and Round Mountains. You will pass by the trail to Round Mountain in the col between the two.

After a climb to the col and a descent over a 1.65-mile section you will pass another trail up Noonmark Mountain, and shortly beyond that you will come to a private driveway. This driveway gives easement to this area; be sure to stay on the marked route. You will only be on the drive for a few minutes before you come out to the AMR Road. Follow here, downhill and right, back to your second car.

Just remember there's nothing that says you have to go all the way through, you can always go as far as you wish and turn around.

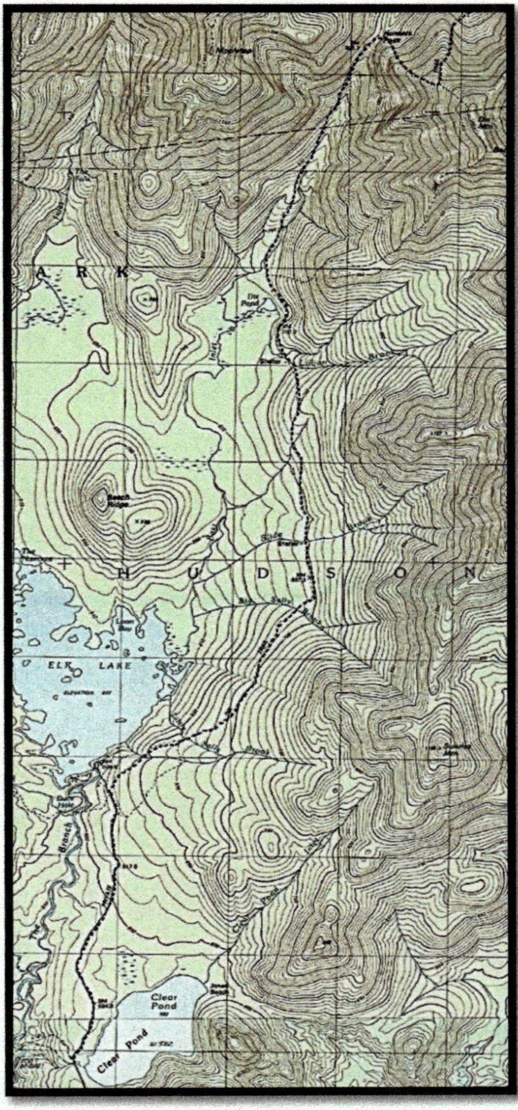

Southern Section

Northern Section

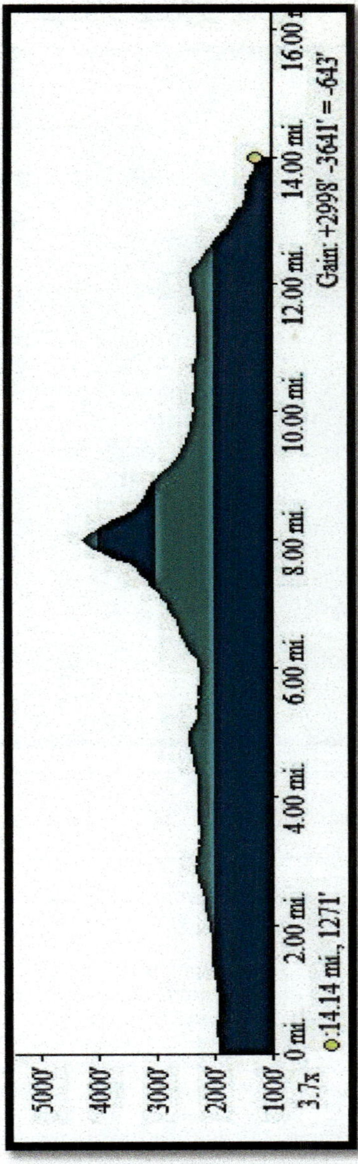
5000'
4000'
3000'
2000'
1000'
3.7x
0 mi.
2.00 mi.
4.00 mi.
6.00 mi.
8.00 mi.
10.00 mi.
12.00 mi.
14.00 mi.
16.00
:14.14 mi., 1271'
Gain: +2998' -3641' = -643'

Heart Lake Loop

Quad:

Keene Valley

Distances:

- **Adirondack Loj parking to Heart Lake Ski Trail-0.5 miles**
- **To Old Marcy Dam Trail-0.5 miles**
- **To Algonquin Trail-0.6 miles**
- **To Whales Tail Ski Trail-0.4 miles**
- **To Marcy Dam-1.1 miles**
- **To Adirondack Loj Parking-2.3 miles**

Total distance 5.4 miles, loop

Directions to Trailhead:

From the intersection of Routes 86 and 73 in Lake Placid follow Route 73 toward Keene Valley. Go just over 3 miles to the Adirondack Loj Road on the right. It is the first right after the Olympic ski jumps. Follow this road to its end, through the toll booth and park in the hiker parking lot to the left.

Trail Conditions:

This run is over lightly used trails, for the first half. With decent footing over most, there are sections of rather difficult footing that can be expected.

Side note

There is paid parking at the Adirondack Loj with reduces pricing for ADK members

Many of these trails are accessed more as ski trails but can simply be used as run loops.

From the parking area you will need to cross the road back by the toll booth and look for the trail to Rocky Falls and Scott Clearing. Following the trail you will have some interesting footing, but not dangerous. There are several large, well-grounded boulders to jump on, over or run around if so desired. You will pass by a trail register and run slightly downhill as you pass by Heart Lake on your left. After a short uphill you will come to the Heart Lake Trail on the left. This section of trail is used almost exclusively as a snowshoe/ski trail, so expect it to be narrow and slightly overgrown.

This trail will spit you out near the base of an old ski slope on ADK property. The trail heads down it along the ski slope and back into the woods. Shortly thereafter the trail will come to an intersection. The trail left leads back to the campground on ADK property and right is the Old Marcy Dam Trail; follow right here.

This trail, again used widely as a ski trail, will bring you uphill to the new Marcy Dam Trail at the intersection with the Algonquin Peak Trail. Follow right toward Algonquin Peak. This trail section is very well-used and pounded very hard - this, of course, builds for some very nice footing. On a mostly continuous uphill you will come to the Whales Tail Ski Trail on the left after a quick 0.4 miles from the last intersection.

Following the ski trail you will find that this will be the roughest footing of the day. This trail gets very little use during non-ski months. It climbs moderately to a pass between Whales Tail Mountain and the Whale. The descent out of the pass is much steeper than the climb and the footing can be a little rough; just use care and a little extra time to make it down safely.

The Whales Tail Ski Trail will exit you at a lean-to at Marcy Dam. Marcy Dam Pond as seen on the map no longer exists. When Hurricane Irene came through, the dam was destroyed and drained the pond and left a wetland with Marcy Brook running through it.

Follow the trail to the left from the lean-to and join the Marcy Dam Trail to the left back toward the ADK Loj. From the site of the dam to the left has been temporarily closed due to the dam being washed out. It may not be as noticeable from this side and it should be used with caution until you regain the open trail - just a couple minutes down the trail. This rumor is that the bridge will be re-built, but the dam will not be. Is this true or just talk? We will have to see. Just keep in mind that it could be reopened and this trail section as well.

The final section from the dam is 2.1 miles and loaded with sweeping turns and rolling hills; this is a very fun section of trail to run. With footing being very good and the terrain not steep you can really pick up the pace and run really hard. You will exit this trail at the Heart Lake parking lot.

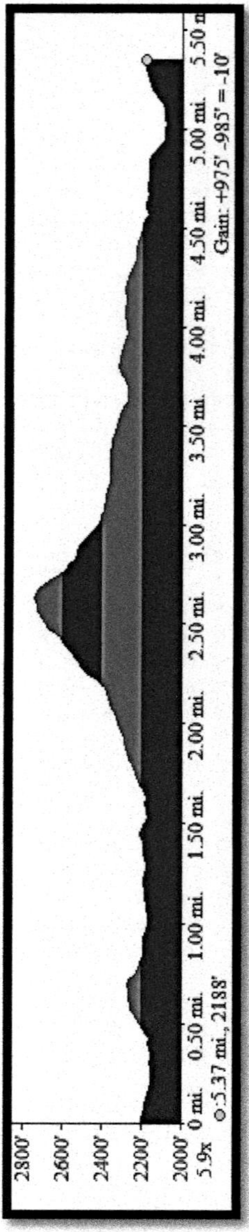

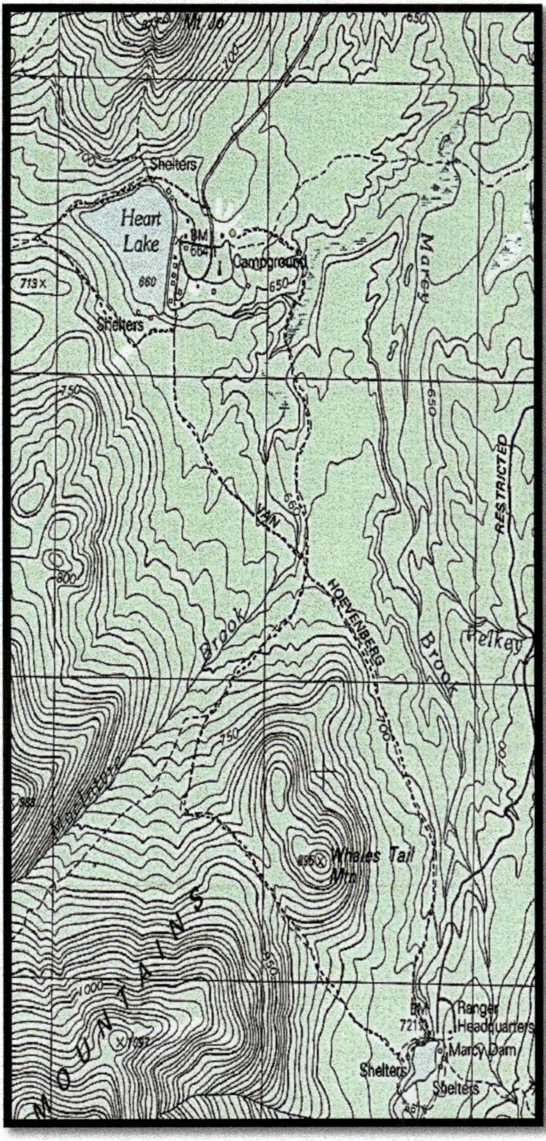
Mt Jo
Shelters
Heart
Lake
BM
Campground
Shelters
Marcy
Brook
RESTRICTED
VAN
HOEVENBERG
Brook
Pelkey
Whales Tail
Mtn
MOUNTAINS
BM
Ranger
Headquarters
Marcy Dam
Shelters
Shelters

JBL Loop

Quad:
Keene Valley

Distances:

- **Garden Parking lot to Southside Trail junction-0.5 miles**
- **To Deer Brook Lean-to-0.6 miles**
- **To Suspension Bridge over Johns Brook-1.8 miles**
- **To Johns Brook Crossing-2.2 miles**
- **To Northside Trail-0.2 miles**
- **Back to Garden parking-0.5 miles**

Total distance 5.8 miles, loop

Directions to Trailhead:
From I-87 take Exit 30, head west along Route 73. Go 10.5 miles to the hamlet of Keene Valley and look for the Ausable Inn on the left. Take Johns Brook Lane. Follow the road for approximately 1.5 miles here to the end, which is the Garden Trailhead parking lot,

Trail Conditions:
Aside from a couple random wet areas this entire loop is pretty dry. There is one crossing of John's Brook at the end of the loop that can pose issues during high water.

Side note

There are sections of landslides on this loop that were created after Hurricane Irene, be aware of the slight trail changes.

High water puts parts of the trail underwater, use of the "high water route" are encouraged during wetter time periods and in the spring.

This is one of our favorite runs in the High Peaks Region. Below is the trail description in a counter-clockwise direction.

From the parking area you will immediately pass by the Big Slide/Brothers Trail and work your way quickly to the base of a small hill. The trail is mostly uphill to the intersection of the Southside Trail, which comes in on your left after 0.5 miles. Continuing uphill - aside from a small dip here and there to cross drainage - you will come to the former area of the Deer Brook Lean-to at 1.1 miles. This may or not be apparent - but no less you are there. Just past here is a continual uphill, but on a moderate to easy grade to Bear Brook Lean-to area. We say area, as this lean-to was moved slightly uphill and away from the trail. Immediately past here is a very steep downhill, at the bottom there are two brook crossings. On the other side of the brook is a steep uphill, but short in distance.

From this point there will be several more ups and down, some slightly steeper than others, but mostly mellow rolling terrain. At about 2.7 miles you will come to some tenting sites on your right, at the top of a modestly sized downhill run. If you have ever hiked in the area, you know the hill I am referring to. The trail is narrow with sharp turns, and as you near the base it gets very tight, with trees that seem to close in. At the base of the hill there is a T-intersection. Right goes to John's Brook Lodge and left to the suspension bridge. Hang a left and pass by the ranger's interior outpost on your right. The suspension bridge is just a few hundred feet further.

Cross the bridge with care and hang a left on the opposite side. In about 0.2 miles you will come to the trail intersection that leads to Wolf Jaw Notch, avoid this by staying straight. Along mostly flat terrain you will shortly cross Wolfjaw Brook, on a rather good-sized bridge. In a little over 0.25 miles from here is Bennies Brook and the slide path caused by Hurricane Irene in August 2011. The trail crosses and regains the old trail just on the other side.

At about 0.4 miles past Bennies Brook, you will come to a high water route on the right. You have the option to take this, but I warn you, it gets little use, developing standing water. The low water route usually poses no issues, but there are trickier sections to run - trickier but more fun. What do I mean by trickier? Usually it's loose rock and slippery conditions as the trail approaches the shore of John's Brook. During high water the trail is usually submerged.

So, back at the intersection of the high water route - in a short span of time you will come to Rock Cut Brook, and that's just what it is too. Here you will have no choice but to stop running. You will have to scale a six foot rock wall - this is actually pretty easy to do, but not at a high rate of speed. From here it is a quick downhill with a sharp right that leads to a much more moderate but steady downhill grade. You will find yourself high above the brook, on a narrow trail before descending to the brooks shore.

Once you leave the shore you will be back in the forest and pulling away from John's Brook. You will then be running on a very gentle downhill, with only a couple small ups that are forgotten just as fast. Just 0.1 miles shy of the Johns Brook crossing you will come to an intersection with a private trail; take a left to remain on the state trail. Before you reach the brook crossing be prepared for a steep drop-off of what looks to be an old berm.

The John's Brook crossing isn't one to take lightly. You should do it as efficiently as possible. Rushing water below you is nothing to mess around with. Be sure to take in mind current and recent weather conditions to evaluate its flow and depth. On the opposite side of the brook you will find a trail with one steep little drop-off before you approach the base of an esker. The trail follows along the esker through an old-growth forest. This is very steep and relentless for a relatively short amount of time. Above the esker the Northside Trail shortly reappears - follow right. From this point its 0.5 miles; mostly downhill back to the parking area.

Garden
Keene Valley
JBL
Rooster Comb
Hedgehog Mtn
The Brothers
Gain: +1120' -1099' = +21'
5.76 mi., 1546'
0 mi.
0.50 mi.
1.00 mi.
1.50 mi.
2.00 mi.
2.50 mi.
3.00 mi.
3.50 mi.
4.00 mi.
4.50 mi.
5.00 mi.
5.50 mi.
6.00 mi.
2400'
2200'
2000'
1800'
1600'
1400'
4.1x

Peninsula Trails

The Brewster Peninsula Trails are located on the shores of Lake Placid and are tucked back on a dirt road. The DEC has worked to use old access roads and selected new trails to develop this year-round destination for short, fun afternoon outings. A destination for cross-country skiers, snowshoers, mountain bikers, trail runners, hikers, family picnics and fishing - you shouldn't be surprised to see all kinds of recreationists. Young and old, novice to experienced - this is a great spot to stretch your legs.

Quad:

Lake Placid

Directions to Trailhead:

From the intersection of Routes 73 and 86 in Lake Placid follow Route 86 toward the center of town and Saranac Lake. Continue 1.6 miles to Peninsula Road on the right. This road is hard to locate as it looks like a driveway to a hotel. It is located just before the Howard Johnsons Restaurant. Follow this steep road which quickly turns to dirt. At the intersection head left and you will see the trailhead for the Brewster Peninsula Trails just a short distance down.

Below you will find descriptions of four trails that can be combined to make for several different loop options.

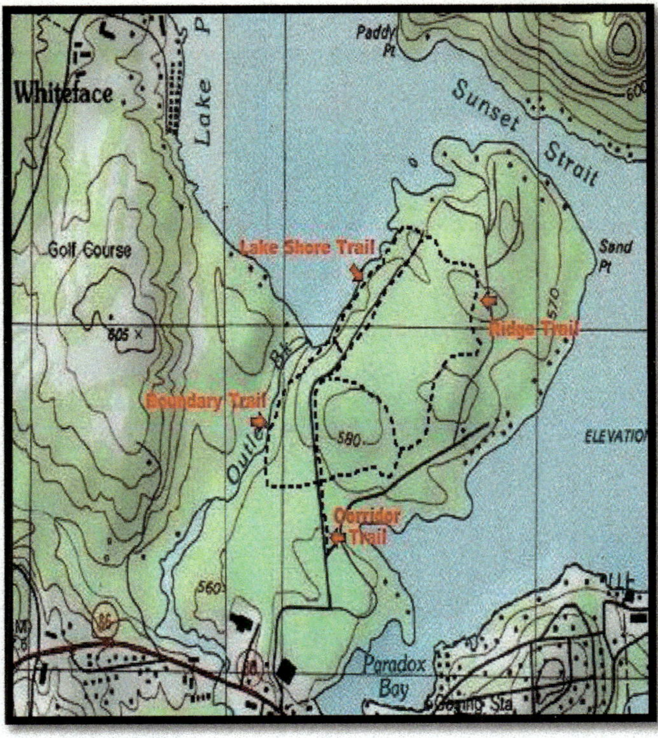

"Success isn't how far you got, but the distance you traveled from where you started."

Brocaw Blazers.org

Distances:

↳ **Total distance 0.75 miles, one way**

Trail Conditions:

Dry and easy to follow; great access route to all other trails in the area

The corridor trail is just that - a trail through the heart of the peninsula and the start for every loop.

From the trailhead, you will pass by a yellow gate and in a matter of feet the trail register. From here it is a light downhill to a rather generous flat section. It is roughly 0.25 miles to your first intersection. This is where the Boundary Trail crosses the Corridor Trail. Just past this intersection the trail begins to climb ever so slightly. You will see a rather large sign as you come around the corner and a picnic table. This is the end of the Ridge Trail.

Just past this section is the start of the Boundary Trail, which I will get to in a second. You will finish off the Corridor Trail in no time as the trail is mostly flat. At the end of the trail you will see the start of the Ridge Trail and the start of the Lake Shore Trail, which is a spur trail that connects the other loops mentioned below.

Lake Shore Trail

Distances:

- **Total distance 0.4 miles, one way**

Trail Conditions:

This trail has exposed rocks and roots and in a couple areas a slight amount of mud - most demanding footwork trail in the network.

Starting at the end of the Corridor Trail where the Ridge Trail also starts, hang a slight left to descend ever so slightly to the shore of Lake Placid. From here you will be running a mostly flat course. Your footwork will need to be in good working order. There are numerous exposed rocks and roots that you will need to work your way through, but it's all good.

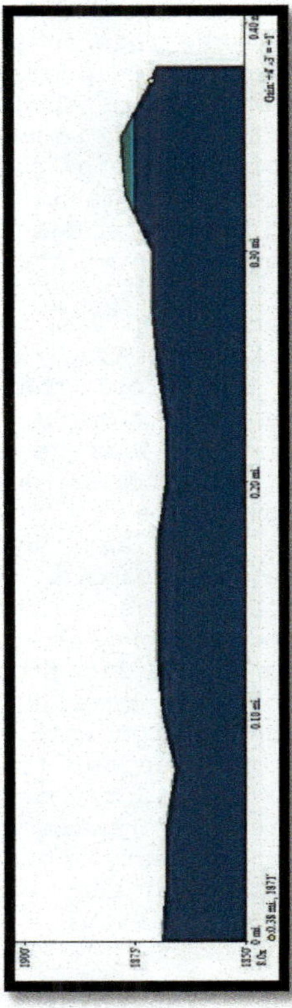

Distances:

↳ **Total distance 0.9 miles, one way**

Trail Conditions:

This trail in part follows the Jackrabbit Trail. It's mostly dry with hardly any issues with wet conditions.

We have started the description for the Boundary Trail at the second intersection along the Corridor Trail. The first very short bit is actually both the Corridor Trail and the Lake Shore Trail.

From the intersection with the Corridor Trail, run a slightly steep trail for a couple hundred feet down to the shore of Lake Placid. At the shore, take a left and run along shore toward the dam. In a very short amount of time you will be at the dam on Lake Placid. It is a smooth, flowing concrete dam with amazing views out over the lake.

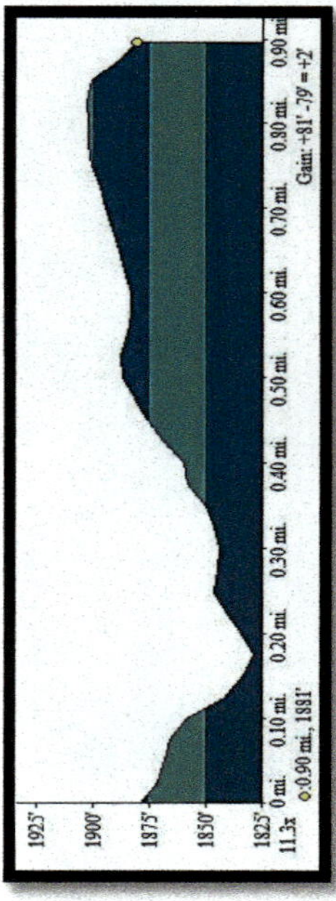

From the dam, follow the Jackrabbit Trail to the left - do not cross the bridge over the dam, this will bring you to the Whiteface Inn Golf Course. Shortly down this section there is a split, take the left and continue along the Jackrabbit Trail. This section has a few fun small swoops along its course, making for a fun section to run. You will come to a four-way intersection with a small tree in the center, take a left to the Corridor Trail and cross here. The remaining section of the Boundary Trail is mostly uphill and ends abruptly along the Ridge Trail.

Ridge Trail

Distances:

➪ **Total distance 0.7 miles, one way**

Trail Conditions:

Being the trail with the most elevation change, it is by far the most sought after. This is a nearly completely dry trail, with great rolling hills.

This trail is the most fun of all the trails on the peninsula. Starting from the end of the Corridor Trail, hang a right and start a semi-decent little climb to the top of the ridge. The top of the ridge is a nice, mellow run with one very steep drop that you will run-off to the hardwoods below.

From this point, it's rolling hills and a few tight turns before it passes by the Boundary Trail on the left. From here it is all downhill back to the Corridor Trail.

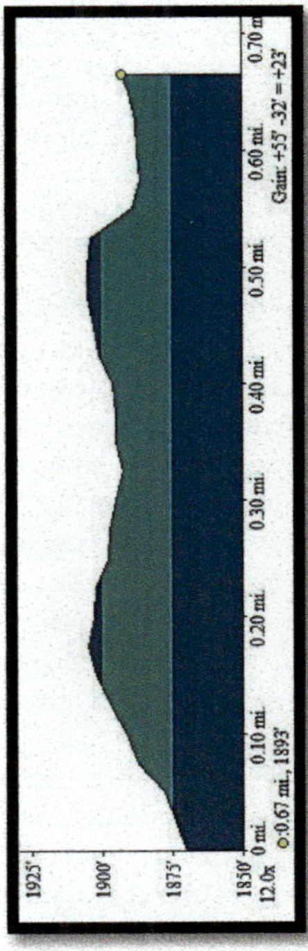

Henry's Woods

Henry's Woods, which is owned and maintained by the Uihlein Foundation, is a community preserve located just outside of the village of Lake Placid. And now for a brief history lesson - not that long ago, this plot of land was relatively undeveloped. Over the course of two years, the directors of the Uihlein Foundation discussed plans for the best utilization of the property. In 2005 the decision was made to develop the property for recreational endeavors (hiking, running, mountain biking, snowshoeing) as Henry Uihlein was an outdoor recreational enthusiast. So it began; trail work in Henry's Woods commenced in 2006 by following an old Bridle Path developed by the Lake Placid Club. In 2008 Henry's Woods opened to the public and in the following year more trails were added with options for loops and more aggressive terrain.

The question is; will Henry's Woods keep growing? Yes, it is seen as an expanding trail system that will continue over the next few years. There are 100 adjoining acres called the "Backwoods" and 600 additional acres referred to as the "Heaven Hill" property. Heaven Hill can be found on most topographical maps and is noticeably an area with amazing land features for recreation. We are very excited to the see what the new trails have to offer as I am sure you will be too; once you see what Henry's Woods already has in store for you.

With all that being said; the caretakers and the Uihlein Foundation ask that you utilize them but be respectful of the property. Use environmental ethics, recreational ethics, respect and the sometimes all too uncommon; common-sense when using them. With Henry's Woods developed for all to use, this is the first time it will be truly be described in a guide book. The property is already getting heavier use than expected so it will take everyone to keep it in the pristine shape that you will find it in when you get there.

We would like to express our sincere gratitude to Jim McKenna for taking his time to answer our many questions; Ray Curran and Craig Cheeseman for supplying us with the trail system map; and everyone at the Uihlein Foundation for permitting us to share this local gem with all of you.

For more information in regards to Henry's Woods Trails you can make contact them at (518)523-3061 or heavenhillfarm@verizon.net

Quad:

Lake Placid

Directions to Trailhead:

From the intersection of Routes 73 and 86 in Lake Placid, follow Route 73 toward Keene. Continue 0.2 miles to Station Street on the right. This road is the first right after you cross the Chubb River. Follow this road for 0.75 miles to Old Military Road. Take a left on Old Military Road and follow for 0.9 miles to Bear Cub Road on the right. The trailhead is a couple hundred feet up on the right.

Below you will find descriptions of the four trails that can be combined to make for several different loop options. The trails are very well marked - with signs at the trail intersections, you will still need to watch for the different-color trail markers to access the individual trails.

Henry's Woods - A Community Preserve

Trail Name	Map Symbol	Miles One-way	Challenge Level	Elevation Gain
Connector	Green	0.3	Easiest	100 feet
Loop	Green	2.0	Moderate	190 feet
Plateau	Yellow	0.9	Easiest	20 ± 40 feet
Switchback	Blue	.25	Moderate	130 feet
Rocky Knob	Red	0.9	Strenuous	320 feet
The "Summit" is 2270 feet		4.4 Miles of Trail	Henry's Woods is 212 acres of forest.	

The **DISTANCE** from "Trail Head" to "Summit" by following "Loop" then "Rocky Knob" and continuing back to "Trail Head" in the same direction on "Loop" is **3.1 miles** with a climb of **450 feet.**

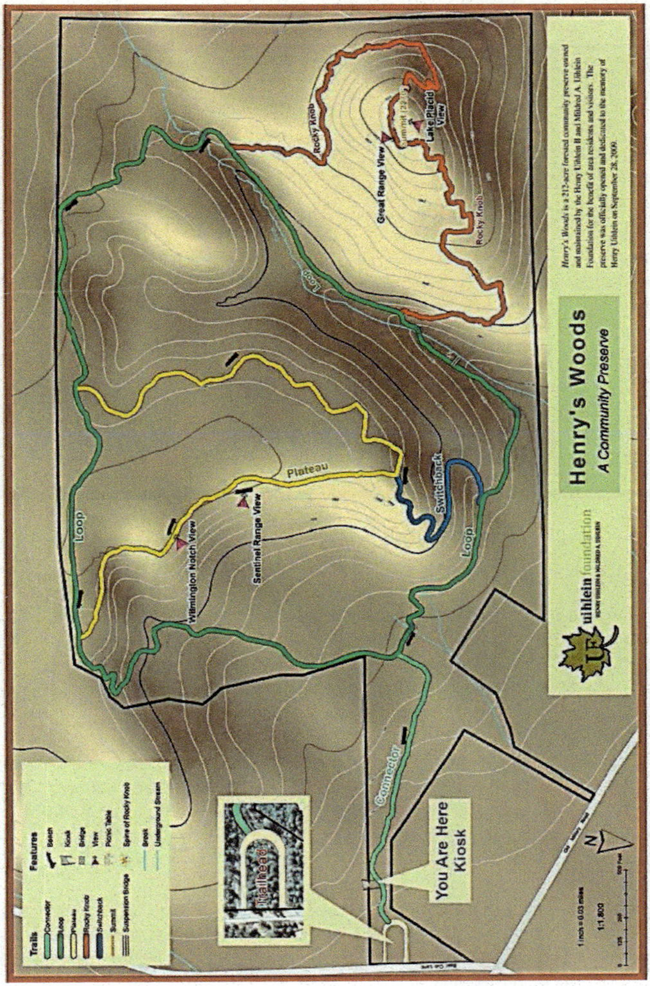

"Map produced for the Uihlein Foundation by Adirondack Information Group -- Ray Curran and Craig Cheeseman, Wilmington, NY."

Connector and Loop Trail

Distances:

- Connector Trail to Green Trail-0.3 miles
- To Switchback Trail Trail-0.25 miles
- To Rocky Knob Trail North-0.4 miles
- To Rocky Knob Trail South-0.25 miles
- To Plateau Trail West-0.4 miles
- To Plateau Trail East-0.2 miles
- Back to Loop Trail split-0.5 miles
- Back to parking-0.3 miles

Total distance 2.6 miles, one way

Trail Conditions:

You will find bridge crossings and steeper hills while running this main corridor route.

The Loop Trail with **green markers** is what you might refer to as the "Corridor Trail." Since it accesses all other trails in the network and is the trail you start and finish on, no matter what loops you desire to experiment on.

The trail marker pictured above is an example of the ones you will see along the trails. Again, be sure to watch for different-colored markers that help indicate trail intersections.

From the trailhead you will begin your trip on the 0.3-mile Connector Trail and pass by a small kiosk on the left. Shortly beyond you will begin to climb a moderate hill to your first intersection.

This intersection is actually a split of the Loop Trail. Following here in a counter-clockwise direction, there is a short downhill that will cross over a bridge and then make a sharp right up a modest hill. Atop this hill you begin a soft descent through a majestic open hardwoods forest. Down in the valley you will pass by the Switchback Trail on your left. Running on you will pass by the Bridge to Nowhere on the right. It truly is a bridge to nowhere, you'll see. In a short distance you will come to the Rocky Knob Trail on the right. Continuing on with the Loop Trail, you will remain on a somewhat flat course and quickly pass by the other end of the Rocky Knob Trail as it rejoins the Loop Trail.

In a short matter of time you will find yourself on the up and up again as you climb moderately - to - steeply up to a height of land. After a couple sharp switchbacks, the trail levels out and follows along a high ridge or plateau with steep slopes to your left. As you move along, be sure to look for the Plateau Trail on the left; it is on the flats of the upper ridge.

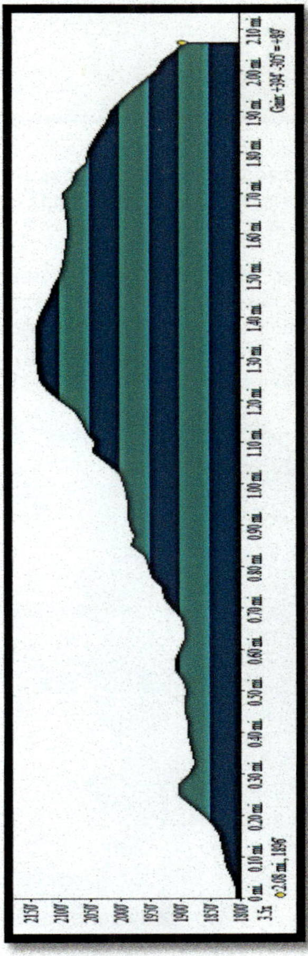

Shortly beyond, the trail will begin to descend and come to the opposite side of the Plateau Trail. Beyond this point, be prepared for a more serious downhill run. This downhill run will continue for most of the remaining portion to the trailhead. On this downhill there is one very sharp dog-leg-left, as a golfer would call it. The remaining down is moderate to slightly steep at worst - or best as some might call it.

Rocky Knob Trail

Distances:

- **From the Loop Trail to Rocky Knob Summit-0.6 miles**
- **Back to Green Trail-0.3 miles**

Total distance 0.9 miles, one way

Trail Conditions:

This is a very steep trail, even with the switch-backs. While a little slippery in spots, it doesn't hold much for water and mud. The height of land on this trail offers great views from Henry's Hill.

The Rocky Knob Trail is a **red marked** trail and it leaves the Loop Trail in a valley and will be the most challenging trail in Henry's Woods. Following in a counter-clockwise direction, begin your course.

From the Loop Trail starting on the northernmost end of the **Red Trail**, start a consistent uphill assault. You start off rather moderately on a side cut before the switchbacks start. There are a couple private trails along this route that you should avoid - all

private trails will be on your right, so bear left and you will be fine.

Through a series of steep switchbacks you will make your way to just below the top of what I have referred to a Henry's Hill - not in any reference to the mobster "Henry Hill." There is a short, narrow and steep spur trail to get you to the top of the hill, which opens up nice views out over the Lake Placid area.

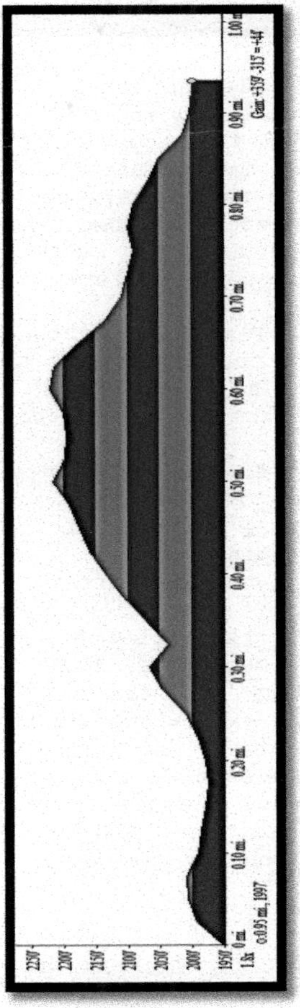

From the spur trail it is quite steep for a split second - but that's all it will take to run right off the edge of a small cliff - not really, but you get my drift, be careful. The trail goes to the edge of the cliff and hangs a very sharp right. Beyond here the trail is very manageable. You first run past a small cliff on the right and work your way down through the forest on a moderate trail. There are a couple sharp turns as you meander down to a smooth run back to the Loop Trail.

Plateau Trail

Distances:

- Loop Trail to Switchback Trail-0.5 miles
- Back to Loop Trail-0.4 miles

Total distance 0.9 miles, one way

Trail Conditions:

This trail follows along an upper ridge with amazing views along flatter terrain.

The Plateau Trail is a yellow marked trail and leaves from the Loop Trail along the high plateau. Starting from the western end of the Plateau Trail begin a gentle run through a very attractive hardwood forest.

The Plateau Trail is a mellow trail, period. You will run hard along the plateau at the top of a horseshoe ridge line, or a kind of bluff. You will enjoy small dips in the trail to put a breeze in your hair and long sweeping turns. Along the way you will partake of some very nice viewpoints out over the valley and off into the mountains. About halfway along the trail you will pass the Switchback Trail on the left, which can be easily missed at a high rate of speed. Eventually you will rejoin the Loop Trail just beyond the plateau.

Distances:

- Total distance from Plateau Trail to Loop Trail-0.25 miles

Trail Conditions:

This is a very short trail with some serious downhill - it makes for a great connector trail between the Plateau and the Loop Trail.

The Switchback Trail is a **blue marked** trail and is located off the Plateau Trail and is the shortest trail, with the most extreme elevation change. From the Plateau Trail you will be passing through an open forest but will soon be faced with tight turns on a steeper slope.

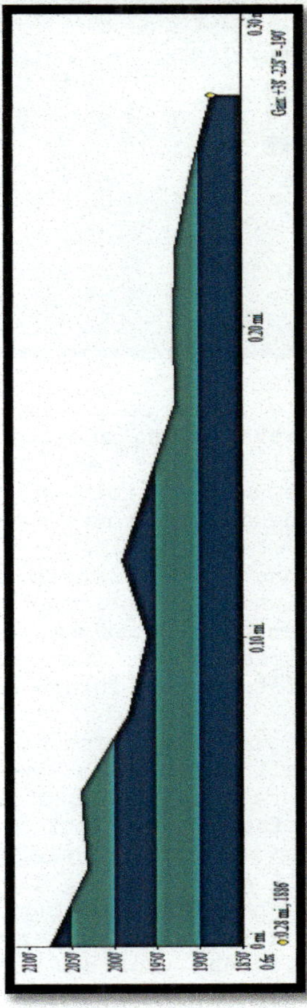

This trail drops down off the plateau and exits in the valley on the Loop Trail. This is actually one of those trails you want to climb and run again and again - it really is a ton of fun, even if your legs aren't totally in agreement.

Quad:

Newcomb

Distances:

- **Great Camp Gate to Moose Pond Trail-2.2 miles**
- **To Newcomb Lake Trail-1.3 miles**
- **To Great Camp Santanoni-0.7**

Total distance 4.2 miles, one way

Directions to Trailhead:

From the intersection of Routes 30 and 28N in Long Lake, follow Route 28N toward Newcomb. Continue for 13.6 miles to the Newcomb Lake Road on the left. Drive down this one-lane dirt road for about 0.3 miles to the trailhead.

Trail Conditions:

This run is over an old access road to one of the Adirondack Park's remaining Great Camps. You can plan on a dry run over a well-graded footing.

This route is a lazy day run (if that really even exists) along a woods road to one of the most historical great camps of the Adirondacks. While there are several rolling hills and long moderate runs, none of this route is steep.

Along this run there are several old buildings, some of which are getting refurbished. Feel free to check them out - most will be locked from access, just be respectful of their history and help sustain their existence for future generations.

As you are finishing off the run you will cross a small bridge with Newcomb Lake to your left and what is called Upper Duck Hole to your right, not to be confused with Duck Hole, located near the Seward Mountains. A couple minutes past this bridge you will come to Great Camp Santanoni. Some of the doors may be open allowing visitors in - it is important to treat this property like your own, which is if you treat your own with care. Be sure to enjoy the views out over the lake and if the weather permits, maybe a small dip in the really cool waters of Newcomb.

Quad:
Saranac Lake

Distances:

- **From Route 86 to the first intersection-0.1 miles**
- **To the second intersection-0.3 miles**
- **To State Property Line-0.4 miles**
- **To old gate-0.2 miles**
- **Back to trail at first intersection-0.5 miles**
- **Back to Route 86-0.2 miles**

Total distance 1.7 miles, loop

Directions to Trailhead:
From the main intersection of Routes 3 and 86 in the Town of Saranac Lake, follow Route 86 toward Lake Placid. Continue for around 2 miles to the crossing of the Adirondack Scenic Railroad. The parking is on the right, just before the crossing.

Trail Conditions:
Initially following an old road, you will be pleasantly surprised by the hard footing. There is a small amount of mud along the trail that parallels the lake, but aside from that small section it's quite dry. The trail is just a few feet down the railroad tracks, on the same side of the road as the parking lot.

You will see a small, narrow trail that enters the woods of tall pines. This is a short loop, nice for a quick loop or two before or after work. Maybe you have an hour or so to kill - perfect.

This trail starts out relatively flat and after 0.2 miles you will pass by a trail on the right - ignore this, you will come out here. Continue for another 0.2 miles to a second trail that comes in on the right follow this one. If you continue straight you will come out closer to Oseetah Lake, but at a dead end with water up to your eyeballs.

Right will bring you through a narrow section of trail that meanders along an old road before it brings you to the southern end of Lake Flower - OR - the northern end of Oseetah Lake. Not that I don't know where I am sending you, it's just a wide section of water between two lakes where they join. Just before and along the lake is where the mud is, and it is limited to just this area. Take in the views as they expand out over the water. Begin here to look for the yellow blazes of the state property line. Once you find this, follow it as it begins to climb. As you approach the shoulder of an unnamed little mountain the property line will head left and the trail will head right up to an old gate. Follow the route to the old gate. Pass by the gate and continue to climb over the top of the unnamed mountain. At this point you will be at over 1,600 feet in elevation.

Past the height of land is a nice run down. The slope is a tad bit steep in small parts, but mostly just a mellow run. The trail tends to be a little narrow, but the woods are open. At the base of the hill, there is yet another intersection. Follow right; left leads to private property. You will quickly be back to the trail you ran in on - less

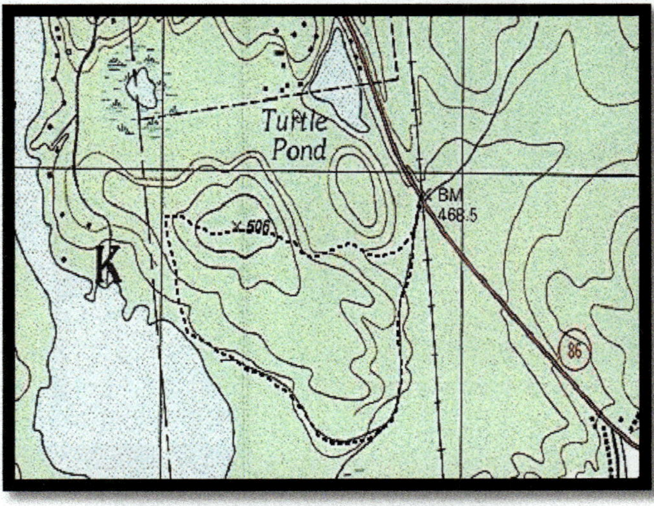

than 0.2 miles from the parking spot.

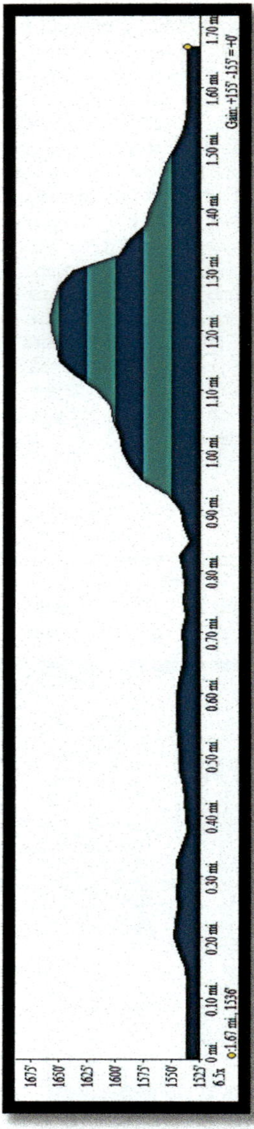

Quad:
Saranac Lake

Distances:

- **Forest Home Road to Lower Saranac Lake-2.1 miles, one way**

Directions to Trailhead:
From the intersection of Routes 3 and 86 in Saranac Lake follow Route 3 toward Tupper Lake. Continue for 0.8 miles to Edgewood Road on the right. Follow Edgewood Road for 0.4 miles to Forest Home Road on the left. Follow Forest Home Road for roughly 3.2 miles to a small rest area/pull-off on the left. At the back of the pull-off is a faint herd path - you are here.

Trail Conditions:
This is an unmarked woods trail, hence the name - path. Most of this course you will be in a dry upland forest surrounding. Since this path is not maintained by any official group or organization, it can have deadfall on or over the path at any point of the year.

Side note

It might be a good idea to bring along a map and compass and the ability to use it on this route, just in case you lose the path.

This is a very simple trail description, or herd path description as the case may be. The hard part is locating the herd path and the correct pull-off, once you do this; the trees are fairly well blazed with paint, not official DEC markers.

You will start immediately through open forest over several very small rolling hills. The course of this herd path stays within the contour lines avoiding any major elevation change - until about 1.2 miles in.

At 1.2 miles the trail starts a slow descent and even mixes in a couple rather more serious downhill runs. Be very careful on the down's that are steeper - there often is a downed tree across the trail. These can be easily skirted.

From this point it is mostly downhill; only a couple short climbs are all that are in your way of reaching Lower Saranac Lake and the site of an old cabin. Large erratic's mark the shore and add some flavor to the already amazing views.

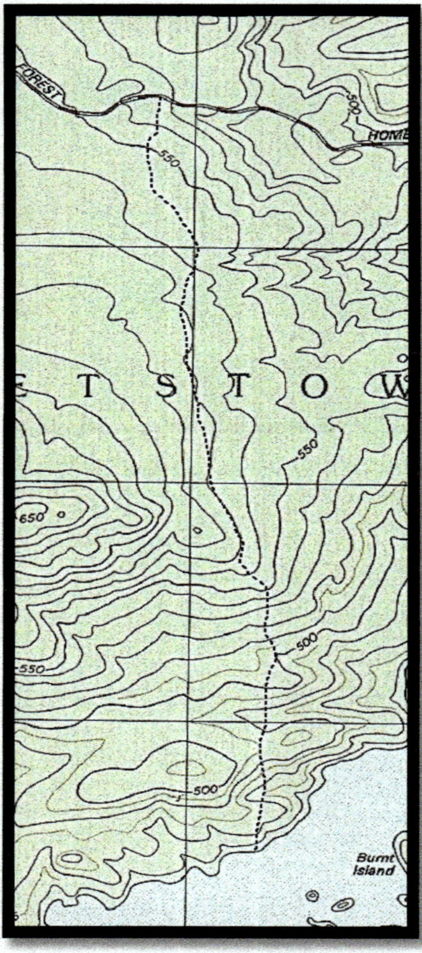

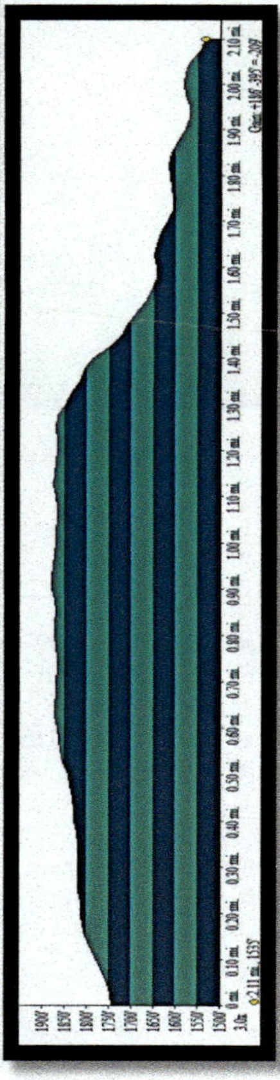

Floodwood Loop

Quad:

Upper Saranac Lake

Distances:

- **Floodwood Road to Fish Creek Campground-3.55 miles**
- **Back to trail-0.1 miles**
- **To Floodwood Road-3.0 miles**
- **Back to trailhead-0.75 miles**

Total distance 7.4 miles, loop

Directions to Trailhead:

From the intersection of Routes 3 and 30 between Tupper Lake and Saranac Lake, follow Route 30 toward Fish Creek. Continue for just under 9.0 miles to Floodwood Road on the left. Follow here for around 3.0 miles to the trailhead, which is a secondary snowmobile trail that gets little use by machines.

Trail Conditions:

This trail has mixed conditions for summer running, but with that being said it's a really good test of endurance and agility. Mud isn't terrible and is not usually what runners focus on. The main focus is the narrow trails and slightly overgrown sections on the return half of the loop.

This trail can be quite a challenge and should not be undertaken without knowing this. The length is not the issue but the lack of use. The trail is designated as a snowmobile trail, but gets very little attention from riders, making the trails much narrower than a typical snowmobile trail. The trails tend to be slightly overgrown in areas and some care might be needed to locate the actual location, slowing the pace a bit. Again, map and compass skills might not be a bad idea.

Starting from the NW trailhead you will start a course through the forest on a moderate terrain. The first pond you will come to is Floodwood Pond where you will be on flat terrain as you navigate along the shores. Making a sharp left you will follow the narrows that lead to Little Square Pond. The trail from here follows Fish Creek and invites you to more rolling hills and a couple decent downs along the way. This section of trail will spit you out on the paved road that goes through the Fish Creek Campground.

Run along the side of the road for 0.1 miles or so and look for the trail to go back into the woods. This first section is very flat with not much action. Echo Pond will be seen through the trees.

Shortly beyond this are Follensby Clear Pond and then Horseshoe Pond. There is a trail that leads into the mouth of the horseshoe which I recommend taking for extra views out over the lake, but a cut-off trail will avoid this. You will run around the northern horn of the horseshoe on a relatively mellow surface and pass between Horseshoe and Little Polliwog ponds. There is a nice hill in this area as well as in the valley between Little Polliwog Pond and Polliwog Pond.

Past here you will be given a few more opportunities to enjoy some more aggressive terrain, but not too aggressive. You will come out onto Floodwood Road about 0.75 miles from your car at the other trailhead. At this point if a second car is not spotted here at this trailhead you will have to run along the side of the road. This is a hard-packed dirt road, slightly softer than pavement, but not much.

Green Pond
Pond of Clear
Follensby Clear
Polliwog Pond
Horseshoe Pond
Middle Pond
Floodwood Pond
Little Square Pond
Whey Pond
Square Pond
Fish Creek Ponds
Fish Creek Bay
Echo Pond
Black Pond
Copperas Pond
Pond
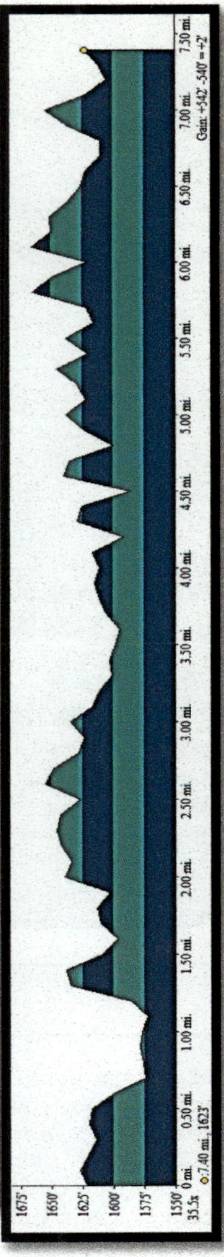
1675'
1650'
1625'
1600'
1575'
1550'
35.5x
0 mi.
0.50 mi.
1.00 mi.
1.50 mi.
2.00 mi.
2.50 mi.
3.00 mi.
3.50 mi.
4.00 mi.
4.50 mi.
5.00 mi.
5.50 mi.
6.00 mi.
6.50 mi.
7.00 mi.
7.50 mi.
7.40 mi., 1623'
Gain: +542' -540' = +2'

Otter Hollow Loop

Quad:

Upper Saranac Lake

Distances:

- **Fish Creek Campground to Black Pond Canoe Carry-0.3 miles**
- **To Copperas Pond Canoe Carry-0.2 miles**
- **To Whey Pond Canoe Carry-0.4 miles**
- **To Little Square Pond-1.1 miles**
- **To Rollins Pond State Campground-2.5 Miles**
- **Back to Fish Creek Campground Trailhead-4.0 miles**

Total distance 8.5, loop

Directions to Trailhead:

From the intersection of Routes 3 and 30 between Tupper Lake and Saranac Lake, follow Route 30 toward Paul Smiths. Continue for 5.3 miles to the Fish Creek Campground entrance on the left. Turn in here and continue for 1.0 miles to the trailhead on the right.

Trail Conditions:

The last portion of this run is through a campground on a roadside. If you prefer to, a second car could be spotted at the northern end of the trail to avoid this section. The trail itself is in decent condition, short of a small section through a wetland area.

****Side note****

Day use fees may be required

Starting your run through a mixture of hardwoods and evergreens you will quickly pass by the short canoe carry to Black Pond on your left and then in another 0.2 miles the canoe carry to Copperas Pond. While remaining on a mostly flat running surface you will come to a third canoe carry, this one to Whey Pond.

From here, for a while it gets a little trickier for solid footing. After a small descent you will come to a wet area also known as a swamp which is part of a couple kettle ponds that lie the east. This section is rather short in length in comparison to the whole picture. You will ascend a touch to get out of the swamp and go over one of the several small hogbacks and bumps you will running over. As you run around Lttle Square Pond you will have a few more rolling pushes before you descend to a cutover trail that leads to the Floodwood Loop, also covered in this guide - just a couple page back if I'm not mistaken.

For the next mile or so you will be running along the shores of Floodwood Pond; be sure to take a second or five to enjoy its amazing graces. So, at about 4.5 miles the foot trail ends and car trail begins. You will pop out at a gate at the north side of the Rollins Pond State Campground. I will be totally up front with you, the next 4.0 miles or so is not the most exciting time you will probably have

exploring the trails in this guide - but since no taxi service shuttles runners or hikers from one end to the other, you don't have too many options.

You can choose to run alongside the road to save your chins, knees, back, feet, quads, sanity - this will be a much softer route. The glory of this section is the never ending views out over Rollins Pond to your right. But be sure to keep your eye on the road a little at least, during open seasons these campgrounds are the busiest in NYS. At a hair under 8.5 you will be back at your car and asking yourself - "what's the closest pizza joint."

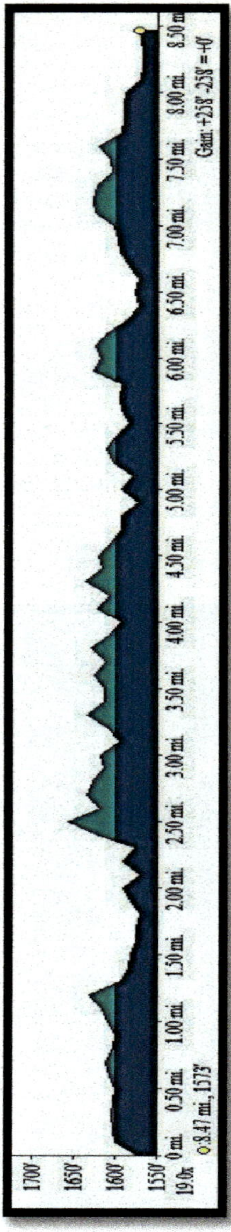

Fish Pond Truck Trail

Quad:

Upper Saranac Lake and Saint Regis Mountain

Distances:

- **Fish Hatchery Road to railroad tracks-0.15 miles**
- **To Fish Pond Truck Trail-0.7 miles**
- **To Grass Pond Trail-3.0 miles**
- **To Fish Pond-1.6 miles**

Total distance 5.45 miles, one way

Directions to Trailhead:

From the intersection of Routes 3 and 30 between Tupper Lake and Saranac Lake, follow Route 30 toward Fish Creek. Continue for just under 11 miles to Fish Hatchery Road on the left. Follow here for around 0.3 miles to Station Road on the left. Drive to the end of Station Road and park near the railroad tracks.

Trail Conditions:

This entire run is over a truck trail, hence the name. With this being the case you can pretty much depend on amazing running conditions over a dirt one-lane woods road.

The start is along an access road leaving from Fish Hatchery Road. This first section is just over 0.1 miles in length and then comes to a railroad track. Following the road alongside the railroad track to the left, you will come to the truck trail on the right. Turning here you will find yourself on an old DEC truck route to Fish Pond.

The start of the trail is rather flat, flowing through a forest of mixed conifer trees. Then at about 1.4 miles you will cross over an outlet where beaver activity has been noticed in the past. Continuing on over a rather flat course you start to see the introduction of some taller pines as you go over a slight rise. You will then drop slightly to a low-lying area where wet conditions can be possible.

On the opposite side of the low area you will begin a climb of 200 feet to the height of land for this trail.

As you descend off the high point you will enter an area where several side trails start to appear. The first of these is the short carry to Saint Regis Pond. Just beyond this trail is a crossing of a outlet with the carry trail to Grass Pond, coming in on the left. Next will be the carry trail to Ochre Pond on the right.

As you pass by this carry trail you will start to descend and come to yet another inlet crossing, this one for the Saint Regis River. From this point the terrain mellows out and you have a nice run for the remaining distance to Fish Pond.

Fish Pond is an amazing backcountry pond nestled in the center of several smaller hidden gems, with a backdrop of small, rugged trailless peaks. Take time to soak it in - take off your socks and soak you feet - then just relax on the shores of the crisp waters of the Adirondacks - just watch out for leaches.

Saint Regis Pond
Little Green Pond
Rat Pond
Fish Pond
Turtle Pond
Boat Ramp

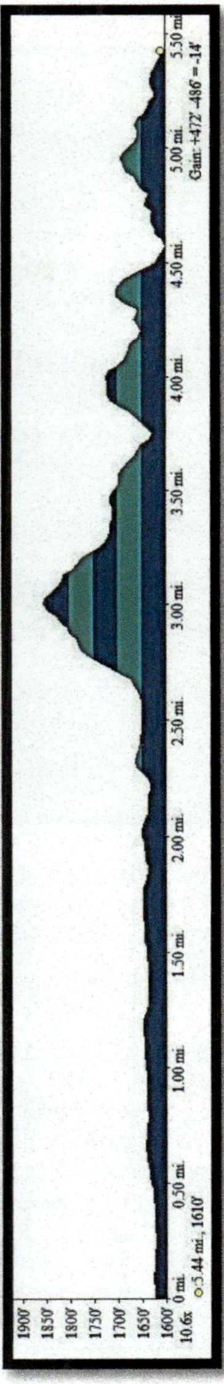
1900'
1850'
1800'
1750'
1700'
1650'
1600'
10.6x
0 mi.
0.50 mi.
1.00 mi.
1.50 mi.
2.00 mi.
2.50 mi.
3.00 mi.
3.50 mi.
4.00 mi.
4.50 mi.
5.00 mi.
5.50 mi
5.44 mi., 1610'
Gain: +472' -486' = -14'

Deer Pond Loop

Quad:
Upper Saranac Lake and Tupper Lake

Distances:

- **Route 3 to side trail-1.2 miles**
- **To Lead Pond Trail-1.7 miles**
- **To west side of Deer Pond-0.3 miles**
- **To Old Wawbeek Road-1.5 miles**
- **To trailhead-2.5 miles**

Total distance 7.2 miles, loop

Directions to Trailhead:
From the intersection of Routes 30 and 3 between Tupper Lake and Saranac Lake, follow Route 3/30 toward Tupper Lake for 0.6 miles to the trailhead on the right.

Trail Conditions:
You will start and finish along an old woods road. Much of the terrain is dry but as usual to many Adirondack trails you will have to fight some wet and muddy sections. The trail has tons of rolling hills and a few more aggressive ones to test your heart rate.

From the trailhead you be running along nearly flat terrain. As you pass along a somewhat narrow trail you will quickly come to the Route 30 trail on the right.

Past this trail lies a much more interesting trail. You will start with moderate rolling hills and a slightly steeper climb to a small shoulder of a height-of-land. Shortly following this point there is a downhill to a brook crossing, returning to an immediate climb. There will be several rolling hills along this section, but at the end, just before Deer Pond itself is a long downhill to the Lead Pond Trail intersection.

If you follow the trail to Lead Pond you will get a better view of Deer Pond from a rock outcropping.

The rock outcropping is just past the brook crossing.

Returning to the Deer Pond Loop continue on to the west side of Deer Pond. Be sure to check out the rarely visited Little Deer Pond to the south; it lies just feet from the trail. The run along the shore of Deer Pond is filled with rolling hills, some of which are a little more aggressive.

After a sizable climb you will be treated with many more rolling hills, some of which are quite steep, but most are just smooth transitions from high points to low points.

Just before Old Wawbeek Road, you will have one last decent down, with a sharp turn at the end. This will exit you to Old Wawbeek Road; follow here to the left. Again, this is a road and not so exciting. You will follow this for the remainder of the run.

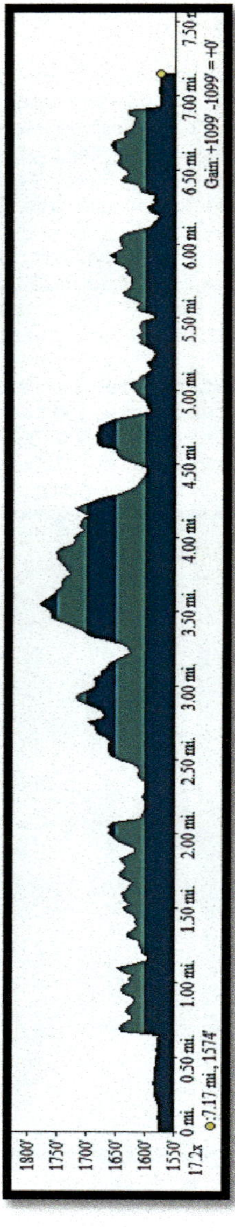
1800'
1750'
1700'
1650'
1600'
1550'
17.2x
0 mi.
0.50 mi.
1.00 mi.
1.50 mi.
2.00 mi.
2.50 mi.
3.00 mi.
3.50 mi.
4.00 mi.
4.50 mi.
5.00 mi.
5.50 mi.
6.00 mi.
6.50 mi.
7.00 mi.
7.17 mi., 1574'
Gain: +1099' -1099' = +0'

Quad:

Saranac Lake

Distances:

- **From the trailhead to the Wanika Falls spur trail-5.2 miles**
- **To Wanika Falls-0.2 miles**

Total distance 5.4 miles, one way

Directions to Trailhead:

From the intersection of Routes 86 and 73 in Lake Placid, take Station Street on the right. The first right after you cross the Chubb River. Follow here, to the intersection Old Military Road at 0.8 miles, cross onto Averyville Road. Follow Averyville Road for just under 1.2 miles to the trailhead for the Northville/Placid Trail, on the left.

Trail Conditions:

This trail has the tendency to be very wet, but when it's not, it's a very nice run. The payoff of this run is a gorgeous waterfall and swimming hole.

This is a fun trail when conditions are good. While it gets its fair share of hikers it also gets a few runners as well.

So, the scoop is when it's good, it's great. There are numerous small rolling hills to succeed and at the end a more substantial hill. At around 4.5 miles you will come to a small bridge over a flume and shortly beyond that is the old and closed section of the NPT. Keep this in mind; it is on the right - avoid it.

In about 0.75 miles from this point is the spur trail for Wanika Falls, but before this is where the climbing begins. In some cases it can be very slippery, and other times dry as a bone, feel it out as you ascend.

The spur trail is very steep in spots and in my opinion, is not really a good run - again, you make the call. You may consider fast hiking for this section, just in case.

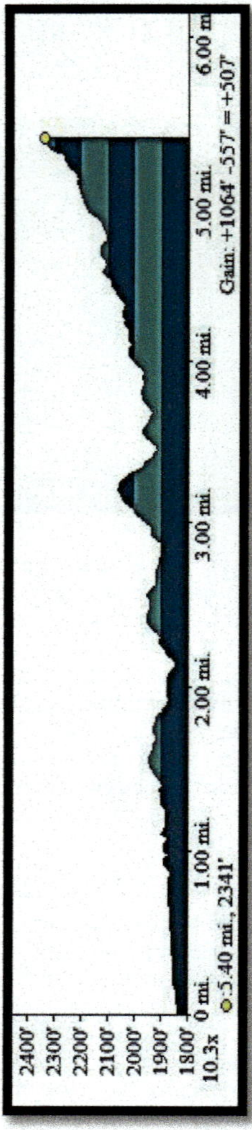

Quad:

Ampersand Lake

Distances:

- **From the trailhead to Pine Pond and Oseetah Lake-7.1 miles, one way**

Directions to Trailhead:

From the intersection of Routes 86 and 73 in Lake Placid follow Route 73 toward Keene. Continue for 0.2 miles to Station Street on the right. The first right after you cross the Chubb River. Follow here to the intersection with Old Military Road at 0.8 miles; cross onto Averyville Road. Follow Averyville Road for just under 4.1 miles to the end, which is the trail for Pine Pond.

Trail Conditions:

This route follows an old Jeep road. The route is now a multiuse trail for snowmobile, ATVs, dirt bikes, hiking, snowshoeing, skiing - you get the point. There are several small sections of mud along the course to Oseetah Lake. With several small rolling hills, the route doesn't have the typical "I'm running along an old road" feel.

This description is rather simple, as is the trail to follow. You know how to get to the trailhead; you basically need to continue following a trail which is essentially a continuation of the road.

You will begin your run along a flat to the base of a modest hill. The run up this hill quickly gets the blood flowing and the heart pumping. Once you crest this initial hill you will have the all-too-obvious descent. A large portion of this trail is relatively calm; some rolling hills welcome you but the going is very pleasant through a forest of some very old growth. Along the route there are a few minor intersections which are quite obviously not the correct direction.

There is one major intersection about halfway in - the route you want goes to the left. Both routes will get modest ATV use so it can be hard to delineate.

Near the end of the trail there is a final major intersection. Right leads to Oseetah Lake - an amazing body of water. Left leads to Pine Pond.

Please be aware that there is private property around the entire area of the lakes; please be respectful. Follow your route in to get out.

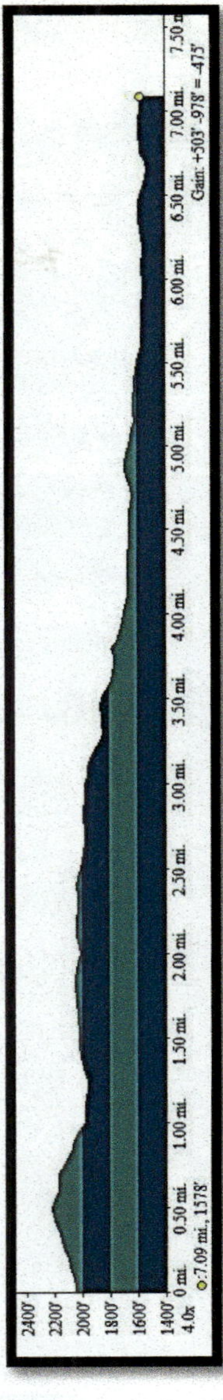
2400'
2200'
2000'
1800'
1600'
1400'
4.0x
0 mi.
0.50 mi.
1.00 mi.
1.50 mi.
2.00 mi.
2.50 mi.
3.00 mi.
3.50 mi.
4.00 mi.
4.50 mi.
5.00 mi.
5.50 mi.
6.00 mi.
6.50 mi.
7.00 mi.
7.50 mi.
7.09 mi., 1578'
Gain: +503' -978' = -475'

Southern
Adirondacks

Long Swing Circuit

Quad:

Paradox Lake and Pharaoh Mountain

Distances:

- **Route 74 to Cotters Pond Outlet-0.6 miles**
- **To Crane Pond Road-1.95 miles**
- **To Crane Pond-0.2 miles**
- **To Glidden Marsh Trail-0.7 miles**
- **To Crab Pond Trail-0.65 miles**
- **To Short Swing Trail-0.5 miles**
- **Back to Long Swing Trail-1.0 miles**
- **Back to trailhead on Route 74-3.85 miles**

Total distance 9.45 miles

Directions to Trailhead:

Using Exit 28 off I-87 and from the intersection of Routes 9 and 74, north of the Town of Schroon Lake, follow Route 74. Continue for 3.9 miles to the trailhead on the right for Crane Pond and Pharaoh Mountain.

Trail Conditions:

With several brook crossings and chances of beaver activity, this trail has the potential to be very wet. If one is careful, however, wet conditions can be avoided. Several rocks are found along this trail, especially in the beginning, care and good footwork will be needed to be successful on this run.

From Route 74 you will head into the woods along a narrow trail with a bridge that is almost immediate. Be careful on this crossing; it tends to be slippery more often than not. After running for a very brief amount of time you will begin to see a beaver marsh to your right and the cliffs of Blue Hill in front of you. As you pass by the opening that the beavers have made you will cross the outlet to Cotters Pond. This next section of trail is very tricky for running and with the numerous scattered rocks in the trail it takes a little finesse.

As you run around the perimeter of the pond you will have a slight ascent followed by a moderate descent to another possible wet area. You will then swing around to a high point between two wetland areas with Pyramid Lake off in the distance to your left.

Immediately following there will be a decent sized hill awaiting your lucky legs. You will ascend the shoulder of an unnamed little bump to your right and descend ever so slightly to a small plateau before climbing again up and over a slightly higher unnamed peak. Why don't we just name it Pyramid Hill for laughs - it has the shape of a Pyramid and it's near Pyramid Lake, so why not? As you crest Pyramid Hill you will descend on a slightly steeper course and exit out onto a dirt road called Crane Pond Road. Following here to the left, you will be running on this road for about 0.25 miles, to where it splits to the Crane Pond Boat Launch site. Passing by the trail to the boat launch on your left; you will again begin to climb above Crane Pond and descend slightly to the Glidden Marsh Trail, which is on the left. Follow the Glidden Marsh Trail as it follows close to the shore. Pass by the intersection for the Short Swing Trail and Oxshoe Pond and continue south along the shore of Glidden Marsh. As you leave the shore, look for the Crab Pond Spur Trail on the left and follow this. This short section of trail has one decent climb in the 0.5 miles to the shore of Crab Pond. At the shore of Crab Pond follow the Short Swing Trail left along the SW shore of Crab Pond. Continue to follow here as you descend to the shore of Oxshoe Pond on your right. After a short climb over a small hogback you will return to the Glidden Marsh Trail. Take a right back to the Crane Pond Road and then a right onto the Long Swing Trail, which swings you back to Route 74 and the trailhead from which you started.

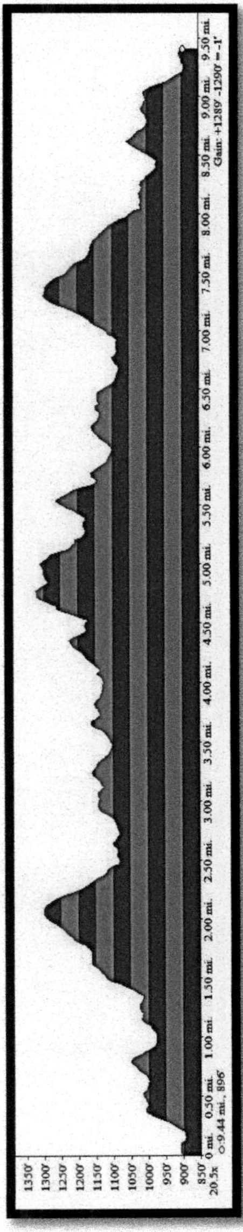

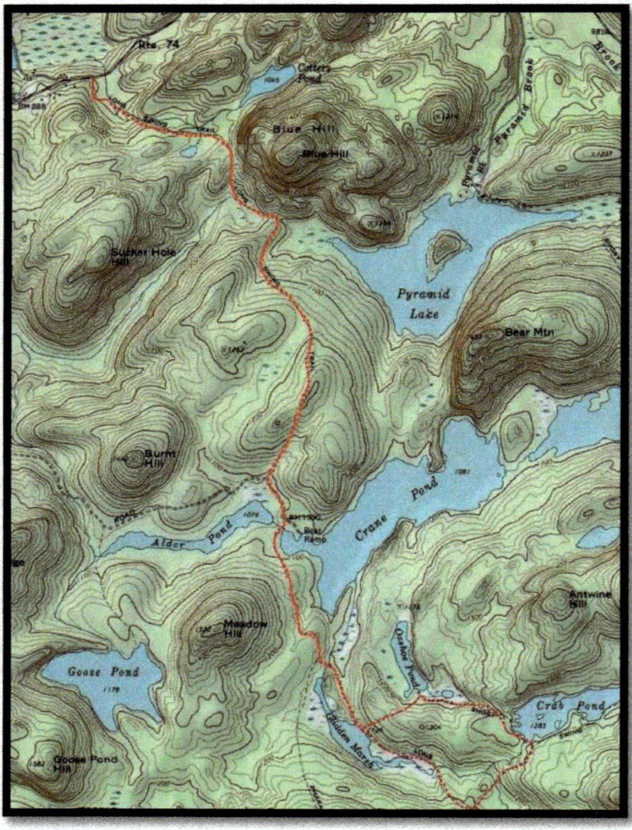
Rte. 74
Cotters Pond
Blue Hill
Blue Hill
Pyramid Brook
Brook
Sucker Hole Hill
Pyramid Lake
Bear Mtn
Burnt Hill
Alder Pond
Crane Pond
Boat Ramp
Antwine Hill
Meadow Hill
Goose Pond
Oxshoe Pond
Crab Pond
Glidden Marsh
Goose Pond Hill

Montcalm Point of Tongue

Quad:

Silver Bay and Shelving Rock Mountain

Distances:

- **Route 9N to Shore Trail-0.45 miles**
- **To Bear Point-1.8 miles**
- **To Montcalm Point-2.8 miles**

Total distance 5.05 miles, one way

Directions to Trailhead:

Get off I-87 at Exit 24 (Bolton Landing) and follow County Route 11 to Bolton Landing-Riverbank Road, east toward Bolton Landing and Route 9N. At the end of the Road (approx. 4.8 miles) you will be at Route 9N, follow here to the left, north. Continue for 4.4 miles to the trailhead on the right. (Clay Meadow)

Trail Conditions:

This trail heads toward the Shore of Lake George and at times moves away just to return on several occasions. The terrain is rough and rocky, but generally dry. There is one significant climb en route, but other than that rolling terrain awaits you, and lots of it.

The trail starts by dropping some elevation to a slippery stream crossing before starting a climb to the intersection with the Five Mile Point Trail.

Following the Point of Tongue Trail to the right you will quickly come to another stream crossing. After you descend closer to a marshy area you will begin a slow descent to the height-of-land along this trail. The trail then begins a more aggressive climb as it gets slightly more washed out due to the steepness of the course. As you pass behind a small knoll you will begin to descend rapidly back toward Lake George. After 2.25 miles you will come to a most amazing spot on the lake, named Bear Point. With a couple more brook crossing and somewhat steeper climbs and descents you come to a killer swim rock at around 2.75 miles. Aside from the never-ending brook crossings there is one frequent wet area at a little over 4.0 miles, but not really significant enough to ruin a day.

One very aggressive climb through a poor footing area will bring you to the second-highest point along this trail, before dropping you back to the shore of Lake George. Following along the shore for a bit longer you can enjoy new vistas around each turn. The junction for the Ridge Trail is soon after. The Point of the Tongue is further down, where you will find some great opportunities for a swim and a snack.

"Whether you believe you can or believe you can't, you're probably right."

-Henry Ford

NORTHWEST BAY
Northwest Bay Bk
Bear Pt
Walker Point
BAY
TONGUE
First Peak
Bass I
Turtle Island
Mohican Island
The Narrows
Uncas I
Pine I
Montcalm Point
The Juanita

575'
550'
525'
500'
475'
450'
425'
400'
375'
350'
325'
300'
20.5x
0 mi.
0.25 mi.
0.50 mi.
0.75 mi.
1.00 mi.
1.25 mi.
1.50 mi.
1.75 mi.
2.00 mi.
2.25 mi.
2.50 mi.
2.75 mi.
3.00 mi.
3.25 mi.
3.50 mi.
3.75 mi.
4.00 mi.
4.25 mi.
4.50 mi.
4.75 mi.
5.00 mi.
5.25 mi.
3.04 mi, 318'
Gain: +328' -420' = -92'

Pilot Knob Preserve

Quad:

Putnam Mountain

Distances:

- Trailhead to first intersection-0.3 miles
- To pavilion and second intersection via northern route-0.2 miles
- To third intersection-0.7 miles
- To top of waterfall-0.1 miles
- Back to third intersection 0.1 miles
- Back to second intersection 0.7 miles
- Back to first intersection via southern route-0.5 miles
- Back to trailhead-0.3 miles

Total distance 2.9 miles, loop

Directions to Trailhead:

From I-87, take Exit 21, follow Route 9 north. Continue for 0.35 miles to Route 9L on the right. Follow here for 7.1 miles to Pilot Knob Road on the left. Follow Pilot Knob Road for 0.7 miles or so to the trailhead for the Pilot Knob Preserve.

Trail Conditions:

This is a fairly new trail network (2000) so it has gotten some decent attention, but still offers a fresh trail with some tread. There are some rocky sections and some steep sections but almost everything is dry and no mud is apparent.

This trail starts off right away by heading directly uphill; no warm-up for you. Before leveling off at the first intersection, the Preserve Trail will switchback across a rocky hillside. Head left at this point and loop your way around to the north. At first following what seems to be an old road; you will soon find yourself on a rocky hill scrambling up to a more level run. There is a short ascent after this that will bring you to a pavilion overlooking Lake George. Just beyond the pavilion is the second intersection.

Taking a left at this intersection you will start on a 0.7-mile run through some very open hardwood forest of hickory, maple and eastern hop-hornbeam. This section of trail is fairly moderate with a mostly steady uphill, but with an occasional downhill section mixed in. There is another short downhill to the third intersection.

Take a left at the third intersection, climb steadily to the top of the ridge and descend slightly to the top of Pilot Knob Falls. The falls are pretty easy to look at from the top but the best views are from the base. Continue along the trail and loop back around to the bottom. The base of the falls is a couple hundred feet upstream and can be seen from the trail. Follow a faint herd path upstream to the base of the falls. Returning to the trail, it is less than 0.1 miles back to the third intersection. Retrace your steps back to the second intersection through the open hardwoods you were in earlier.

Once back at the second intersection hang a left and follow the old paved road as it meanders down the steep slopes. The road eventually stops at a gate and a foot trail veers off to the right and connects back up rather shortly to the first intersection. Retrace your steps downhill on the initial 0.3-mile leg of the trip back to the trailhead.

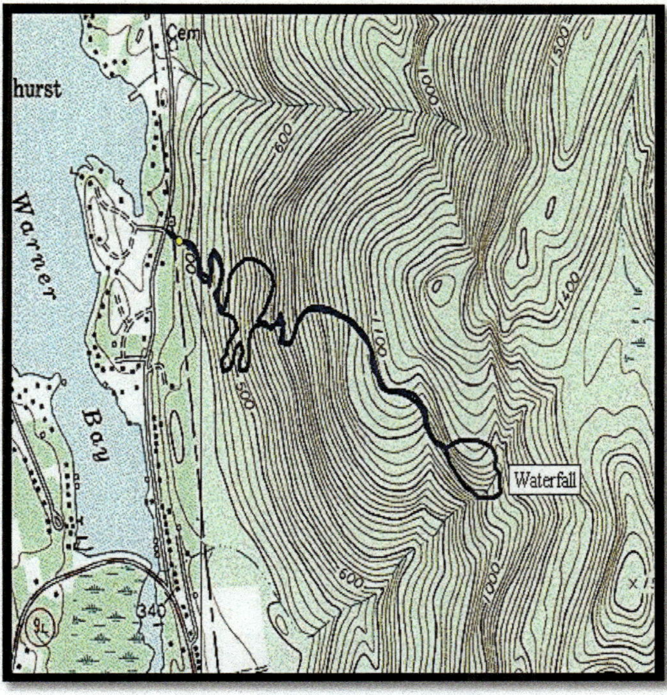

Some days all I want to be is a missing person!

T-shirt

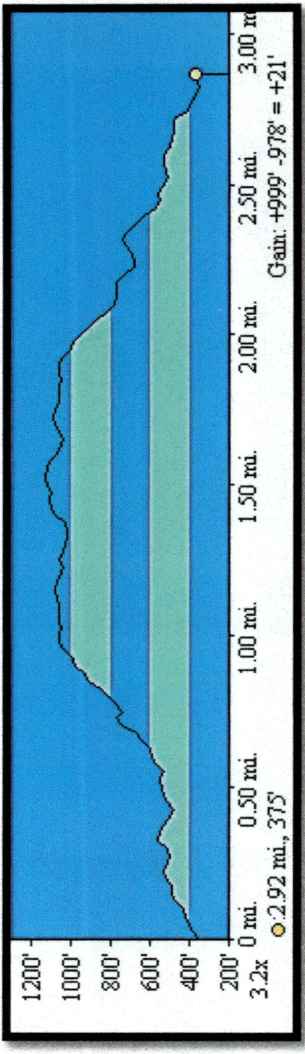
1200'
1000'
800'
600'
400'
200'
3.2x
0 mi.
0.50 mi.
1.00 mi.
1.50 mi.
2.00 mi.
2.50 mi.
3.00 m
2.92 mi., 375'
Gain: +999' -978' = +21'

Quad:

Shelving Rock

Distances:

- **Pike Brook Road to Black Mountain intersection-1 mile**
- **To Lapland Pond shelter-0.85 mile**
- **To Round Pond-0.4 miles**
- **To Black Mountain Pond-0.45 miles**
- **To Black Mountain Trail-0.30 miles**
- **To Black Mountain-0.75 mile**
- **To trailhead-2.35 miles**

Total distance 6.1 miles, loop

Directions to Trailhead:

From the intersection of Routes 74 and 22 in the Town of Ticonderoga follow Route 74 south. Continue for just over 19 miles to County Route 6 or Huletts Landing Road. Follow here for just under 2.6 miles to Pike Brook Road. Follow here for 0.8 miles or so to the trailhead for Black Mountain on the right.

Trail Conditions:

Initial start is along a road which is normally dry. The foot trails around Black Mountain have wet sections but nothing too crazy. The back side of Black Mountain is a steep run, or hike, depending on what you want to do. The descent on the north side is a typical Adirondack trail, meaning steep and rocky.

The trailhead for this loop starts right off Pike Brook Road from a rather large parking area. Initially you will follow a dirt/gravel road as it climbs up to a height-of-land. It slowly levels off and passes by a small marshy area before leaving the road and entering the woods as a foot trail on the right. You will pass by a private camp on the left as you make your beginning steps into the woods. The trail at this point is mostly flat and remains so up to the intersection with the Lapland Pond Trail. The Black Mountain Trail continues on to the right.

Following the Lapland Pond Trail you will find yourself slightly descending and crossing a small brook over a bridge. A small marshland is located directly to your right. Past the bridge the trail starts a moderate but steady climb up to the eastern shoulder of Black Mountain. The shoulder is very wide, making for a relatively moderate hike over mostly flat terrain. There is a slight descent at the end to approach the northern shore of Lapland Pond. Just before shore the trail splits and heads right toward Black Mountain ponds and left to the lean-to on the east side of Lapland Pond. The run over to the lean-to is short and sweet and highly recommended, as the view of the pond is much grander.

Back at the intersection; take that turn toward Black Mountain ponds to continue the loop. A short distance down this trail you will come to yet another intersection. This intersection is easy to miss as the signs are 12 feet up in a tree, placed there by The Jolly Green Giant himself. This trail is 1.2 miles to the lean-to on the southeast shore of Millman Pond. The right is what you want for the loop.

In 0.4 miles from this intersection you will be at Round Pond. Round Pond isn't labeled as such on the maps, but according to the sign a half-mile up a tree, it is indeed Round Pond. On most maps it is labeled as one of the Black Mountain ponds. Either way it's the same pond, and indeed is roundish in shape.

Round Pond is very tough to impossible approach in most cases. The grass is very tall along the shore, which is also along the trail; it rustles loudly in the steady winds so often found here.

Another 0.4 miles or so beyond Round Pond is Black Mountain Pond, another very pleasant backwoods gem. You will come to a very nice slab rock landing on the pond with the lean-to located above on the hill. The trail continues on the other side of the rock slab. After a slight incline you will be at an intersection. Left leads to Black Mountain Point on Lake George, and straight is the trail up and over Black Mountain; head straight toward Black Mountain.

You might as well get a peak in today while you're out there - why not Black Mountain. This small peak is home to a fire tower and some of the finest views of Lake George one can find. However, you will have to earn this one as it's a three quarter to a mile section of trail to the summit. The one nice thing about this trail is that it has switchbacks, something much of the Adirondacks do not have. This trail is rocky and footing is a little tricky in spots, but the never-ending outcroppings and views will take your mind off how hard you are working.

Once on the summit, take some time to refuel as you soak in the outstanding views of Lake George and the numerous mountains that make up its shoreline. Unfortunately, the tower is being used as a relay station or weather tower or something and cannot be climbed. This is only a minor issue though, as the views from the open rocks are just as superb and the radiation is just as effective.

The descent off Black Mountain is steep in spots, and can be very slippery. There is one confusing intersection on the way down not far below the summit. At this point take a left and you will be heading in the right direction. From here the trail becomes slippery as much more rock starts to appear and remains so for much of the descent to more stable ground. The next intersection you will encounter is at 1.25 miles from the summit; the Lapland Pond Trail that you used earlier in the day. In another easy 0.3 miles or so the dirt/gravel rock will be underfoot. This trail leads back to the trailhead and if you thought ahead, a six-pack of cold beer and a slice of day-old pizza.

Pike Brook Road
Round Pond
Lapland Pond
Shelter
Black Mtn Ponds
Black Mtn
Lookout Tower

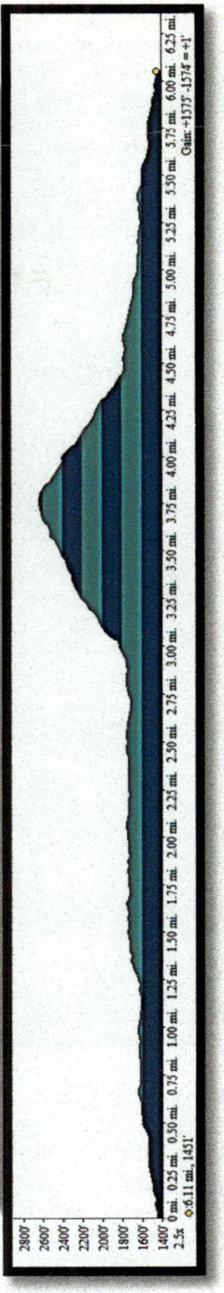
2800'
2600'
2400'
2200'
2000'
1800'
1600'
1400'
2.5x
6.11 mi, 1451'
Gain: +1575' -1574' = +1'

Quad:

Johnsburg

Distances:

- **Trailhead to Crane Mountain-0.85 miles**
- **To Crane Mountain Pond-0.65 miles**
- **To Putnam Brook Trail-0.75 mile**
- **Back to trailhead-0.95 miles**

Total distance 3.2 miles, loop

Directions to Trailhead:

From I-87, take Exit 23 follow Route 9 into Warrensburg. At just under 1 mile, look for Route 418 on the left. Follow here over the Hudson River for 3.5 miles or so to Athol Road on the right. Follow here for just over 0.9 miles to a stop sign, where the road becomes the Glen/Athol Road. Follow here for 2.3 miles to Valley Road on the left. Follow here for 3.7 miles to its end at South Johnsburg Road. Take a right here for 0.85 miles to County Route 6, also called Garnet Lake Road. Follow here for 1.2 miles to Ski Hi Road on the right. Follow here to its end and the trailhead for Crane Mountain. There are several signs along this multiple-turn route that point to Crane Mountain Trailhead, but it's always best to have a road map with you as you drive, as road signs change and become missing on occasion, and, most of all, this is a very tough trailhead to find.

Trail Conditions:

You will find mostly decent conditions on this trail. A little steep and slippery off the summit of Crane and a couple ladders to contend with, but that's most of the extent of it.

From the parking area, follow the Crane Mountain Trail into the woods on a moderate approach. The trail has a small steep section only a couple tenths of a mile into the hike. At around 0.5 miles you will come to a small side path to an open rock ledge with excellent views. Shortly beyond this view there is a trail intersection. Left is the Crane Mountain cutoff trail and right is the summit of Crane Mountain. The cutoff trail will bring you directly to Crane Pond in 0.4 miles on a steady but fairly moderate downhill pace, through a very unique draw. Use this to side-step the actual peak.

Continue on by following the right path to the summit of Crane Mountain on a moderate ascent. In another 0.2 miles you will be at a short ladder that gets you over a small rock shelf. Above this shelf you will be on a very flat traverse to a very tall ladder that gets you up an aggressive rock face. At the top of the rock cliff the trail goes over a few large boulders to the summit at 1.4 miles from the trailhead. The views from here are quite breathtaking, especially on a clear, cool day after a heavy rain storm. Heavy rains tend to clear the humidity out of the air opening up distant views to far of mountain ranges. Also, cooler air holds less moisture than hot air, making the views less obstructed by humidity.

Continuing over the top of Crane Mountain a trail will lead you to shore of Crane Mountain Pond. A little over 0.25 miles from the summit there is an excellent lookout over Crane

Mountain Pond - your first real glimpse of the body of water. The pond is 1.2 miles from the summit after an at times very steep and slippery descent. This descent has some issues with heavy erosion, which makes it a little tougher than it should be. Water seems to be on the rocks very frequently. Just shy of the pond a side trail leads left to a camping area. Right leads to the pond in another 0.1 miles.

Following the trail to your left you will run along the south side of the pond to complete the loop. In 0.15 miles from where you reached the pond you will come to the other end of the Crane Mountain Cut-off Trail on the left. You can use this uphill short run of 0.4 miles to loop back to the trail you followed earlier in the day. Head right around the pond and in 0.2 miles you be heading away from the pond and down toward the Putnam Brook Trail.

A blast from the past; this is an early 1900s photo of hikers on Crane Pond Mountain.

The descent from the pond to the trail is a very steep one with boulders, rock ledges and numerous views to enjoy. At just shy of the trail there is a natural rock bridge that you will be crossing. Be sure to take the time to drop down on the right and look. If you are comfortable enough you may wish to shimmy yourself inside for a very cool break. Shortly beyond there you come to an intersection where the Putnam Brook Trail leads right and left. Left is the way you want to go to get back to the trailhead. The trail starts out on a slight descent before starting a very gentle climb along a wide and very open trail. In 0.9 miles you will be back to your car at the trailhead.

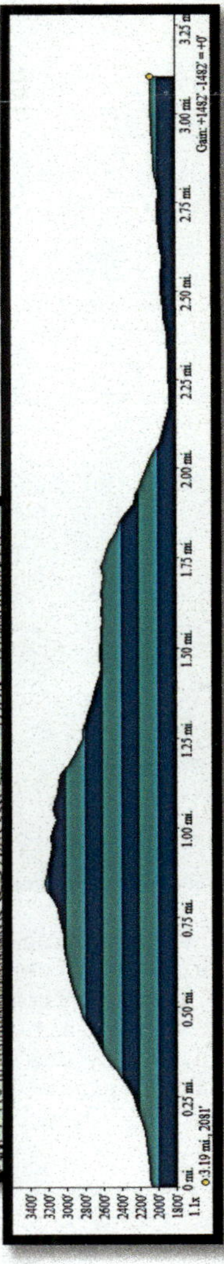

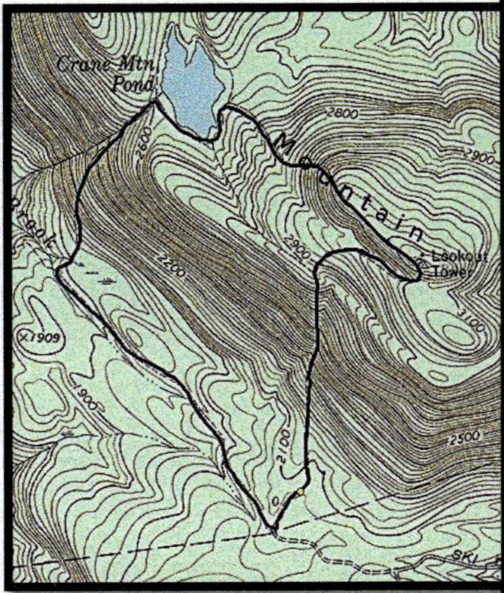

Mud Lake and Tamarack Vly

Quads:

Lassellsville and Canada Lake

Distances:

- **State Land barrier to Mud Lake-1.7 miles**
- **To Tamarack Vly-1 miles**
- **Back to gate-1.5 miles**

Total distance 4.2 miles, round trip

Directions to Trailhead:

From Route 29 in the small town of Lassellsville look for North Road or County Route 119 on the north side of Route 29. Follow here for 3.1 miles to Dempster Corners where the road turns into Gleason Road. Gleason Road is still considered County Route 119. Continue on Route 119 to Crystal Lake Road on the right at approximately 2.8 miles. On the corner of Crystal Lake Road and Route 119 there is a state trailhead sign. Follow Crystal Lake Road and keep bearing left along this road. The road becomes narrow, rough and muddy in spots but eventually ends at the State Land Barrier. It may be required to walk or run this section, if your vehicle is unable to pass. Just be sure to park well off the road so as to not impede traffic.

Trail Conditions:

This run is along an old woods road, which is now considered a snowmobile trail. Most of the tread is in decent condition, but some mud does exist. The trail is wide, making the mud avoidance easier than other trail runs.

The beginning portion of the run is rather uneventful and is very quick to cover ground. After roughly 1.0 miles from the barrier there is an obvious split in the trail - at this point there is a "carry it in, carry it out" sign on a tree. Left leads to Mud Lake, right to Tamarack Vly. Head left at this point; you will return to this spot later.

Following the trail left you are still on a well-used road, very wide and well-marked. In a rather short amount of time, you will be above Mud Lake and a short left spur trail to its shore. It is a very steep drop to the shore of Mud Lake - you may not want to run this spot. This drop will bring you to the base of some small cliffs, near an old dock and an equally old row boat. There is an excellent view over the pond from the tops of the cliffs.

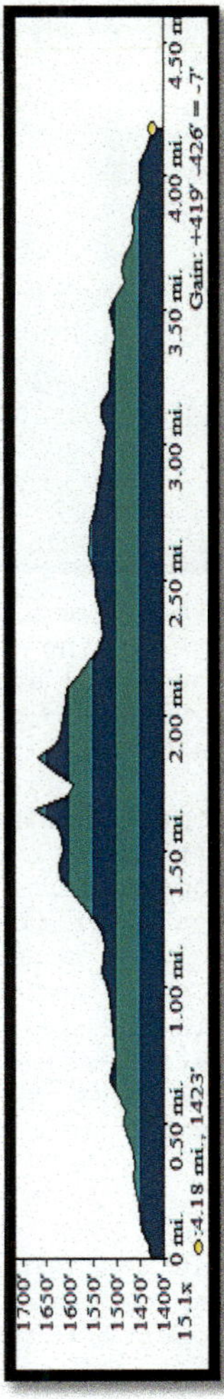

Returning to that fork we talked about a minute ago take the other spur and head slightly downhill to the shore of Tamarack Vly for about 0.1 miles. At the south end of the Vly there is a small bench and a beaver dam. To return to the gate just retrace your steps.

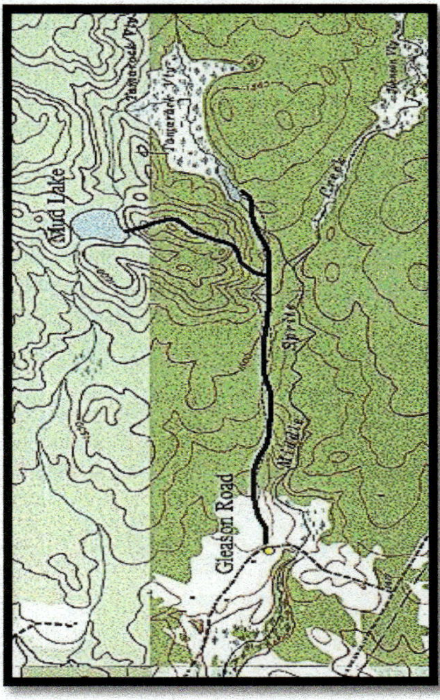

Hillabrandt Vly

Quad:

Lassellsville

Distances:

- **Glasgow Road parking to Glasgow Mills Pond-1.5 miles**
- **To Hillabrandt Vly-1.75 miles**
- **To bridge over outlet-0.25 miles**

Total distance 3.5 miles, one way

Directions to Trailhead:

From Route 29 in the small town of Rockwood, follow Route 10 north toward Caroga Lake. Go 2.75 miles to Glasgow Road, on your left. Follow a dirt road named Glasgow Road for 0.4 miles to the parking area.

Trail Conditions:

This run is along an old woods road which is now designated, in part at least as a snowmobile trail. Conditions are mixed from dry to wet. The footing is a little tricky in spots as well.

This snowmobile trail (old woods road) starts at the back of the parking area. However it is not usually plowed and sometimes blocked well into spring so you may need to park off Route 10 and walk/run the extra few hundred feet to the trail.

Almost immediately you will pass a small pond on the left and climb slightly uphill. You will follow a property line with state land on your left and private land on your right. After roughly 0.25 miles you will come to a bridge and an intersection with a second snowmobile trail that comes in on the right. This one is private, and marked as such. Follow the state marked snowmobile trail to the left. Soon you will pass by a gate and the start of a moderate climb over very unsettled terrain.

It is roughly a 250-foot climb to Glasgow Mills Pond. Once at Glasgow Mills Pond you will notice that the buildings on the map are no longer there; they may have been removed when the state gained the property, but that's simply a guess. The snowmobile trail follows the north side of the narrow pond, giving visitors many opportunities to approach the water's edge.

The terrain is now relatively flat for about 0.5 miles before you start to climb again. At this point the snowmobile trail leaves the route found on the map and may have been rerouted to avoid the marsh to the west of Glasgow Mills Pond. No matter the reason, you will be climbing to a height-of-land along the trail about 200 feet higher than the pond. Once at the height-of-land you will enjoy a continual descent for the remaining part of the run to Hillabrandt Vly. The vly is actually more of a pond, and quite a sizable one at that. Small campsites are visible along shore. There is a bridge over the outlet of the vly at the west end, giving an absolutely awesome view down the vly's narrows. Return via your route in.

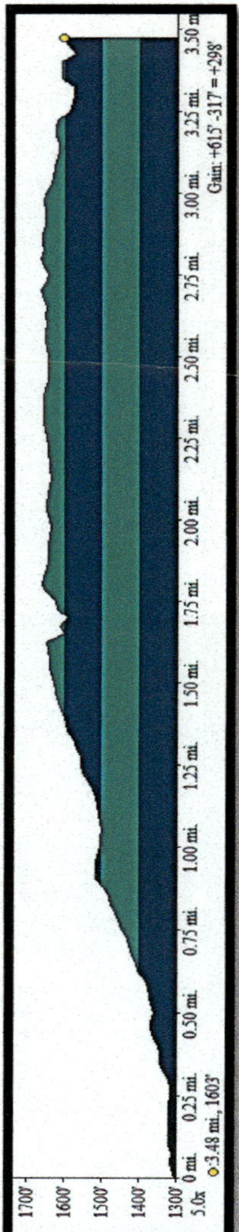

Never take life seriously; no one gets out alive

~anonymous

Big Pond

Quad:

Schroon Lake

Distances:

- **Hoffman Road to Lower Big Pond-0.45 miles**
- **To Big Pond-1.0 miles**

Total distance 1.45 miles, one way

Directions to Trailhead:

From I-87, Exit 28, head east toward Route 9. Drive south along Route 9 through Schroon Lake. Just outside the village of Schroon Lake begin to look for Hoffman Road on the right. Follow Hoffman Road for about 2.25 miles. The trailhead is on the right, but not marked with the typical DEC brown-and-yellow trailhead sign. The trailhead offers parking for a half-dozen cars. The trail is located on the left hand side of the parking area.

Trail Conditions:

This is a decent trail. Hardly any water issues exist, only your usual suspects in depressions along the trail; otherwise, no issues of concern.

This trail is part of an old woods road and is very wide in spots. The beginning is flat, with several smaller wet spots, and these can remain wet until an early winter cold snap. At 0.4 miles you will be at a height-of-land overlooking Lower Big Pond. There is a slight descent along the east side of the pond that leads to a bridge over the outlet of Lower Big Pond. Here you have a nice view of the pond, but more viewpoints can be had on the other side of the bridge.

After the bridge the trail slowly climbs a few feet before descending and climbing again. At 1.4 miles you will be at a good spot to take a heading toward Big Pond. You should be able to see the pond from the trail at this point. It is a short push downhill to it. No real trail leads to the shore, but the forest is very open, and it's only about 200 feet or so. The size of this pond shows where its name comes from. Return via the way you came.

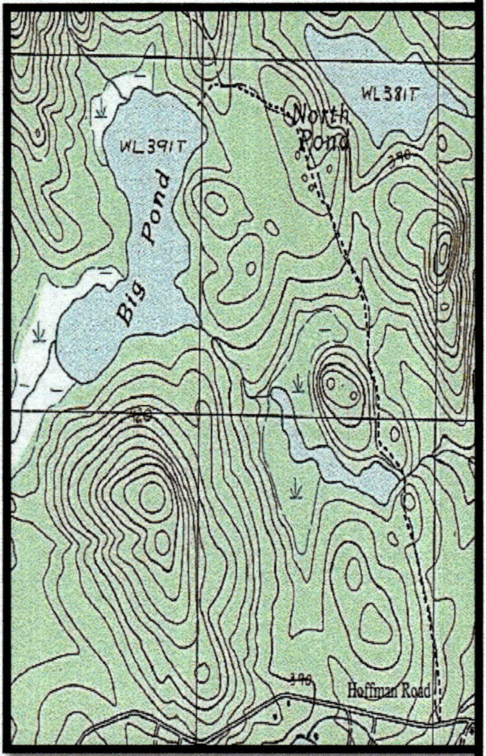
WL381T
North Pond
WL391T
Big Pond
Hoffman Road

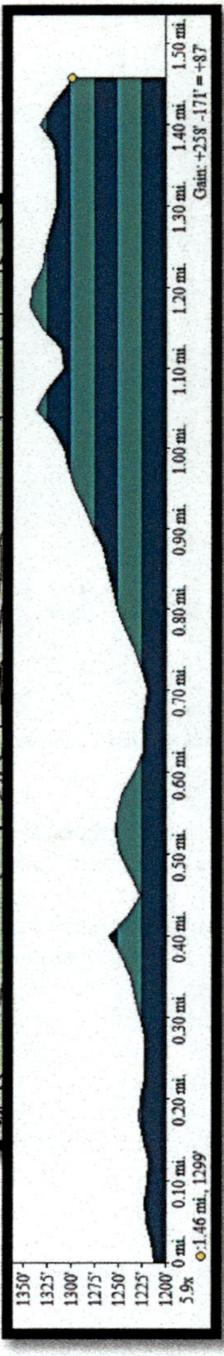
Gain: +258' -171' = +87
:1.46 mi., 1299'
0 mi.
0.10 mi.
0.20 mi.
0.30 mi.
0.40 mi.
0.50 mi.
0.60 mi.
0.70 mi.
0.80 mi.
0.90 mi.
1.00 mi.
1.10 mi.
1.20 mi.
1.30 mi.
1.40 mi.
1.50 mi.
1350'
1325'
1300'
1275'
1250'
1225'
1200'
5.9x

Central
Adirondacks

Hitchins Marsh and Pond

Quad:

Piercefield, Little Tupper Lake

Distances:

- **Gate to sand pit near marsh-0.8 miles**
- **To end of marsh-0.2 miles**
- **To bushwhack point-0.4 miles**
- **To Hitchins Pond-1.25 miles**

Total distance 2.65 miles, one way

Directions to Trailhead:

From the intersection of Routes 30 and 3 in Tupper Lake, follow Route 30 south toward Long Lake. Continue for 8.8 miles or so to Route 421 on the right. Route 421 starts out as a paved road then become dirt on the southern side of Horseshoe Lake. Continue on the dirt portion, driving much slower, as the road is rough in spots. The road will take you past the campsites on Horseshoe Lake and cross railroad tracks. Continue following the road at the next intersection. There is a yellow gate on the left fork, park here. The route is the left fork.

Trail Conditions:

This is a woods road still used on occasion by authorized motor vehicles. This run is very dry and compact as well as a little hard on the knees.

This run starts along a jeep road in a well-wooded area for only a short distance before the marsh starts to show its face. The road stays fairly close to the marsh with a line of tall trees between, so the views of the marsh are quite obstructed at first. At about 0.6 miles you will start to see more of the marsh as it reaches across both sides of the road.

At 0.75 miles the road makes a sharp left in a more southerly direction. This is where the true view of Hitchins Marsh comes out and you can see the massive expanse for the wetland that it is. Looking out over the marsh you can see tamaracks, pitcher plants, cotton grass, and several species of goldenrod, to name a few.

Once around the marsh you will enter a wooded area again across an inlet of Hitchins Pond. Continue on the road and quickly you will notice a small ridge growing on your left. At the same time another small wetland will come in on the right. Once the ridge to your left ends, you will be at a crossing of an inlet of Hitchins Pond.

The road stays very well used and hard under foot. You will experience a few smaller wetland areas along this route. Slowly the road begins to taper back toward Hitchins Pond. Shortly you will be at Lows Upper Dam and a short access road to Hitchins Pond.

This route is an old road that

accessed a few camps from the Low's Upper Dam. The camps are no longer there, but their footprint is. In a couple places there are foundations, walls, and even a fireplace. This route is on the north side of the Lows Lake outlet.

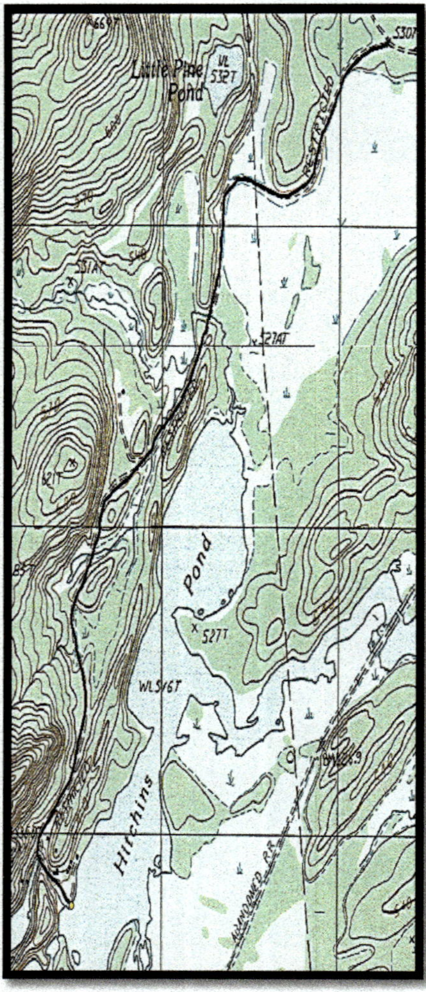

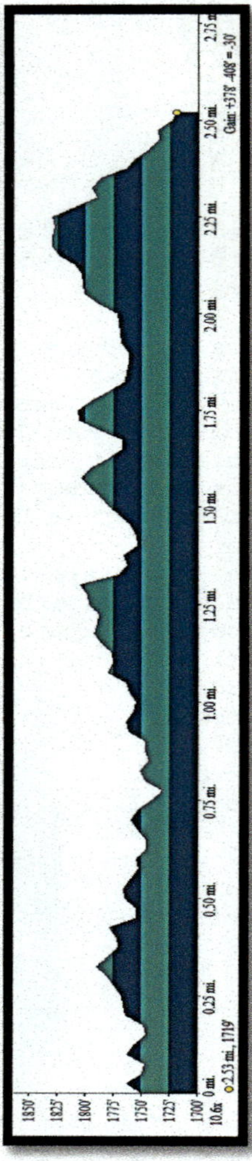

Quad:

Wakely Mountain

Distances:

- **Moose River Plains Road to Cellar Pond-1.75 miles, one way**

Directions to Trailhead:

From the intersection of Routes 30 and 28 in Indian Lake, head west toward Blue Mountain Lake. Go a little over 2.0 miles to Cedar River Road, which will be on the left, just past the golf course and cemetery. Follow Cedar River Road to its end at the campsite and ranger cabin (approximately 12 miles). This is where the Moose River Plains Road starts (beyond the gate). Follow here for around 3.5 miles to a small Jeep trail, slightly grown up. The Jeep trail is not marked or signed. Park someplace off the road or take your chances driving in a ways.

Trail Conditions:

This is a tough little trail and depending on how much trail maintenance it gets, running can be a challenge. There is a little bit of blowdown scattered across the trail. The last part of the trail is a little tight but can be run with some care; it would be more like a jog than a run to be safer for the eyes.

From the start of the Jeep road you have a choice - run it, or try to drive part of it. It is passable in some respects, but only to high clearance four-wheel drive vehicles and only for a very short distance - my suggestion is to run it. Last time I was in there it was only passable for about 0.3 miles, and at that point it was tough to turn around. The road is very narrow, making it difficult to maneuver to turn around.

The road is very easy to run in the beginning - mostly flat, wide for foot travel and very easy to navigate. At 0.25 miles you will pass by the remnants of an old cabin. Shortly beyond that, you will notice that the road will be impassable by vehicles other than a small tank. Washouts start to occur, trees downed and it's getting wet - quite a mess in spots; agility will be the key. At this point you should be able to see the steep slopes of Cellar Mountain to your left. The Jeep road will start to climb along the side of Cellar and eventually top out on the ridge north of Cellar.

The trail will then slowly descend through a much narrower passage; then loop around the west side of a small bump. This section gets a little help from someone, but is still slowed down by downed trees and wet conditions. This is where you should start looking for old artifacts of logging past - a possible old logging village.

Once the pond is in sight, just head for it and bushwhack a hundred feet or so to the shore. Deer and moose paths are also around leading to the water's edge. From the pond, if you waited around long enough, you may have the luck of spotting a moose. Loons dot the water, diving and reappearing hundreds of feet away. The shore is grassy and bushy with some nice boulders housing dry spots for relaxing.

None of us are as smart as all of us

~Proverb

Cellar Pond
Cellar Mtn
4WD

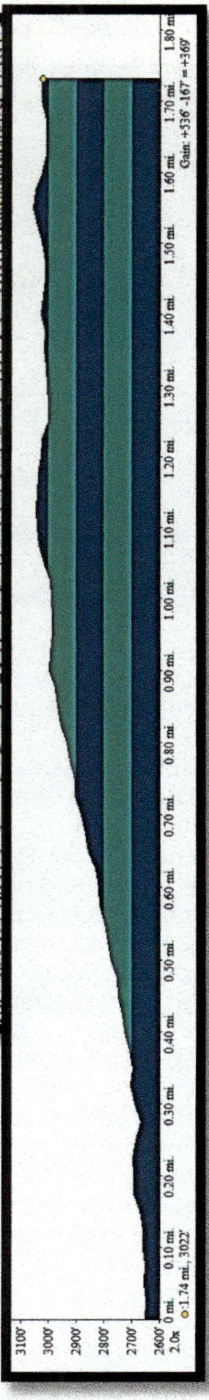

Blue Ledge on the Hudson

Quad:

Dutton Mountain

Distances:

- **North Woods Club Road to Blue Ledge-2.2 miles, one way**

Directions to Trailhead:

From the intersection of Routes 28 and 28N in North Creek, follow Route 28N toward Newcomb. Continue for just under 9.5 miles to North Woods Club Road on the left. Follow here for 6.5 miles to the trailhead on the left.

Trail Conditions:

There are a couple brook crossings but overall this is a very attractive trail with decent conditions.

From the trailhead you almost immediately cross an inlet of Huntley Pond and shortly after you will have excellent views out over the water.

Shortly past Huntley Pond you will start a soft climb to a height-of-land. Once you get your heart under control from this little uphill you can descend slightly to a second brook crossing at a little over 0.6 miles. Don't get your hopes up, though - there is an immediate climb on the opposite side of the stream. This climb will bring you to the highest point along this trail. As you crest this high point you will swing around the north side of the ridge on a slow descent. As you swing around the west side of the ridge you will come to a nice lookout ledge that peers across the Hudson below. As you are high on the ridge you get the sense that the river is near as it echoes in your ears through the valley. You will reach the river in about 0.3 miles from the lookout - that is, after you do a descent run to its shore. The 300-foot ledges on the opposite side are quite the sight. Just upstream is a nice swim-hole, most of the rapids are downstream. BEWARE - the water is ice cold, which has a tendency to make certain areas quite bashful.

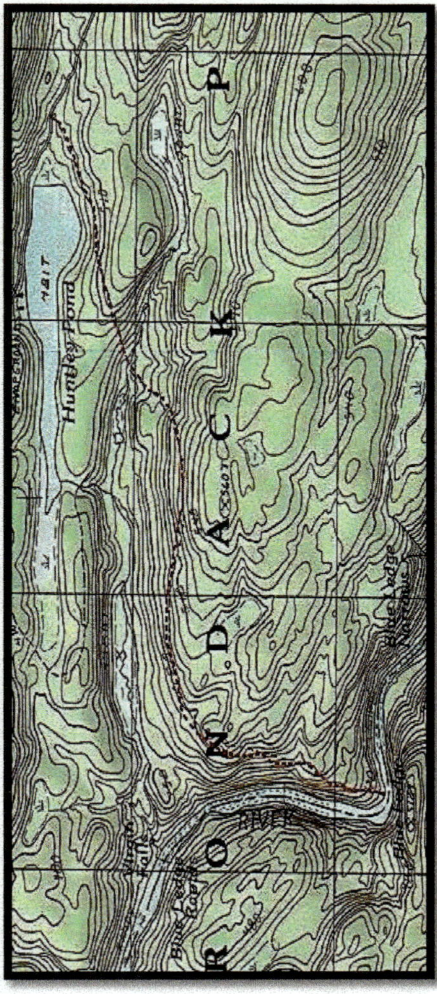
Huntley Pond
RIVER
Blue Ledge Narrows
Blue Ledge
Virgin Falls
Blue Ledge Rapids

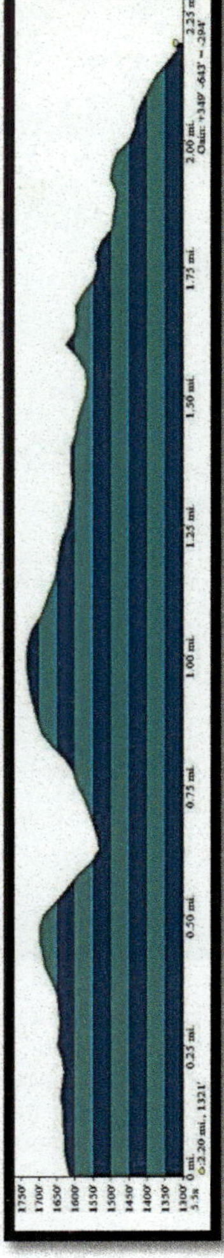
0 mi.
0.25 mi.
0.50 mi.
0.75 mi.
1.00 mi.
1.25 mi.
1.50 mi.
1.75 mi.
2.00 mi.
2.25 mi.
1300'
1350'
1400'
1450'
1500'
1550'
1600'
1650'
1700'
1750'

Puffer Pond Loop

Quad:

Thirteenth Lake

Distances:

- **From King's Flow Parking to Carol Brook-0.8 miles**
- **To the John Pond Trail intersection-0.65 miles**
- **To the shoulder of Bullhead Mountain-0.3 miles**
- **To Puffer Pond-0.35 miles**
- **To the King's Flow Trail-1.5 miles**
- **To the trailhead-1.45 miles**

Total distance 5.05 miles, loop

Directions to Trailhead:

From the intersection of Routes 28 and 30 in Indian Lake follow Route 30 toward Lake Pleasant. Continue for just under 0.5 miles to Big Brook Road. Follow here for 7.8 miles to King's Flow Parking Area. This is the trailhead for Chimney Mountain, Johns Pond and Puffer Pond. This is pay-to-use parking, very informal; pay the small fee at the small kiosk.

Trail Conditions:

Variable trail conditions exist throughout on this loop run. The run up and over the shoulder of Bullhead Mountain is rigorous, and footing can be difficult.

From the parking lot at King's Flow find the trail for John Pond and Puffer Pond on the west side, just above the parking area. You will quickly cross a bridge, and not long after start a gradual uphill climb. At about 0.8 miles in you will come to Carroll Brook, which can be tricky to cross, depending on how much mischief the beavers have been up to lately. Once across the brook you will follow its shores for 0.2 miles before you turn away and start a rather steep climb to the shoulder of Bullhead Mountain. A little over 0.6 miles from Carroll Brook there will be a trail intersection - left is John Pond; you want to continue straight. This climb you are about to undertake is a rather aggressive one. The footing is poor and the trail is eroded in spots. Once at the top of the pass on the shoulder of Bullhead Mountain you will lose 200 feet in elevation to the shore of Puffer Pond and its lean-to. The descent isn't terrible, but again it is steep in areas. The trail forks here; go right toward the southwest end of the pond. It will be a little over 0.3 miles to the end of Puffer pond.

The trail now follows along Puffer Pond Brook, which will be to your left. Over a large portion of this section of trail the brook can be heard but not seen. However, on occasion you will have the pleasure of seeing some small cascades. This section of trail is an old wagon route, so the grade was built to allow for easy passage with horse and buggy. With that being said, it is relatively flat, even when the forest around you is not. You will be at the intersection with the King's Flow Trail after 1.5 miles from the Puffer Pond Lean-to.

Once you pass the intersection you will continue on a fairly level course before dropping to an old fisherman's trail on the left. Continue on the marked trail toward King's Flow and the grassy field. Running through the grassy fields can be wet, especially after recent rains or spring thaw. This trail will bring you back to your car, hopefully where you parked it a few hours ago.

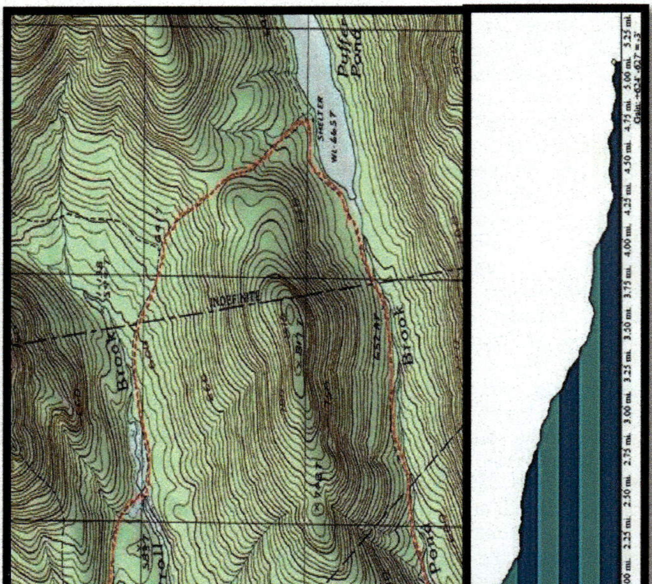
Puffer Pond
Kings Flow
Carroll
Brook
Pond

Big Brook Loop, Lake Eaton

Quad:
Deerland

Distances:

- **Trailhead to Walker Road-0.7 miles**
- **To old road intersection-0.2 miles**
- **To Route 30-0.4 miles**
- **To Owls Head Trail-0.8 miles**
- **To Lake Eaton Campground-0.9 miles**
- **To Start-0.6 miles**

Total distance 3.6 miles, loop

Trailhead Directions:
From the intersection of Routes 30 and 28 in the center of Long Lake head down Route 30 toward Tupper Lake. Continue 2.5 miles to the entrance of Lake Eaton. Parking for the trail is located here on the left.

Trail Conditions:
This trail is, simply put, seasonal - a snowmobile trail, with limited use in the off-season. To make a long story even longer - this trail, as with most snowmobile trails, is wide and the footing is wet and unsettled. Much of the trail, especially in the spring, has areas of low and flat ground where water tends to settle so expect wet conditions in most seasons, wide trail-ways, tough footing and moderate course - what's for dessert?

From the trailhead parking, there is a bridge over the drainage along the road-side - across the road is the gated trail.

Once on the trail, you will notice just how moderate this run is. The trail is also quite wide to accommodate the use of snowmobiles, in season.

The first section of trail goes over the shoulder of a small knoll, which you will hardly notice. A small marshland will be to your right; it can be a little wet here. After 0.7 miles the intersection with Walker Road will come in on the right; after this intersection, you will climb over a more significant knob. The tread up this knob is a little tricky for running and in most cases wet and slippery. From the top it's a low grade downhill to the edge of Route 30. An old section goes left but the trail goes right and passes through a red pine stand; the trail is lined on both sides, very picturesque.

After a short distance of running perpendicular to Route 30, you will come to a crossing of Route 30. There is an old semi-paved road across the way. Follow here until you come to a gate. To the left just before the gate is the continuation of the loop. Here you will do a slight climb before it becomes very flat and meets up with the Owl's Head Mountain Trail that comes in on the right. Follow the signs to Lake Eaton Campground, which is 0.9 miles away.

From this intersection it's mostly a downhill run to the campground. You will be at the backside of the campground and need to navigate the road system back to the car; not a big deal. Just keep left and you will be back to Route 30.

Only when the last tree has died and the last river has been poisoned and the last fish has been caught will we realize we cannot eat money.

~Cree Indian Proverb

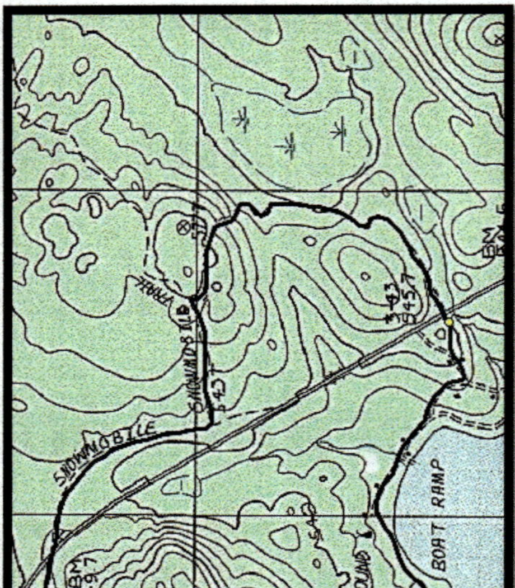
SNOWMOBILE
SNOWMOBILE TRAIL
CAMPGROUND
BOAT RAMP
RESTRICTED
SNOWMOBILE TRAIL

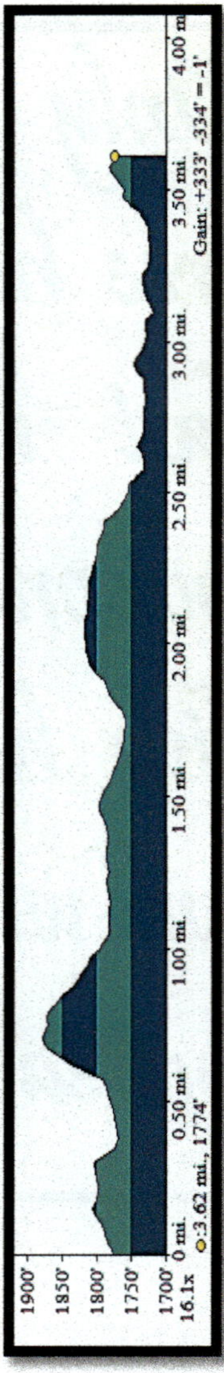
1900'
1850'
1800'
1750'
1700'
16.1x
0 mi.
0.50 mi.
1.00 mi.
1.50 mi.
2.00 mi.
2.50 mi.
3.00 mi.
3.50 mi.
4.00 mi
:3.62 mi., 1774'
Gain: +333' -334' = -1'

Trout Pond and Lows Lower Dam

Quad:

Little Tupper Lake

Distances:

- Snowmobile parking to Low's Lower Dam Trail-0.3 miles
- To Lows Lower Dam-0.7 miles
- Lows Lower Dam Trailhead to Trout Pond-1.15 miles

Total distance 2.15 miles, one way

Trailhead Directions:

From the intersection of Routes 30 and 3 in Tupper Lake, follow Route 30 south toward Long Lake. Continue for 8.8 miles or so to Route 421 on the right. Route 421 starts out as a paved road, and then becomes dirt on the southern side of Horseshoe Lake. The road turns from paved to dirt and the Lows Dam road will come in on the left, shortly beyond. Drive to the parking located at the end.

Trail Conditions:

This is a mostly dry trail with decent footing. This trail also gets limited use from hikers and fisherman, and with what seems to be limited trail maintenance it can become a little overgrown in some areas.

From the parking area you will hike down a few feet to the trail register just beyond it's only a couple hundred feet to Lows Lower Dam. The trail is across the dam. The trail enters the woods on a short uphill grade before it levels off on a flat plateau. You will quickly pass by a small wetland on your right before you start a steady but easy uphill climb to almost 2000 feet in elevation. This trail is designated as a snowmobile trail so it is designed to be very wide. After about 0.75 miles from the dam you will crest the height-of-land on a long ridge that runs down the north side of Trout Pond. You will continue over the hill and start a slow to modest descent to the shore of Trout Pond.

You will be at the east shore of Trout Pond looking west down a very long and narrow strip of water. This is designated for snowmobiles to travel the pond to access Sabattis. As a runner, I don't believe you could run fast enough to make it, so, you will have to designate this run as an out-and-back.

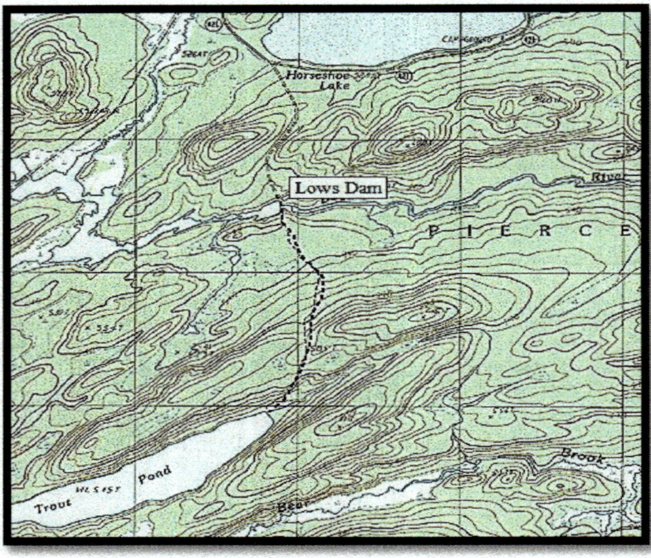

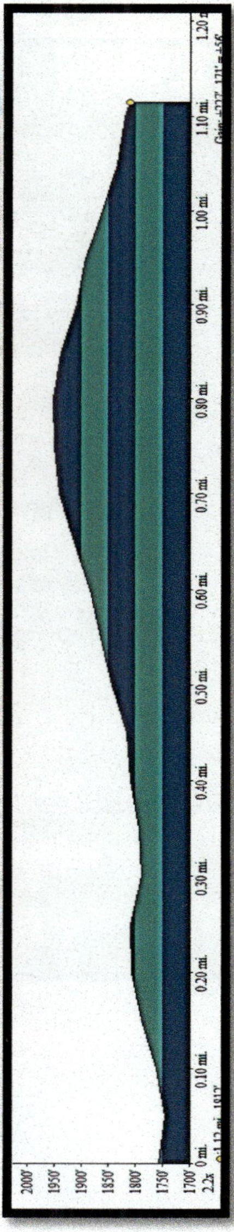
2000'
1950'
1900'
1850'
1800'
1750'
1700'
2.2x
0 mi.
0.10 mi.
0.20 mi.
0.30 mi.
0.40 mi.
0.50 mi.
0.60 mi.
0.70 mi.
0.80 mi.
0.90 mi.
1.00 mi.
1.10 mi.
1.20 mi.

Sargent Ponds Loop

Quad:

Raquette Lake

Distances:

- Trailhead to Upper Sargent Pond-1.25 miles
- To intersection with Grass Pond Trail-1.7 miles
- To Lower Sargent Pond and back-0.1 miles
- To Grass Pond-0.6 miles
- To second trailhead-1.2 miles
- Back to vehicle-1.5 miles

Total distance 6.35 miles, loop

Trailhead Directions:

You can find these two trailheads off the Forked Lake Road in Long Lake. Start at the three corners in Long Lake drive south toward Blue Mountain Lake on Route 28N/30. North Point Road will be on the right, in 3.0 miles - drive down North Point Road. There will be a fork in the road a few miles in; right leads to Forked Lake Campsite, left to the trailheads. The trailheads will both be marked with state DEC signs on the left side of the road. The first trailhead is at 3.1 miles from the intersection with Forked Lake Road; 1.5 miles separate the two trailheads.

Trail Condition:

Expect mixed conditions on this loop. There is a moderate chance of periodic deadfall as well as small mud pits. Tricky footing in areas always makes for a fun adventure, with a short, easy run at the end along the North Point Road.

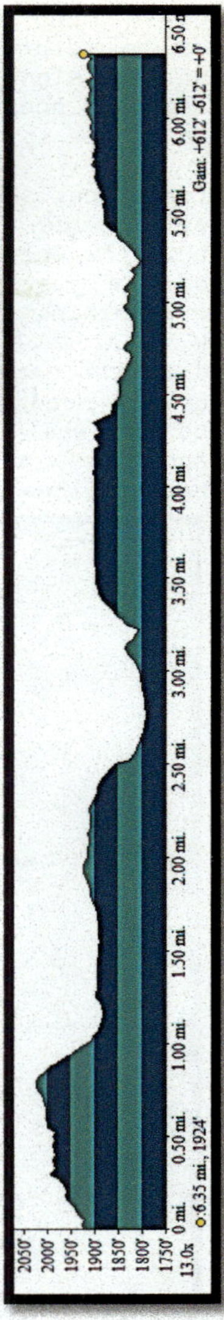

This is a very straightforward run through a large tract of hardwood forest. Starting the loop from the east trailhead, begin a very gradual run over a well maintained but narrow trail. This is considered a snowmobile trail, but gets little use by the machines. After a quick 1.2 miles you will come to a trail intersection, with only one sign. The sign pointing right leads to Lower Sargent Pond; left and unmarked is a 0.1-mile trail to the shore of Upper Sargent Pond. Upper Sargent is worth the short spur run, if for no other reason than to just look over the placid waters.

Returning back to the junction, make the left turn toward Lower Sargent Pond. This section of trail is a little more demanding with small ups and downs, possible wet crossings, and sections of trail that are very narrow and getting overgrown. Along this route you will see a long marshy area to your left which is part of Middle Sargent Pond but not actually the pond itself. After 1.7 miles you will come to an intersection - right is to Grass Pond (the trail you will need to return to) and left is to Upper Sargent Pond. The sign reads Upper Sargent Pond 0.1 miles. A trail continues along the shore to a lean-to if you wish to see it.

Retrace your steps to the intersection and follow it over a wide, well-maintained trail toward Grass Pond. It's only about 0.6 miles to Grass Pond, whose shore is just that, grass-covered, wet and mossy. The remaining 1.3 miles to the road is a nice, mellow run. Small rolling hills dot the landscape and add to the experience. Once at the North Point Road you will need to get back to your vehicle if a second car-was not available. It's a 1.5 mile run along the windy, well-traveled road, back to the other trailhead.

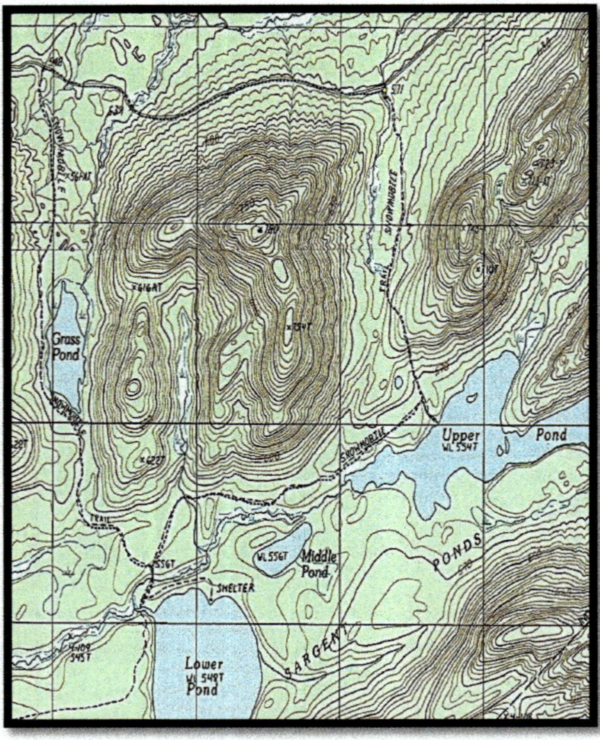

Trombley Landing

Quad:
Tupper Lake

Distances:

- From the trailhead to Trombley Landing-1.5 miles, one way

Directions to Trailhead:
The trail is directly across the road from the intersection of Routes 30 and 3, between Tupper Lake and Saranac Lake.

Trail Conditions:
Mostly dry with one major hill along the way to crest. This is a wonderful low-land trail through an evergreen forest.

Down-up-down-up-down, that's the course of the day, or few hours as the case may be. You will immediately head downhill on a decent clip to the crossing of a small brook. On the other side - an ascent over the top of a small unnamed little bump. The descent down the opposite side is rather fun. Not terribly steep but there is a sharp little turn or two in there.

You will soon enter an evergreen forest and run on mostly flat terrain until you reach the shore of the Raquette River at Trombley Landing. There is a lean-to off to the left - a very nice spot to relax and maybe enjoy a little afternoon nap.

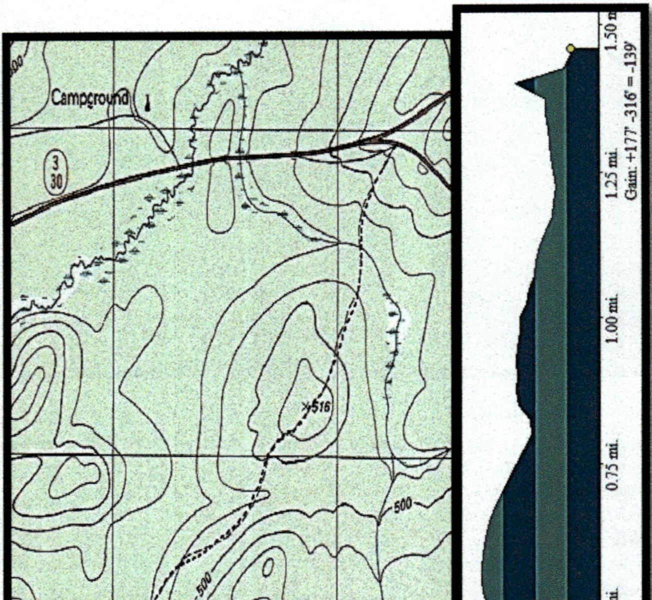
Campground
Shelters
Trombley
Landing
516
532
500
1700'
1650'
1600'
1550'
1500'
5.9x
0 mi.
0.25 mi.
0.50 mi.
0.75 mi.
1.00 mi.
1.25 mi.
1.50 mi.
:1.47 mi., 1545'
Gain: +177' -316' = -139'

Kempshall Point on Long Lake

Quad:
Deerland and Kempshall Mountain

Distances:

- **Trailhead to Catlin Bay Lean-to's-1.0 miles**
- **To Kelly Point-2.75 miles**
- **To Kempshall Bay-0.5 miles**

Total distance 4.25 miles, one way

Directions to Trailhead:
From the intersection of Routes 30 and 28N follow Route 28N toward Newcomb. Continue for 1.5 miles to Endion Road on the left. Follow here for 0.7 miles to the Northville/Placid Trail parking on the right. The trailhead is about 100 feet further down the road on the right.

Trail Conditions:
Wet in a few areas with a couple slippery bridges and boardwalks - this trail is one very interesting section of the NPT. You will start on an initial downhill but level off to several small rolling hills.

Immediately you will run downhill and quite steeply at times as well. This will continue to a small bridge over a fork of Sixmile Brook - a hair short of 0.5 miles.

Along this route you will be challenged with numerous rolling hills - a couple are a tad bit more extensive than others. However, while you will be working so hard to get to Kempshall Bay, you will be blessed with numerous opportunities for views and vistas out over Long Lake.

Passing by a few shelters along the way you have ample opportunity to rest and relax. Kempshall Bay is a short spur trail that leads northwest to the shore of Long Lake. This is located at a four-way intersection. Straight is a continuation of the NPT and ends at Lake Placid. Right is the closed trail to Kempshall Mountain. The Kempshall Mountain trail is very difficult to follow. Once the fire tower was removed, the views ceased almost as fast as the visitors. Your left will be the very short spur trail to Long Lake.

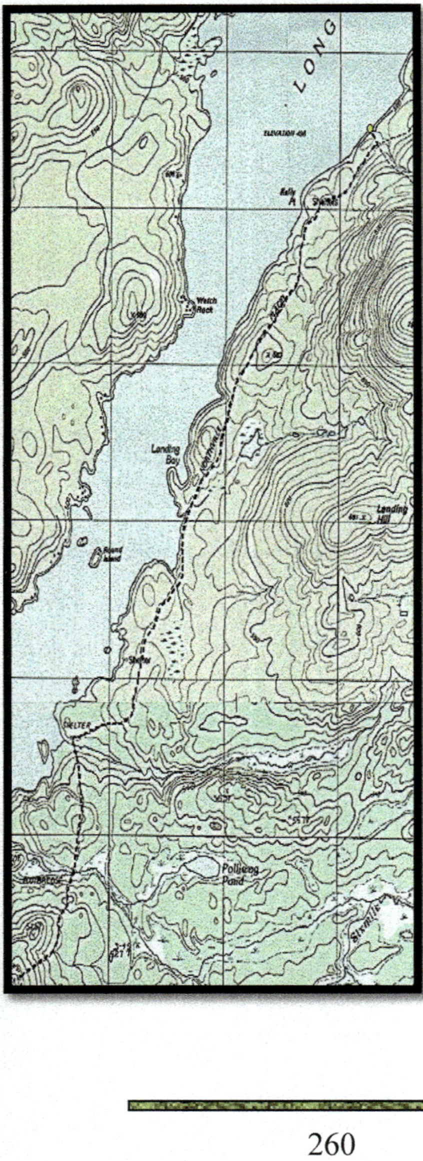

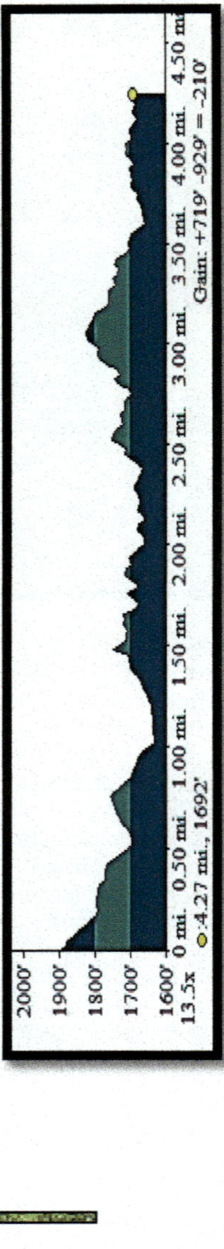

Kempshall Point on Long Lake

Quad:
Deerland and Kempshall Mountain

Distances:

- **Trailhead to Catlin Bay Lean-to's-1.0 miles**
- **To Kelly Point-2.75 miles**
- **To Kempshall Bay-0.5 miles**

Total distance 4.25 miles, one way

Directions to Trailhead:
From the intersection of Routes 30 and 28N follow Route 28N toward Newcomb. Continue for 1.5 miles to Endion Road on the left. Follow here for 0.7 miles to the Northville/Placid Trail parking on the right. The trailhead is about 100 feet further down the road on the right.

Trail Conditions:
Wet in a few areas with a couple slippery bridges and boardwalks - this trail is one very interesting section of the NPT. You will start on an initial downhill but level off to several small rolling hills.

Immediately you will run downhill and quite steeply at times as well. This will continue to a small bridge over a fork of Sixmile Brook - a hair short of 0.5 miles.

Along this route you will be challenged with numerous rolling hills - a couple are a tad bit more extensive than others. However, while you will be working so hard to get to Kempshall Bay, you will be blessed with numerous opportunities for views and vistas out over Long Lake.

Passing by a few shelters along the way you have ample opportunity to rest and relax. Kempshall Bay is a short spur trail that leads northwest to the shore of Long Lake. This is located at a four-way intersection. Straight is a continuation of the NPT and ends at Lake Placid. Right is the closed trail to Kempshall Mountain. The Kempshall Mountain trail is very difficult to follow. Once the fire tower was removed, the views ceased almost as fast as the visitors. Your left will be the very short spur trail to Long Lake.

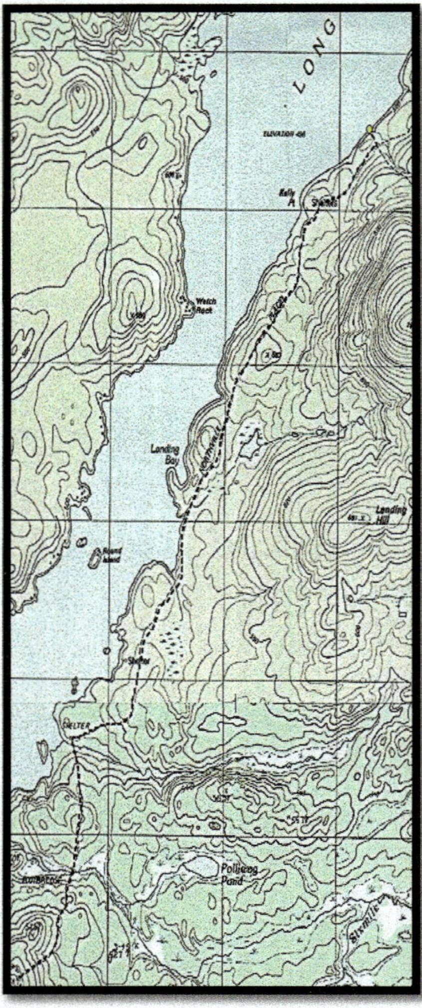

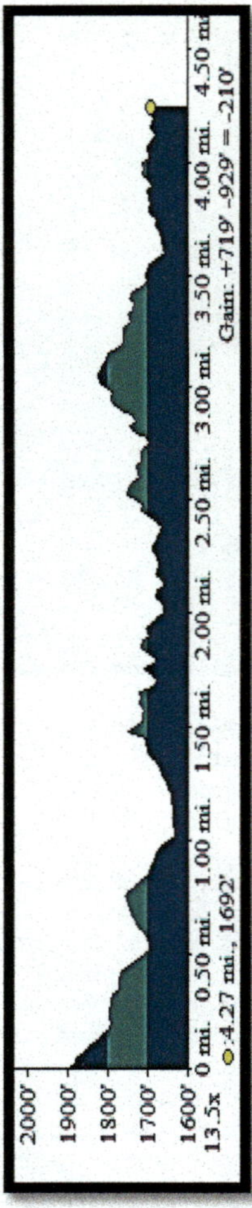

Wilson Pond

Quad:

Blue Mountain Lake

Distances:

- **Forked Lake Road to Grassy Pond-0.3 miles**
- **To Wilson Pond-2.5 miles**

Total distance 2.8 miles, one way

Directions to Trailhead:

From the intersection of Routes 28 and 30 in Blue Mountain Lake follow Route 28 toward Raquette Lake. Continue for 2.75 miles to the Grassy Pond Trailhead on the left.

Trail Conditions:

There can be a few wet areas to fight your way through, with one marshy area that is hard to cross - but in full, it's an excellent run in an area that gets light use.

The start of this trail is mostly flat with a couple small hills. The run to Grassy Pond is very fast, but you may need to hunt a little for perfect views.

Past Grassy Pond you will find the terrain get a little trickier. After you pass by a marshy area on the right you will run over moderate terrain for a little longer and then drop short and steep to the shores of Loon Brook. This crossing can be a little bit of a pain in the neck, depending on the conditions and your idea of fun. Be aware you may need to go up-or down-stream to find the best crossing. Chances are, if you follow the trail that others use to cross, it should get you to a decent point.

Once across you will follow the brook's side along a tight trail. The terrain at this point gets steeper along a slight side hill course. After you top off here you can depend on that this is not all of the adventure for the day. As you pass through some very attractive hardwood forest there are several more small hills, before you reach the shore of Wilson Pond. The lean-to is on the north side of the pond overlooking a majestic body of water.

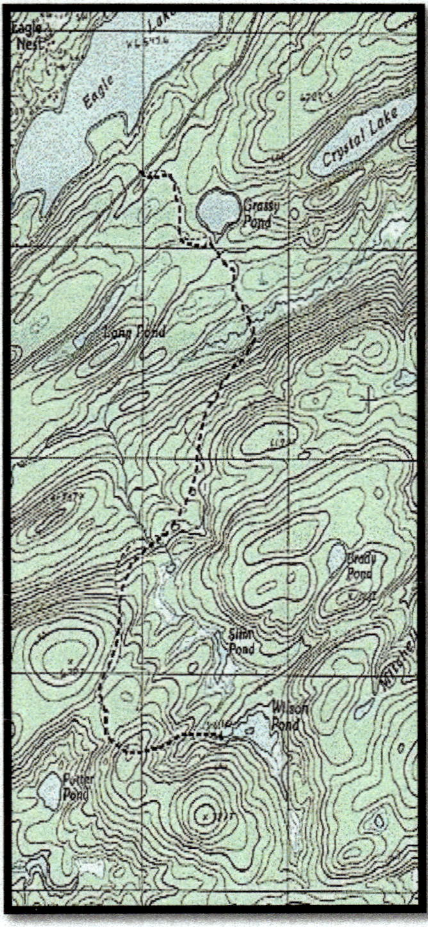
Eagle Nest
Eagle
Crystal Lake
Grassy Pond
Brady Pond
Wilson Pond
Potter Pond

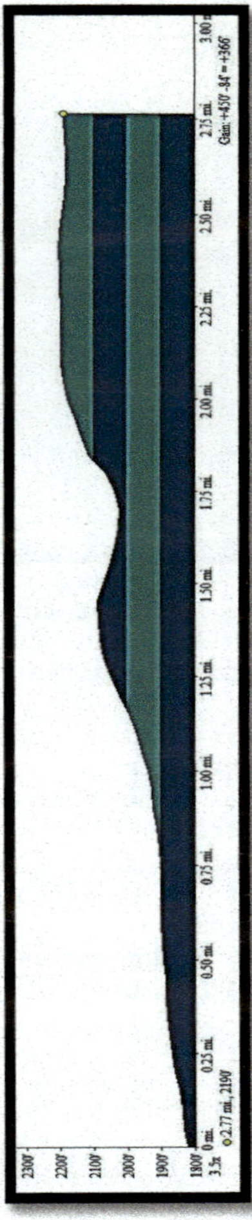

Tirrell Pond

Quad:

Blue Mountain Lake and Deerland

Distances:

- **Blue Mountain Trailhead to Jeep road-1.3 miles**
- **To Northville/Placid Trail-1.5 miles**
- **To Tirrell Pond Lean-to-0.3 miles**

Total distance 3.1 miles, one way

Directions to Trailhead:

From the intersection of Routes 28 and 28N/30 follow Route 28N/30 toward Long Lake. Follow here for 1.4 miles to the Blue Mountain Trailhead on the right. The trailhead is at the top of a long, winding hill.

Trail Conditions:

Sections of this route can be slightly overgrown and a bit rough. Water isn't usually a huge factor. Once on the NPT, the trail is better beaten.

Standing at the trailhead you may not even notice that a second trail leaves this rather large landing zone. While the Blue Mountain Trailhead is to the back, the Tirrell Pond Trail is to the north end of the trailhead and begins alongside Route 28N/30.

This trail, while mildly used does offer a nice run through the woods - the destination does attract larger groups as Tirrell Pond is a very attractive body of water.

The first section of this trail is a bit overgrown. The steep slopes of Blue Mountain come down to your right while the main highway roars off in the distance to your left. At 1.3 miles from the trailhead you will come to a private dirt road, which the trail crosses. From this point the trail is mostly on a downhill slope. The trail is slightly wetter than the other section of trail. This portion of the trail ends at the NPT. Follow right on the NPT for a little over 0.25 miles to the lean-to on Tirrell

Pond. The NPT is a heavier use trail and follows along the entire south side of Tirrell Pond.

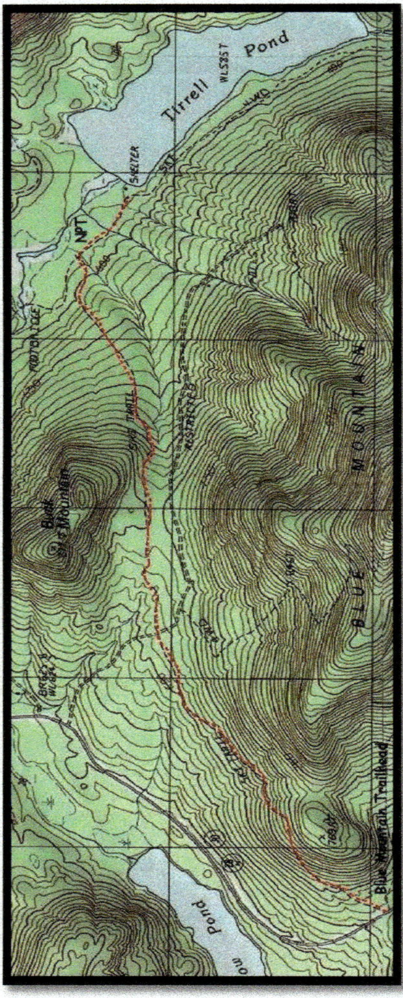

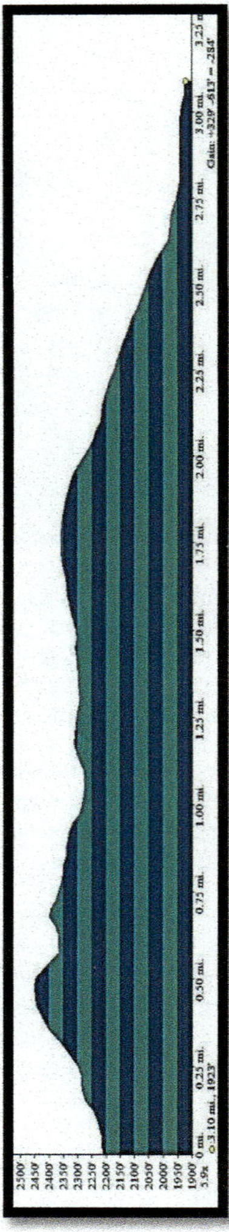

Glossary of Terms

Bluff- Formed steep hillside usually found along the edges of a body of water or in an area for which water once existed.

Bog- A wetland area - which in some cases can be floating. A bog is also considered a fragile environment.

Bump- A small summit or peak, usually found on a ridge of a much taller peak; can be of various sizes and shapes.

Bushwhack- The act of walking through the woods without the aid of a path or trail to follow.

Canopy- The natural coverage of the forest floor by the trees and their vegetation.

Col- Also known as a valley or a pass between two peaks.

Corduroy- Logs placed side by side to help form woods roads or trails through a wet or muddy section.

Cripplebrush- A band of thickly studded growth, usually found at higher elevations.

Drainage- An intermittent streambed which in many cases can be dry, but it's an impression in the landscape deep enough to carry water.

Draw- Referred to as drainage or small valley between two hogbacks.

Easement- A term used to define permission from the land owner or manager to use their land.

Erratic- A large rock or boulder placed by a glacier.

Esker- A ridge created by glacier forming a boundary between two bodies of water or streams.

Hogback- A small hill, usually one that is traversed along a path or trail.

Kettle (pond) - A body of water formed in a depression of land that was created by slow glacial melt. These ponds, over time create bogs and ecosystems of their own.

Non-conforming Structure- A structure or piece of equipment placed in a wilderness area, which is not naturally part of the area. Fire towers and canisters are often seen as non-conforming structures.

Old Growth Forest- A forest structure made up of older generation trees, free of logging for decades.

Quad or Quadrangle- A portion of land laid out on a contour map. The land boundaries are different sizes and resolution. They are normally named for the most prominent feature within those boundaries.

Slide- An open avalanche track, often steep and exposed.

Tread- Another name for the surface of a trail or road used for foot travel.

Vly- Also known as marsh or meadow.

Abbreviations

ADK- Adirondack Mountain Club

ADKS- Adirondacks

AMR- Adirondack Mountain Reserve

ATIS- Adirondack Trail Improvement Society

ATV- All-terrain Vehicle

DEC- Department of Environmental Conservation

FT- Feet

GPS- Global positioning system

JBL- John's Brook Lodge

MTN- Mountain

N/A- None Available or Not Applicable

NPT- Northville/Placid Trail

NYS- New York State

RT- Round trip

TNC- The Nature Conservancy

USGS- United States Geological Survey

VIC- Visitors Interpretive Center

Published 2007
By
Dacksdescents
Publishing

Published 2011
By
Inca-Pah-Cho
Wilderness
Guides

INCA-PAH-CHO WILDERNESS GUIDES

Guiding Strong Since 2004

We are a local guide service as well as a self-publishing organization, revolving our efforts around recreation and the great outdoors. For additional information and specialized trips contact us via our website www.incapahchowildernessguides.com or by phone at (607) 267-3474

Our promise to you

To provide a safe and memorable outdoor experience and adventure that fits your every expectation and aspiration.

Our certifications

- √ **New York State Licensed Guides**
- √ **Wilderness First Aid/CPR**
- √ **Emergency Medical Technician (EMT)**
- √ **Avalanche Safety**
- √ **Water Safety**
- √ **Wilderness Orienteering**
- √ **Search and Rescue Certified**
- √ **Winter Survival**
- √ **Degrees in Forest Technology and Recreation with Minors in Forest Ecology and Wildlife**

A sample of what we offer

- **Hiking/Backpacking**
- **Slide Climbing**
- **Winter Camping**
- **Winter Mountaineering**
- **Bushwhacking**
- **Navigation Training**
- **Route Finding Development**
- **Kayaking/Canoeing**
- **Long Distance Paddling**
- **Scenic Tours**
- **Ski Touring**
- **Trail Running Excursions**